Portable DBA

SQL Server

Damir Bersinic
and
Stephen Giles

McGraw-Hill/Osborne

New York Chicago San Francisco
Lisbon London Madrid Mexico City Milan
New Delhi San Juan Seoul Singapore Sydney Toronto

The McGraw·Hill Companies

McGraw-Hill/Osborne
2100 Powell Street, 10th Floor
Emeryville, California 94608
U.S.A.

To arrange bulk purchase discounts for sales promotions, premiums, or fund-raisers, please contact **McGraw-Hill**/Osborne at the above address. For information on translations or book distributors outside the U.S.A., please see the International Contact Information page immediately following the index of this book.

Portable DBA: SQL Server

1234567890 DOC DOC 01987654

ISBN 0-07-223016-9

Publisher   Brandon A. Nordin
Vice President & Associate Publisher   Scott Rogers
Editorial Director   Wendy Rinaldi
Project Editor   Jody McKenzie
Acquisitions Coordinator   Athena Honore
Technical Editors   Todd Meister, Deborah Bechtold
Copy Editor   Emily Hsuan
Proofreader   Susie Elkind
Indexer   Valerie Perry
Composition   John Patrus, Jean Butterfield
Illustrators   Kathleen Edwards, Melinda Lytle, Michael Mueller
Series Design   Peter F. Hancik, Lucie Ericksen, Elizabeth Jang
Cover Series Design   Pattie Lee

This book was composed with Corel VENTURA™ Publisher.

This book is dedicated to the patience and understanding
of my ever-loving wife, Visnja, and my boys, Anthony and Matthew.
Thanks (once again) for putting up with me and my crazy schedule. It is
most likely not the last time, so I'll apologize in advance for shutting myself
in my home office and writing until the crazy hours of the morning,
and thank you for letting me do it. That, and so many other reasons,
is why I love you all so much.

—Damir Bersinic

Writing time often encroaches on family time, so having an understanding
family is indispensable. Therefore, I'd like to dedicate this book to
my wife, Antonella, and my daughter, Olivia Rose, for all their
patience, love, and support.

—Stephen Giles

About the Authors

Damir Bersinic is an infrastructure consultant with Trecata Corporation, a system integration consultancy in Toronto, Canada. He has more than 20 years of industry experience and has worked with every SQL Server version since 1.11a in one way or another. He holds several Microsoft certifications including MCSE, MCDBA, and MCT, and has also provided assistance to Microsoft in the development process of MCP exams. Damir has authored a number of titles on SQL Server, Oracle, Windows, and Active Directory. He is also a database columnist for www.certcities.com and a regular contributor to *MCP Magazine*. He can be reached at dbersinic@hotmail.com.

Stephen Giles, MCSE, MCDBA, MCSA, MCT, CTT+, is a consultant, trainer, and author. He is currently a partner at AllianzWeb, an Application development and IT consulting company based in Toronto, Canada (www.allianzweb.com). He has worked extensively with SQL Server since the early beta days of SQL Server 7. Stephen is the author of several books on Windows, Oracle, and SQL Server. When not working, Stephen spends as much time as he possibly can with his wife, Antonella, and his daughter, Olivia Rose. Stephen can be reached at stephen@allianzweb.com.

CONTENTS

ACKNOWLEDGMENTS

The people you work with make or break the success of a project. At times I'm sure Wendy Rinaldi, the fantastic leader of the editorial team for this book, asked herself "How did I get myself into this?" But, in the end, it all worked out. It is with her belief in Steve and I that this book is in print today, and her enormous contribution needs to be acknowledged. The other members of the editorial team—Jody, Athena, Todd, Emily, and Deborah—were invaluable in making sure things are as they are supposed to be. Finally, thanks to my bud Steve for helping on yet another book to make it a success.

—Damir Bersinic

Thanks to the fantastic editorial staff at Osborne for keeping us on the straight and narrow, especially Jody McKenzie and Wendy Rinaldi. This book wouldn't have been done without you. Thanks also to Todd Meister, for keeping me honest, and Emily Hsuan, for finding all my favorite typos (over and over…).

Thanks to my partner Phill for not commenting on my afternoon five-minute "power naps" the day after a chapter was due.

And thanks, finally, to Damir for keeping this little writing partnership going (next year we go for three!).

—Stephen Giles

INTRODUCTION

As a DBA, I wanted to find a resource that would give me most of what I needed in a small package that was easy to carry. Books Online is a good resource but has a number of bugs. As a result, Microsoft has had to issue updates to correct the documentation on Books Online. Besides, you can't always have a computer handy when you want to refresh your memory on how SQL Server works on a cluster or the command-line options for the DTSRUN command. This book is designed to solve those problems by providing information on the common tasks performed by database administrators in a concise package.

In this title you will not find detailed explanations on every single option for every single Transact-SQL command—other books and Books Online give you this in spades. What you will find is enough information to be able to do your job effectively, including how to program in SQL Server—something all DBAs should understand at a basic level. Topics covered include security; understanding how SQL Server works; creating databases and database objects; performing backups and restores; automating administration and data extraction, transformation and load; monitoring and tuning SQL Server; distributed transactions and replication; and clustering and log shipping. For any DBA involved with the day-to-day administration of SQL Server and making it work in enterprise environments, this book will give you what you need, but not overwhelm you.

One of the more helpful things that we wanted to include, unlike with Books Online and most books on SQL Server, is coverage of SQL Server 2000, 7, and 6.x. In this way *Portable DBA: SQL Server* is a good reference for anyone who needs to work with more than one version of SQL Server.

—Damir Bersinic

Chapter 1

SQL Server Overview

The first step in administering SQL Server is knowing what it is and what it is supposed to do. In its simplest form, SQL Server is a relational database management system or RDBMS. That, and 25 cents, will get you a phone call in most jurisdictions.

Defining SQL Server

SQL Server is a client-server-based RDBMS, which means that it receives requests to process data from client applications, performs the work to process those requests, and sends the results back to the client. This general architecture includes a number of key elements to ensure its success and efficiency (as shown in Figure 1-1):

- **A relational engine** Processes client requests and ensures the consistency and integrity of the data. The relational engine also parses Transact-SQL (the language used by SQL Server) requests, optimizes and executes the execution plans, enforces security, and maintains the declared relationships between data in the database.

- **A storage engine** Communicates with the Windows file system and manages the reading and writing of SQL Server database files and transaction log files, and ensures that all writes take place properly. The storage engine also performs database backup and restore

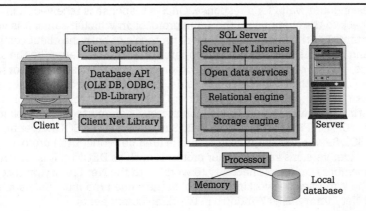

Figure 1-1. SQL Server architecture

operations when requested, recovering data to a consistent state should some of the data files be damaged, and manages the database buffer cache.

- **Networking components**   Allow a client application (client) to communicate with SQL Server and provide a way for SQL Server to receive and respond to requests from clients.

SQL Server Communications

The networking side of SQL Server includes both client components and server components. Client components allow a client application to properly formulate requests to be sent to SQL Server. These requests use a database API to communicate with a client Net Library, which in turn uses the client operating system network interfaces to pass the requests on to the server. The client database APIs and Net Library are shipped with SQL Server, but can also be downloaded from Microsoft as part of a series of data access drivers known by the acronym MDAC (Microsoft Data Access Components). The most recent version of MDAC can be found at:

http://msdn.microsoft.com/library/default.asp?url=/downloads/list/dataaccess.asp

A client application can communicate with SQL Server using a number of technologies including Open Database Connectivity (ODBC), OLE-DB, DB-Library (for backward compatibility with earlier releases of SQL Server and Sybase, or for Unix-based clients), as well as XML, or by using the SQL Server .NET Data Provider.

On the server side, SQL Server receives requests through network protocols supported by the Windows computer on which it runs. The Net Library then passes the request to Open Data Services (ODS), the API equivalent residing on the server, which then submits it to the relational engine for processing and waits for a response. Once a response is received, it is sent back to the client using the same protocol on which it came. It is very important that the underlying network protocols of both the client computer sending requests and the server computer running SQL Server be the same (that is, TCP/IP on both computers), otherwise communication cannot take place. On both the client and server side, the Net Library component passes requests from the database API layer or ODS to the network protocol of the operating systems. The more common protocols supported include Named Pipes, TCP/IP, IPX/SPX, and AppleTalk. Support varies by SQL Server release, with SQL Server 2000 supporting storage area network (SAN) protocols while older versions support other protocols such as DECNet. It is important to remember that for connectivity to work, both the Net Library protocol and the Windows networking protocol of the same type *must* be installed, since Net Library uses Windows networking components.

Transact-SQL: The Language of SQL Server

For SQL Server to understand the commands that are issued to it, the command must be issued in the language that SQL Server understands—Transact-SQL. Transact-SQL is a combination of the Structured Query Language (SQL), for which an international standard has been adopted along with some SQL Server–specific enhancements to allow for additional functionality and the inclusion of procedural language elements such as conditional logic (IF blocks), looping, and variable declaration and manipulation.

SQL Server and the Windows Family of Servers

SQL Server is closely integrated with Microsoft Windows and other Windows server products. This includes taking advantage of operating system features of the installed Windows operating system version, as well as integration with other .NET servers such as Exchange or Internet Information Services (IIS) to provide functionality.

SQL Server will take full advantage of the capabilities of the Windows operating system (OS) to provide the best overall performance. Aside from using the networking components of Windows, SQL Server also makes use of multiple CPUs, large memory, file storage features such as encryption and security, clusters, and so on. SQL Server also uses the Windows event logs to place critical messages in the application log, as well as to facilitate the alerting of operators and the execution of jobs to correct problems as they arise. However, not all editions of SQL Server support all features, so installing the proper edition of SQL Server on the right OS is critical. For maximum functionality on Windows server platforms, SQL Server Enterprise Edition is required.

An important integration element is SQL Server's use of IIS to support HTTP access of SQL Server databases and XML data interchange. IIS also provides the File Transfer Protocol (FTP) that can be used in SQL Server replication. Finally, SQL Server can publish data in HTML format for viewing on web sites by using the Web Assistant Wizard.

SQL Server security model also uses Windows global groups and user accounts in protecting and configuring access to SQL Server data and services. Windows System Monitor (referred to in versions prior to Windows 2000 as Performance Monitor) monitors the performance of SQL Server, and it creates the performance logs. SQL Server also integrates with System Monitor to allow SQL Server to fire an alert when a Windows performance threshold, such as CPU utilization or use of disk space, is reached. In terms of Windows server integration, one of the more important relationships is that between SQL Server and Exchange. SQL Server uses Exchange (5.5 or later) to send e-mails to operators when an alert has taken place, as well as to respond to e-mail messages that contain a Transact-SQL statement in the message body. Integration with Exchange is not automatic and requires that a MAPI-compliant e-mail client (such as Microsoft Outlook) be installed on the SQL Server computer and a mail profile be created.

Many Windows server products also use SQL Server as their data repository. These include Microsoft Operations Manager, Microsoft Commerce Server, Microsoft BizTalk Server, Content Management Server, Microsoft Project Server, Host Integration Server, and Systems Management Server. Host Integration Server can also be used to access data residing on IBM and other host platforms including DB2. Systems Management Server can also be used to manage installations of SQL Server or to automate the installation of updates and service packs.

SQL Server Editions and Components

Microsoft has a number of SQL Server editions available, depending on what you expect to use SQL Server for and your expected database and feature requirements. The list of editions has been relatively consistent since SQL Server 6.5 and includes the following:

- **SQL Server Standard Edition** For small- to medium-sized organizations with typical database management requirements supporting up to four CPUs and 2GB of RAM.

- **SQL Server Enterprise Edition** For those organizations requiring more robust database functionality and support for up to 32 CPUs and 64GB of RAM. The database features only available in Enterprise Edition include the following:
  - Support for active/active and active/passive clustering
  - Log shipping allowing the creation and maintenance of a standby database
  - Parallel DBCC execution
  - Support for parallel execution of CREATE INDEX commands
  - Enhanced read-ahead and scan capabilities for increased query performance
  - Indexed views
  - Federated database server support allowing tables to be logically partitioned over several SQL Servers
  - Storage Area Network (SAN) support allowing SQL Server database files to reside on SAN storage devices
  - Support for Microsoft Windows 2000 Datacenter Server and Windows Server 2003 Datacenter Edition operating systems

1

- **SQL Server Personal Edition (SQL Server 2000 only)** With functionally similar to Standard Edition, Personal Edition is limited in scalability and includes a workload governor that degrades performance after five concurrent Transact-SQL batches. It does not support being a publisher in transactional replication and is intended for mobile users who spend time away from the workplace.

- **SQL Server Developer Edition** Supporting the same features as Enterprise Edition, Developer Edition is limited to 15 client connections and is used for development and testing of SQL Server applications. Using it in a production environment is specifically prohibited according to the terms of the End User License Agreement (EULA).

- **SQL Server Desktop Engine (MSDE)** First released with SQL Server 7, MSDE provides basic database functionality without the administration tools shipped with other SQL Server editions. It is designed as an alternative to the Microsoft Jet Engine found in Microsoft Access for the development and deployment of desktop applications. The database size and functionality is limited to only the core database elements.

- **SQL Server Windows CE Edition** Allows for the execution of SQL Server applications on devices that use the Windows CE or PocketPC operating system, such as handhelds (HP Ipaq, for example). This allows developers to use SQL Server to develop applications that work on PCs as well as handheld appliances since SQL Server Windows CE Edition is programmatically compatible with other SQL Server editions.

Microsoft also offers SQL Server Evaluation Edition, which is equivalent to SQL Server Enterprise Edition but limited to only 120 days of operation, thereby allowing you to test SQL Server prior to buying it. To remove the 120-day restriction, you will need to install a full-fledged licensed version of SQL Server, after backing up your databases to prevent any data loss.

SQL Server Components

When you install SQL Server, a number of components are installed at the same time. Additional components can be separately installed. SQL Server components include the following:

- **SQL Server Relational Database Engine (RDBMS)** Responsible for processing user requests submitted using Transact-SQL or XML and sending back the results.

- **SQL Server Replication** Allows SQL Server database data to be automatically distributed to other SQL Servers or foreign data sources. Replication provides for a loose-consistency of database data on one or more SQL Servers or external sources. SQL Server supports transactional, merge (introduced in SQL Server 7), and snapshot replication, with or without the ability to update replicated data.

- **SQL Server Data Transformation Services (DTS)**   Provides for a graphical interface to define the import and export of data from many different data sources including SQL Server, Oracle, or any OLE-DB or ODBC data source. DTS was introduced in SQL Server 7 and makes the building of data warehouses, operational data stores, and migration of data into and out of SQL Server easier than in previous releases. An interesting feature of DTS is that neither the data source nor the destination needs to be SQL Server to use DTS—only the computer hosting DTS needs to have SQL Server installed.

- **SQL Server Analysis Services (SSAS)**   Introduced in SQL Server 7 (and called OLAP Services at the time), SQL Server Analysis Services provides for the easy creation, maintenance, and access of multidimensional data sources used for data warehousing. SSAS allows you to create the dimensions, measures, and hierarchies for your data mart or data warehouse and then specify and manage a storage structure in multi-dimensional (cube) form or by using a relational engine, such as SQL Server.

- **SQL Server English Query**   Also introduced in SQL Server 7, English Query is designed to allow you to create an application that would provide users with the ability to ask for data using natural English (yes, only English is supported) syntax. For example, if you entered **Show me a list of customers in alphabetical order by customer name who purchased more than $1000 of product last month**, English Query would convert this to the appropriate Transact-SQL statement as follows:

```
SELECT CustomerID, CustomerName FROM Customers c
   WHERE 1000 <= (SELECT SUM(od.ExtendedPrice )
      FROM Orders o INNER JOIN OrderDetails od
        ON o.OrderID = od.OrderID
        WHERE o.CustomerID=c.CustomerID)
    ORDER BY CustomerName
```

Of course, the real work within English Query is educating the query engine to translate from English to Transact-SQL, which in itself is no small feat.

- **SQL Server Meta Data Services**   Provides for a way to store and manage metadata (defined as data about data) about your applications, components, or other information system components. It allows for a standard repository that developers can write to and store and retrieve metadata information. This component can also be used by DTS to store DTS packages and their modification history.

- **SQL Server Network Libraries**   As discussed previously, SQL Server Network Libraries facilitate communication between SQL Server client applications and SQL Server by using the network protocols supported by the host operating system as a conduit for communication.

- **SQL Server Database Drivers**   OLE-DB and ODBC drivers allow SQL Server, its components, and clients to communicate with various data sources. DTS and the replication engine use them if the data source or target is a database other than SQL Server.

	Enterprise Edition	Standard Edition	Personal Edition	Developer Edition	MSDE	WinCE Edition
RDBMS	Available	Available	Available	Available	Available	Available
Replication	Available	Available	Most functionality	Available	Limited functionality	Merge replication only
DTS	Available	Available	Available	Available	Not available	Not available
Analysis Services	Separate install / enhanced features	Separate install	Separate install	Separate install / enhanced features	Not available	Not available
English Query	Separate install	Separate install	Separate install	Separate install	Not available	Not available
Metadata Services	Available	Available	Available	Available	Available	Available

Table 1-1. SQL Server Components and Their Availability in the Various Editions of SQL Server

Not all features of the available components may be enabled in all editions of SQL Server. Table 1-1 provides a list of features and their availability in the various SQL Server editions. Networking and database access components of SQL Server are shipped with every edition or are part of MDAC.

SQL Server Services

Once you install SQL Server onto a computer running any Windows operating systems except Windows 9x, WindowsCE/PocketPC, or Windows ME, a number of SQL Server services will be available. Some of these services will need to be running to access the core database features of SQL Server, while others are only required when using some of the more advanced or management features of the product. The available services include the following:

- **MSSQLServer service** This service is the core database engine and needs to be running to access SQL Server data and databases. In SQL Server 2000 you may also have services with names in the format of *MSSQL$<instance>* where *<instance>* represents a unique name for an instance of SQL Server on the computer. Multiple instance support was introduced in SQL Server 2000 to support multiple SQL Server or MSDE installations on the same computer. It was not available in SQL Server 7 or previous releases. Multiple instance support can also be used to upgrade SQL Server 7 or 6.5 to SQL Server 2000 without having to shut down the previous release.

- **SQLServerAgent service** Used to create and manage alerts, jobs, and operators. If alerts, jobs, or operators are configured and SQL Server

agent is not started, they will not be executed. If multiple instances of
SQL Server are installed, additional SQLServerAgent services will be
configured with names in the format *SQLAgent$<instance>*.

- **MSDTC service**   The Microsoft Distributed Transaction Coordinator
  (MSDTC) service allows client applications to perform transactions that
  include data from several SQL servers. It is the responsibility of the
  MSDTC service to ensure that that transaction and its data remain
  consistent on all instances of SQL Server where the data is being
  modified.

- **Microsoft Search service**   Allows for the creation and maintenance
  of full-text indexes that allow users to execute full-text queries against
  SQL Server databases and text-type columns configured for them.

- **MSSQLServerADHelper** (SQL Server 2000 only)   When SQL Server
  replication is configured, the list of publications on a SQL Server
  computer can be propagated to Active Directory so that subscribers
  can more easily find these publications. The AD Helper assists in the
  propagation of publication information to Active Directory.

- **MSSQLServerOLAPService**   This is the Analysis Services multi-
  dimensional database engine to query and manage Analysis Services
  cubes, dimensions, hierarchies, and measures. Unlike the MSSQLServer
  services, there can only be one instance of MSSQLServerOLAPService.

SQL Server Databases

Once SQL Server is installed, each instance of SQL Server will contain
a number of databases used to store data. Databases in SQL Server are
roughly divided into two types: system and user. When a SQL Server
instance is installed, six databases (four system and two user databases)
will be installed by default, as shown in Table 1-2.

Database	Type	Description
master	system	Contains configuration information about the SQL Server instance, as well as information about the other databases created on the server, including file locations, error messages, and other critical server-wide information. The MSSQLServer service cannot start if it cannot open the **master** database.
model	system	Used as a model (hence the name) or template for all user-created databases for this SQL Server instance. When a new database is created, a copy of **model** is made.

Table 1-2.   SQL Server Databases Available after Installation of a SQL
Server Instance

Database	Type	Description
tempdb	system	A temporary storage area for temporary tables, sorting, and other temporary structures.
msdb	system	Used by the SQLServerAgent service to store information on jobs, alerts, operators, database backup history, replication information, and so on.
pubs	user	Sample database used for learning or problem resolution. Microsoft Product Support will frequently ask you to test a problem you have encountered against the pubs database to determine if it is a genuine SQL Server problem or a problem with the application code.
northwind	user	Sample database used for learning or problem resolution in much the same way as **pubs** is used (available in SQL Server 7 and 2000).

Table 1-2.   SQL Server Databases Available after Installation of a SQL Server Instance *(continued)*

If you have configured your instance to be a distributor in replication, a **distribution** system database will also exist, though it is not installed by default. It is not possible to drop any system database from SQL Server, except **distribution**, provided you have turned off publishing and distribution replication on that instance.

SQL Server instances typically include many other databases, each with different names designed for a specific purpose. These are all considered user databases and can be created and dropped as needed.

SQL Server Tools

Once you install SQL Server on a computer, or if you install the SQL Server client software on a workstation, you will be provided with a number of graphical (GUI) and command-line tools for the administration of SQL Server and development of SQL Server applications. The most commonly used tools include the following:

- **SQL Server Enterprise Manager**   A Microsoft Management Console (MMC) snap-in that is the primary administrative tool for one or more SQL Server instances in an organization. Enterprise Manager allows for the creation of SQL Server Groups to logically organize SQL Server instances for administration. For each instance, you can administer all aspects of SQL Server, including setting configuration options; creating and managing databases and options; configuring jobs, alerts, and operators; implementing and managing replication; and much more. Enterprise Manager also allows for the invocation of other GUI tools from its Tools menu, as well as the addition of other user-specific tools. It is also possible to share Enterprise Manager configuration and settings with others so everyone has a common administrative structure.

- **SQL Server Query Analyzer**   The primary tool for executing and analyzing Transact-SQL statements against a SQL Server instance. Developers and administrators use it to execute Transact-SQL scripts and view statistical information and execution plans of those statements. It supports multiple query windows and saving queries and results for later execution or review.

- **SQL Profiler**   GUI tool used to capture SQL Server activity for later analysis and auditing. It is useful for determining SQL statements that may be performing poorly or monitoring the activity of the server.

- **SQL Server Service Manager**   GUI tool to start, stop, and pause SQL Server services on a local or remote computer. It is automatically installed in the Notification area (bottom right, normally) of the Windows toolbar on the computer where SQL Server is installed.

- **Server Network Utility**   A GUI tool used to configure support of network protocols to be used by SQL Server to listen to requests from client applications and to communicate responses.

- **Client Network Utility**   A GUI tool used to configure communication support from the client applications with SQL Server instances. It is also used to create aliases for SQL Server named instances for clients that do not support this functionality of SQL Server 2000.

For text-based administration and execution of scripts from within Windows BAT and CMD files, a set of command-line utilities are also provided. These are outlined in Table 1-3.

Tool	Description
osql	Tool to execute Transact-SQL scripts and statements against the database. It uses ODBC to communicate with SQL Server.
isql	Similar in functionality to osql, isql uses the Sybase-compatible DB-Library data interface to communicate with SQL Server. isql is being phased out and may not be available in future releases.
bcp	The Bulk Copy Program is used to export data from and import data into SQL Server. Its functionality has been incorporated into the Bulk Insert task of DTS, but it is still used to support legacy SQL Server installations and the quick and easy export of SQL Server data to ASCII.
dtswiz	Used to invoke the DTS Import/Export Wizard from the command line.
dtsrun	Used to execute a DTS package from the command line.

Table 1-3.   SQL Server Command-line Utilities

Tool	Description
rebuildm	Used to rebuild the **master** database in the case of catastrophic loss (if there is no backup). In versions prior to SQL Server 7, you would need to run SQL Server Setup to perform this action.
isqlw	Launches a pre-configured version of SQL Server Query Analyzer to execute a specific script with or without invoking the interactive used interface.
itwiz	Invokes the Index Tuning Wizard interactively.
makepipe	Creates a named pipe for testing connectivity to SQL Server using named pipes. Not installed by default in SQL Server 2000.
readpipe	Used in conjunction with makepipe to test named pipe connectivity. Not installed by default in SQL Server 2000.
odbcping	Tests the connectivity between a client and SQL Server using ODBC. Largely replaces makepipe/readpipe in SQL Server 2000.
scm	Command-line version of Service Control Manager. Can be used to interactively stop, pause, or start SQL Server services.
sqlagent	Used to start the SQLServerAgent service from the command line.
sqldiag	Used to gather SQL Server statistics and configuration information for submission to Microsoft Product Support for resolution of critical SQL Server problems. It can also be used to document your SQL Server configuration to keep track of known good settings.
sqlftwiz	Used to execute the Full-Text Indexing Wizard interactively.
sqlmaint	Invokes the SQL Server Maintenance Wizard tasks to perform backups, reorganize data, create and update database statistics, and more.
sqlservr	Used to invoke the MSSQLServer service from the command line including starting, pausing, and stopping the service.
vswitch	Used to switch between SQL Server 6.5 and the default instance of SQL Server 7 or SQL Server 2000.

Table 1-3. SQL Server Command-line Utilities *(continued)*

SQL Server also includes a number of wizards that are accessed from the Tools | Wizards menu of Enterprise Manager though some may also be invoked interactively from the command line, as indicated previously. Most of those available in SQL Server 2000 (the majority of which are also in SQL Server 7) have names that are self-explanatory and are broken down by functionality, as shown in Table 1-4. Each wizard will be covered in greater detail in later chapters.

Category	Wizards Available
Database	Create Database Wizard Create Index Wizard Create Login Wizard Create Stored Procedure Wizard Create View Wizard Full-Text Indexing Wizard
Data Transformation Services	DTS Import Wizard DTS Export Wizard
Management	Backup Wizard Copy Database Wizard Create Alert Wizard Create Job Wizard Database Maintenance Plan Wizard Index Tuning Wizard Make Master Server Wizard Make Target Server Wizard Web Assistant Wizard
Replication	Configure Publishing and Distribution Wizard Create Publication Wizard Create Push Subscription Wizard Create Pull Subscription Wizard Disable Publishing and Distribution Wizard

Table 1-4.   Wizards Available from Enterprise Manager in SQL Server 2000

Chapter 2

Installing, Configuring, and Upgrading SQL Server

Many DBAs using SQL Server believe that installing the product is a snap. True, the actual installation process is relatively straightforward, assuming you're not performing a remote or unattended install. However, the most important part of installing SQL Server is not running the SETUP program—it is planning the installation itself and being aware of the pros and cons of the planned installation. Granted, you can change many properties of SQL Server after you install it (especially true with SQL Server 2000), but it is always a good idea to get it right the first time.

Hardware and Software Requirements

Depending on the version of SQL Server that you are installing, you will have differing hardware and software requirements. Table 2-1 provides a listing of the minimum requirements for SQL Server 7 and 2000, as well as those that I would recommend as practical for a small- to medium-sized installation. The actual hardware requirements will vary greatly depending on the number of users supported, expected size of the databases, and so on.

When installing SQL Server it is also very important to consider the operating system that you will run it on. Table 2-2 provides a matrix of the 32-bit operating systems supported by SQL Server 7 and SQL Server 2000. You may notice that Windows 2003 Server is not listed in the table, which is by design.

Component	SQL Server 7.0 Minimum	SQL Server 2000 Minimum	Recommended
Processor	Pentium 166MHz	Pentium 166MHz	Pentium II 300MHz
Memory (RAM)	32MB (NT 4.0) 64MB (Windows 2000)	64MB (Windows NT 4.0) 256MB (Windows 2000)	256MB (Windows NT 4.0) 512MB (Windows 2000)
Hard Disk Space (Not including user databases)	72MB Compact 82MB Tools Only 175MB Typical	100MB Client Tools 250MB Typical 270MB Complete	512MB
File System	NTFS or FAT	NTFS or FAT	NTFS
Browser	Internet Explorer 4.01 SP1 or later	Internet Explorer 4.01 SP1 or later	Internet Explorer 5.5 SP1 or later

Table 2-1. SQL Server Hardware Requirements

Edition	Windows 2000 Server Windows NT Server	Windows 2000 Professional Windows NT Workstation Windows XP	Windows 98 Windows ME	Windows CE
SQL Server 2000 Enterprise	Yes	No	No	No
SQL Server 2000 Standard	Yes	No	No	No
SQL Server 2000 Developer	Yes	Yes	No	No
SQL Server 2000 Personal	Yes	Yes	Yes	No
SQL Server 2000 WinCE	No	No	No	Yes
SQL Server 7 Enterprise	Yes	No	No	No
SQL Server 7 Standard	Yes	No	No	No
SQL Server 7 Developer	Yes	Yes	No	No
SQL Server 7 Desktop	Yes	Yes	Yes	No

Table 2-2.   SQL Server 32-bit Version Operating System Compatibility

If you would like to run SQL Server on Windows Server 2003 operating systems, your only choice (as of this writing) is SQL Server 2000 with Service Pack 3 or later. Future versions of SQL Server (Yukon, for example) will run on Windows Server 2003 but Microsoft will not support earlier versions of SQL Server on this operating system. For more information on SQL Server versions and support for Windows Server 2003, visit http://www.microsoft .com/sql/howtobuy/windowsnetsupport.asp.

NOTE   *Microsoft also offers a 64-bit version of SQL Server 2000 that can only be run on 64-bit versions of Windows 2000 or Windows Server 2003 operating systems.*

Preparing to Install SQL Server

Although you now have the necessary hardware and software to install SQL Server, you're not ready to run the installation program yet. During the course of the install you will be asked several questions. You may need to research some of your answers thoroughly, prior to installation, to ensure that license agreements and other elements will not be violated, and to avoid installing the software with incorrect settings. SQL Server 2000 allows you to change many, but not all, options after the software is installed. Earlier versions of SQL Server may not.

Understanding Licensing

2

Often one of the most confusing things you will have to deal with when installing any software is the licensing of the software that is being used in the enterprise. Microsoft SQL Server is no different, and to make things more interesting, depending on which version you have, more than one option may be available. To make things even more confusing, the terminology may change between versions. The valid licensing modes in SQL Server include the following:

- **Processor license** Purchased for each physical CPU (that is, an actual chip rather than any virtual processor available as a result of Intel's Hyper-Threading or similar technology) on the computer that is running SQL Server and that SQL Server is configured to use. This means that if you have a four-CPU system and configure SQL Server to only use two CPUs, you only need to purchase two Processor licenses. A Processor license allows an unlimited number of clients to connect and use SQL Server. The Processor license also allows the use of SQL Server Personal Edition or MSDE on a client workstation, in addition to accessing the server edition of SQL Server.

- **Per-Seat/Server license** Allows you to install SQL Server on a computer but does not allow clients to connect to it. It can run DTS packages that reside on the SQL Server computer, but does not allow any clients to use the databases on the SQL Server. If you would like clients to connect to it, you must purchase Client Access licenses (CAL) for each workstation that connects to the server.

- **Per-Server license** Specifies the number of simultaneous workstation connections allowed to access a specific SQL Server. If you select this mode and have ten users, you will need ten Per-Server licenses for the first SQL Server computer. The license will *belong* to the SQL Server computer and is not transferable. If you add a second SQL Server and want the same ten users to have access to the second server, you will need to purchase an additional ten Per-Server licenses, or convert to a Per-Seat/Client Access license mode. Microsoft only allows one license conversion that cannot be reversed.

- **Per Seat/Client Access license (CAL)** Allows a workstation to connect to *any* instance of SQL Server in the organization. The CAL is *assigned* to a *specific* workstation computer by the administrator who must document which workstations have a CAL and which don't. While there is no technical barrier to creating *floating* CALs, this is not permitted in the SQL Server CAL agreement and is frowned upon by Microsoft. If you are using the Processor license mode, you do not need a CAL for the

SQL Server using the Processor license mode, but you *do* need a CAL for a server using the Per-Seat/Server license mode or the Per-Server license mode. The CAL also allows the use of SQL Server Personal Edition or MSDE on a client workstation, in addition to accessing a server edition of SQL Server.

- **Developer license** Available with the Developer Edition of SQL Server, this license limits you to 15 simultaneous connections to your copy of SQL Server and cannot be upgraded. The Developer Edition is designed to allow software developers to design software that uses SQL Server. Using it in a production (that is, nondevelopment and testing) environment is prohibited.

- **Internet Connector license** Allows an unlimited number of clients to access SQL Server data through the Internet. A key stipulation of the license is that only individuals who are not employees or affiliates of the organization holding the license will access the data. Additionally, the data can only be available via a publicly accessible web site and not through an intranet or extranet. The idea behind this license was to offer a cheaper license for Internet and e-commerce sites without requiring them to purchase a CAL for each person browsing the products available. You need to purchase an Internet Connector license for each CPU of the computer running SQL Server. This license has been replaced in SQL Server 2000 by the Processor license.

As mentioned earlier, not all versions and editions of SQL Server support all license modes. Table 2-3 provides a listing of the available license modes and SQL Server editions and versions. More information is also available at the SQL Server licensing FAQ web page located at http://www.microsoft .com/sql/howtobuy/faq.asp.

License Type	SQL Server 2000	SQL Server 7.0	SQL Server 6.5
Processor	Standard, Enterprise	Not Available	Not Available
Per Seat /Server	Standard, Enterprise	Not Available	Not Available
Per Server	Not Available	Standard, Enterprise	Standard, Enterprise
Per-Seat CAL	Standard, Enterprise	Standard, Enterprise	Standard, Enterprise
Developer License	Developer Edition	Developer Edition	Developer Edition
Internet Connector	Not Available	Standard, Enterprise	Standard, Enterprise

Table 2-3. SQL Server Licenses and Valid Version/Edition Combinations

A fine point that needs to be remembered regarding licensing and SQL Server 2000 deals with multiple instance support. When purchasing any license type for SQL Server 2000 there is no restriction on the number of SQL Server instances that the license may apply to on a given computer. This means that if you purchase a Per-Processor license, you can use that license on a single computer running as many instances of SQL Server as you are technically able to. If you selected a Per-Seat/Server license for a computer, you may still run multiple instances of SQL Server but each client workstation connecting to the physical computer hosting the SQL Server instances will need a CAL.

Character Sets, Sort Orders, and Collations

One of the pitfalls of SQL Server versions prior to SQL Server 2000 was lack of thought given to the selection of a character set and sort order. This was a major problem in situations where the character set and sort order chosen did not meet the requirements of the organization, such as in a multinational corporation. The problem with versions prior to SQL Server 2000 was that once a character set and sort order had been chosen for the server, these choices applied to all databases on the server. The only way to change the selection was to reinstall SQL Server, which required that you export all the databases prior to reinstalling SQL Server and import them afterwards. This limitation was removed in SQL Server 2000 so that choices made for collation and sort rules (the new terminology) in SQL Server 2000 select the defaults for the server and system databases. In SQL Server 2000 you can select a collation and sort rule for a database at creation time, or for a character column of a table when you create the table. You still cannot, however, modify these values after the database or table has been created, but must re-create them to make the change. All in all, choosing the appropriate character set, collation, sort order, or rule at installation time is a critical decision that needs to be made wisely, taking into consideration the requirements of the databases and applications.

Let's backtrack a bit and deal with the questions that must be at the top of your head: What is a character set? Collation? Sort order or rule? Simply put, the choices made for these SQL Server options determine how data will be stored and displayed to the user, as well as which characters will be supported in string/text-based columns of SQL Server. A choice must be made because the entire world does not speak one language or use the same set of characters. Consider that if you pick up a newspaper in Moscow and another in New York on the same day, even if the paper carries the same story, the way it looks will be different because of where the newspaper is published and the language in which it is written. The alphabets used are different and must be represented differently. Even if the locations are Berlin and Paris, because different characters are used to write and read in German and French, the character sets are different.

A character set is a set of 256 (single-byte) or 65,536 (double-byte) letters, digits, and symbols that SQL Server recognizes in the character-based columns of your databases. The first 128 characters of all character sets are the same. If you use only English, and will never have a need for any other language, these first 128 characters will work for you. However, since the world today is very much intertwined, you will likely need additional characters. By choosing a character set you are telling SQL Server which characters to store in the database and display when retrieved.

A sort order or sort rule determines how character data in the database will be sorted. This is important because different parts of the world sort their alphabet differently. For example, the letter x appears very late in the English alphabet and is sorted accordingly, whereas in Spanish it actually sorts much closer to the front. Someone from Spain looking at data sorted using English sorting rules will find that the data does not make sense for them.

A second consideration regarding sorting is whether an uppercase letter (A, B, C) is treated the same or differently than a lowercase letter (a, b, c). In many cases the answer is yes, but if the data needs to be retrieved according to binary order, then the case of the letters becomes significant. Choosing a case-sensitive sort order will have an impact on the way that the data is retrieved since users will now need to make a distinction between Bob, bob, BoB, and BOB when querying the database because each is, in fact, a different string. Using a case-insensitive sort order would retrieve all four instances of Bob no matter how the query was formulated. By the way, character sensitivity, if selected, also holds true for the names of database objects. Generally, unless absolutely necessary, case-sensitive sort orders should be avoided.

In SQL Server 7 and previous releases, because you cannot change the character set and sort order after installation, and because all databases and character columns will use only one character set and sort order combination, it is important to choose the one that most closely reflects the requirements of the enterprise. As a general set of rules, consider the following:

- Choose a character set that contains the characters of the languages you will use to store your data in and that users operate in. The default in SQL Server 7 is Code Page 1252, which incorporates the characters used most often in western European languages such as English, French, and Spanish. If broader western European support is required (for example German or Dutch), Multilingual Code Page 850 is a good choice. Code Page 437 (American English) is a poor choice since it only includes English characters.

- Use the same character set for all instances of SQL Server, unless the data is geographically dispersed and used only within a specific region. In other words, no need to use Code Page 1252 in China if only users in Beijing will access the database.

2

- SQL Server 7 includes support for Unicode character data types (**nchar**, **nvarchar**), which can allow you to store data in a Unicode character set as well as a regular character set. Select and use the appropriate Unicode collation sequence for the language of the locale where the data will be read and stored.

- If you do not need to support Unicode data different from your character data, choose a Unicode collation similar to your character set choice to ensure efficient storage and reduce the possibility of clients not being able to see data in the **nchar** and **nvarchar** columns.

In SQL Server 2000, Microsoft changed the terminology and ways in which character sets and sort orders are used. Instead of committing to a character set and sort order at the time you install SQL Server and not being able to change them easily after the fact, SQL Server 2000 asks you to select a default collation and sort rule.

When choosing collations, you have the choice between Windows collations, which correspond to code pages defined by a Windows locale similar to what you would select using the Regional and Language Options in Control Panel in Windows XP, and SQL collations, which roughly correspond to the character set and sort order used in previous versions of SQL Server. The default is to use the Latin1_General code page to support the Latin alphabet, 33 western European–based locales, and dictionary order case-insensitive sorting. For the majority of the Western hemisphere, this should offer broad character support and compatibility.

Using SQL collations may be necessary in SQL Server 2000 during the transition from earlier releases and when using replication. In any situation when your application is expecting to manipulate data in versions prior to SQL Server 2000, and that data is stored in SQL Server 2000 as a result of an upgrade, you will need to designate a SQL collation to maintain backward compatibility. This also holds true if SQL Server 2000 will be participating in replication with a SQL Server 7 or 6.x server. To ensure compatibility with the default character sets and sort orders used in previous SQL Server releases, the default SQL collation used by SQL Server 2000 is SQL_Latin1_General_CP1_CI_AS, which corresponds to code page 1252, dictionary sort order, case-insensitive sort order, and General Unicode collation—the default used in SQL Server 7.

If you do not select a collation and sort rule when installing SQL Server 2000, defaults will be chosen for you and include the following:

- A Windows collation based upon the regional settings of the computer on which SQL Server 2000 is being installed

- A SQL collation that is compatible with previous releases of SQL Server according to the locale of the computer on which SQL Server 2000 is being installed

It is important that the defaults chosen by the SQL Server 2000 installation program match the reality of the databases and other SQL Servers in the organization. This minimizes any potential problems with replication and application behavior. However, it is also important to remember that the collation and sort rule selected at installation time will be applied to all of the system databases on that server (more on system databases in Chapter 4), and cannot be changed without rebuilding the system databases and any other databases created using the existing values. One of the advantages of SQL Server 2000 over previous releases is that, during database creation time, you can specify a collation and sort rule for the database being created that is different from the server default. In essence, a single SQL Server instance can host many databases, each with a different collation. It is also possible to have character-based columns within a single table that use a collation and sort rule different from the database in which it is created, although this can be hard to manage and should be avoided.

Simple rules that will make your life easier when dealing with collations and sort rules in SQL Server 2000 include the following:

- Pick a default collation for the server that matches the character data to be stored in the majority, if not all, of the databases on the server.

- When creating a new database, use the server's default collation unless the character data to be stored differs widely from the server's default, such as storing Japanese data on a SQL Server in Paris.

- Avoid specifying a collation at the column level as this may necessitate application modifications to support it, or create replication issues, especially with previous releases of SQL Server.

- Unless you have a really good reason not to use it, select the default collation presented by the SQL Server setup program—it usually works.

If, after reviewing these simple rules, you find yourself asking questions about the nature of your data or application, answer them before installing SQL Server. Rebuilding databases is not necessarily a fun job, although having the ability to install more than one instance of SQL Server on the same computer may make it easier.

Multiple Instance Support in SQL Server 2000

Prior to SQL Server 2000, when you installed SQL Server on a computer, that was it—only one copy of SQL Server was allowed on a single computer at one time. Only one copy of the MSSQLServer service could run on a single computer since the Windows registry only contained one set of configuration entries for SQL Server services. If you needed to have separate buffer pools or procedure caches to allow some databases more memory than others, you had no way of doing this except to install a copy of SQL Server on a second computer, acquire the necessary licenses, and move the databases over. With hardware advances increasing and prices dropping, the investment made in server hardware was not being well-utilized since the computer was able to do more than was being asked of it. SQL Server 2000 solved this problem by introducing support for multiple instances of SQL Server on the same computer.

SQL Server 2000 supports two types of instances on a computer—the default instance, which can be SQL Server 2000, SQL Server 7, or an earlier release; and a named instance, which is always a SQL Server 2000 instance. An instance of SQL Server is a copy of the memory structures and executables used to run all aspects of SQL Server under a different name. Support for this happens by having each named instance create and use an MSSQL$*instancename* service, which corresponds to the MSSQLServer service used by the default instance. It is possible to run up to 16 named instances on a single computer, in which case you have enabled multiple instance support.

Clients accessing a named instance must support the syntax to connect to it. When a client connects to the default SQL Server instance on a computer, it needs to only provides the *computername* to the MDAC client components and it will be connected. However, when connecting to a named instance, the format of what to connect to is *computername\ instancename*. MDAC 2.5 or later provides support for named instances; however, your applications may also need to be modified to accept the new *computername\instancename* format. In cases where the application does not support using that new format, you will need to use the Client Network Utility on the client computer to configure an alias for the named instance using the old *computername* syntax, after upgrading MDAC on the client computer to the latest release.

There are several advantages provided by multiple instances, including the following:

- Ability to carefully configure memory and other configuration settings to provide a specific level of service for databases
- SQL Server 2000 and a previous release can co-exist and operate simultaneously on the same computer during SQL Server upgrade and database migration
- Ability to create a test environment to implement changes before rolling them out onto production data
- Enhanced support for Windows Clustering and more robust active/ active cluster configurations
- Easier testing of the effect of SQL Server service packs and patches by creating a second instance and duplicate database to apply them to before rolling them out in production
- Lessening the impact of an instance crash by only having databases on the crashed instance affected while allowing others to continue
- Ability to run servers with different collations on the same computer

It is important to remember that multiple-instance support brings many benefits but can also cause problems if not implemented carefully. Specifically, monitoring of memory and CPU allocation to each instance becomes critical, and being aware of the effect of configuration changes of one instance on all the other instances will prevent problems.

SQL Server Startup Account Selection

Another choice you will be faced with is whether to have the SQL Server services startup using the Local System Account or a domain account that you have configured. Although this is relatively easy to change after installation, it is good practice to make the determination at the outset and not necessarily accept the default of starting SQL Server services with the account used to run the setup program. The choice can easily be decided by answering a simple question: Will SQL Server need to communicate with other programs or services not on the local computer? If the answer to this question is "No," you can configure SQL Server to use the Local System Account. Otherwise, you will need to have at least some of the services startup using a domain account.

In order to answer client requests for data, SQL Server only needs to deal with the local computer's hard disk, memory, and other resources handled by the Windows operating system. However, many organizations configure replication, or the ability to transfer and receive e-mail from SQL Server, or configure and use multi-server jobs. In such cases, the security context of the SQL Server services used to perform these tasks must allow them to access resources on other computers on the network. The easiest way to enable this is to start these services using a domain account.

Configure a domain account to use to start SQL Server services with the following characteristics:

- Set the options Password Never Expires and User Cannot Change Password. Asking SQL Server services to change passwords will cause the services to fail to start.

- Allow all logon hours so that SQL Server is able to authenticate and the services able to be re-started at off-peak hours in case of failure.

- Have access to resources in all domains in which services that SQL Server needs to communicate with reside. This is less of an issue in Active Directory forest configuration where all domains share transitive trust relationships, but in Windows NT domains it is important to ensure that the domain in which the startup domain account was created is trusted by computers with which SQL Server services will need to communicate.

- Specify the Logon Locally and Logon as a Service rights.

- Be a member of the Administrators group on the computer on which SQL Server is installed. This is not the same as making the domain account a member of the Domain Admins group for the domain, which should *not* be done. SQL Server services will need read/write access to the file system and registry entries.

If you decide not to make the SQL Server service startup account a member of the Administrators group on the local computer, you will need to ensure that the domain account used has appropriate read/write permissions to the file system and registry. At the file system level, the domain account must be granted full control permissions to all folders where SQL Server files are installed during the setup process, as well as any folders that will be used to store data and log files, or files used for replication.

The domain account chosen as the SQL Server services startup account must also have read/write permissions to the following registry keys:

- HKEY_LOCAL_MACHINE\Software\Microsoft\MSSQLServer (for the default instance)
- HKEY_LOCAL_MACHINE\Software\Microsoft\Microsoft SQL Server\ *instancename*
- HKEY_LOCAL_MACHINE\System\CurrentControlSet\Services\ MSSQLServer (for the default instance)
- HKEY_LOCAL_MACHINE\System\CurrentControlSet\Services\ MSSQL$*instancename*
- HKEY_LOCAL_MACHINE\Software\Microsoft\Windows NT\ Current Version\Perflib
- HKEY_LOCAL_MACHINE\Software\Clients\Mail

Because of the complexity of maintaining permissions at the registry and file system level, you will most likely configure the SQL Server services startup domain account as a member of the local Administrators group (but *not* Domain Admins).

One final point on this topic is that you have the option to choose a different startup account for each SQL Server service, though most DBAs choose to have all services startup using the same account, for simplicity's sake. In fact, you can have the core database engine (MSSQLServer service or MSSQL$*instancename*) use the Local System Account while SQL Server Agent (SQLAgent$*instancename*) uses a domain account if the MSSQLServer service does not need to communicate with other computers directly. This configuration is common when e-mail for operator notification is the major reason for a domain startup account.

Authentication Mode Selection

One of the most important security-related decisions during installation of SQL Server is the choice of an authentication mode. This selection determines how clients will be authenticated when attempting to connect to SQL Server. You have two possible choices in SQL Server 7 and 2000, and three choices in SQL Server 6.*x*. They are as follows:

- **Windows Authentication Mode**   Also known as Trusted Authentication in previous releases, this authentication mode instructs SQL Server to use the security mechanism of the Windows operating system to validate a user attempting to connect to the server. If the user successfully logs in to the operating system, then he can connect to SQL Server. SQL Server itself simply asks the OS if the user has been validated and trusts the OS to advise it properly. Windows Authentication Mode requires all clients connecting to SQL Server to have a valid Windows account.

NOTE   *How authentication modes fit into the security framework of SQL Server and SQL Server security itself are covered in detail in Chapter 3.*

- **Mixed Authentication Mode**   In situations where you have clients other than Windows that need to connect to your SQL Server databases, you will need to use Mixed Authentication so that you can manually create SQL Server logins for those users. Users connecting to SQL Server will now have the option to be authenticated by Windows (if they have a valid Windows account), or use a SQL Server login and password (if connecting from a non-trusted domain or another operating system such as Linux or Novell NetWare). Note that you will need to maintain SQL Server logins yourself to ensure that access to SQL Server is not compromised.

- **Standard Security Mode**   Prior to SQL Server 7, a third option was available which allowed you to require that all users have a valid SQL Server login and not use Windows Authentication. The benefits of doing so included the ability to separate SQL Server access administration from network user administration, which Windows Authentication Mode imposes, and more precise control over who can access the data. However, the overhead of maintaining duplicate credentials, and the annoyance experienced by users having to supply one username/password combination to access the network and a second login/password combination for SQL Server, made Standard Security less attractive and it was dropped in SQL Server 7. Besides, it was always possible to connect to SQL Server 6.*x* servers using Windows Authentication if you were a member of the local Administrators group on the SQL Server computer—a feature designed to allow access if the **SA** login password was lost or forgotten.

If you selected Mixed Authentication Mode during the setup process of SQL Server 2000, you will be asked to supply a password for the SA login. SA is the *super user* login for SQL Server and has full permissions to all aspects of the server. Select a password that is difficult to hack, but one you can remember, so you can use it if needed, but do not select a blank password (even though you are presented with the option). Prior to SQL Server 2000, the password for the **SA** login defaulted to blank (") and the setup program offered no option to change it. You would be surprised how many SQL Servers out there are running with a blank SA password, a situation which was recently exploited by a virus/worm that gave hackers access to many SQL Servers around the world. Always be sure to change the SA password to something other than blank to secure your server.

2

Networking Library Selection

You will need to choose which network libraries to enable for the server during installation. The SQL Server setup program will default to installing the Named Pipes and TCP/IP sockets network libraries for communication. This ensures broad compatibility with previous releases and the most common client implementations today. The SQL Server management tools, such as Enterprise Manager and Query Analyzer, will use TCP/IP to communicate with SQL Server 2000 instances, but also can use Named Pipes, if needed, to communicate with previous releases of SQL Server that used Named Pipes as the default. Aside from the defaults, SQL Server also supports other network libraries, as outlined in Table 2-4.

Network Library	Supports	SQL Server 2000	SQL Server 7	SQL Server 6.x
Named Pipes	Named pipes over any Microsoft protocol, including NetBEUI	Yes	Yes	Yes
TCP/IP Sockets	Any client using TCP/IP protocol including Windows, Macintosh, Unix/Linux, and so on	Yes	Yes	Yes
NWLink IPX/SPX	Novell NetWare clients using Novell client software, and any other clients running this protocol	Yes	Yes	Yes
Banyan VINES	Banyan VINES network clients or any clients using the VINES Sequenced Packet Protocol (SPP)	Yes	Yes	Yes
AppleTalk ADSP	Apple Macintosh clients using the native AppleTalk protocol (not TCP/IP)	Yes	Yes	Yes
Multiprotocol	Allows clients to use one or more protocols at the same time to communicate with SQL Server	Yes (no longer recommended)	Yes	Yes

Table 2-4. Network Library Purpose and Support in SQL Server

Network Library	Supports	SQL Server 2000	SQL Server 7	SQL Server 6.x
VIA ServerNet II SAN	Allows clients to use the virtual interface architecture of a ServerNet II storage area network (SAN) for communicate between servers or clusters of servers	Yes	No	No
VIA GigaNet SAN	Similar to ServerNet II, allows clients to use the GigaNet SAN protocol	Yes	No	No

Table 2-4. Network Library Purpose and Support in SQL Server *(continued)*

When deciding on which network libraries to use, keep the following in mind:

- The corresponding network protocol must be installed and configured on the computer hosting SQL Server, otherwise communication cannot take place. This means that if you choose AppleTalk as a SQL Server network library, make sure that you also install and configure AppleTalk in Windows.

- If you use Windows Authentication mode, you will need to install TCP/IP and/or Named Pipes for authentication to take place with domain controllers.

- If using SQL Server 2000's Secure Sockets Layer (SSL) encryption for more secure communication between clients and the server, TCP/IP must be installed.

- Multiprotocol encryption is not supported on named instances in SQL Server 2000, so the Multiprotocol library cannot be used in this case.

- Keep it simple and reduce overhead. If all computers in your network use TCP/IP and all applications can communicate with SQL Server using that protocol, don't select others because you *might* need them at some point in the future. This creates unnecessary work for Windows and SQL Server. You can always configure them later.

Installing SQL Server

Having done all your planning, you are now ready to install SQL Server onto your Windows server. You can perform the installation by running the SQL Server Setup program from a CD or network share, perform an unattended setup based upon a script, or perform a remote installation on a different server.

SQL Server Attended Installation

The most common way to install SQL Server is to insert the CD-ROM into drive and select the option to install SQL Server from the menu that is presented when Autoplay runs. If your operating system is Windows 98 or Windows NT, you should also install the SQL Server prerequisites by selecting that option from the menu. Once you choose to install SQL Server, you have three installation types to choose from—Minimum, Typical, and Custom. Many DBAs choose Custom because of greater control available in selecting the location of key files, but the Typical installation will usually suffice. Choose Custom if all you need to install are the management tools or network connectivity. You can also use Custom to modify your installation and add or remove components (which can also be accomplished from Add/Remove Programs in Windows). Choose Minimum when all you need to install is the SQL Server database engine and related components and you do not require support for full-text search or need the client tools installed. Table 2-5 provides a listing of the components that are installed by each installation type.

NOTE *You will not be able to install SQL Server 7 or 2000 until the prerequisite software is installed.*

During the course of installation you will be asked where you would like to place the SQL Server data files, log files, and program files. If available, place the database and log files on separate disks to minimize data loss in the case of disk failure, and to improve performance of the databases. When installing SQL Server, place the program files on a disk separate from the

Component	Minimum	Typical	Custom
Database server	Yes	Yes	Optional
Upgrade tools	No	Yes	Optional
Replication support	Yes	Yes	Optional
Full-text search support (SQL 7 and 2000 only)	No	Yes (SQL 2000) No (SQL 7)	Optional
Management tools	None	All	Optional
Client network connectivity	Yes	Yes	N/A
SQL Server Books Online	No	Yes	Optional
Development tools	None	Debugger	Optional
Sample code	None	None	Optional
Collation settings (SQL Server 2000 only)	Yes	Yes	Optional

Table 2-5. SQL Server Installation Types and Components Selected by Default

operating system files or paging files to minimize any performance impact. While the location of database and log files can be changed later, program files can only be moved by removing and reinstalling SQL Server, so ensure that these are placed in the best location at the outset.

If you are installing SQL Server 2000, one of the screens will ask whether you want to install a default or named instance of SQL Server. If you will be upgrading from SQL Server 6.x or 7, choosing a named instance will allow both versions to co-exist on the same computer at the same time. This can make the process of upgrading smoother since you can run SQL Server 6.x or 7 while migrating databases to the named instance, and testing the upgrade process while allowing the live system to continue. If a default instance of SQL Server 2000 already exists, you will only have the option to install a named instance. Each named instance must have a unique name on the computer, and up to 16 named instances of SQL Server 2000 are supported on a single server.

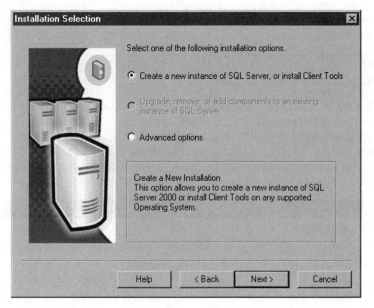

Automating SQL Server Installation

When you have many installations of SQL Server to perform, or if you have found a set of installation options that make sense across the enterprise (for example, management tools and network connectivity only, replication and full-text search support), it may be easier to run the installation unattended without any user intervention. This will ensure that each SQL Server instance has the same settings and is more likely to result in a working configuration. SQL Server accomplishes this through the use of setup initialization (ISS) files.

When you install SQL Server on a computer, a file called SETUP.ISS with the settings that you selected and installed is created and placed in the Install folder of your SQL Server installation (in SQL Server 2000 typically C:\ Program Files\Microsoft SQL Server\MSSQL\Install). Microsoft also ships additional ISS files with SQL Server 2000 and SQL Server 7 to help automate installs. ISS files contain instructions on which SQL Server components to install, and other information such as the CD key used for the installation, to whom the software is registered, installation paths, and so on. You can create your own ISS file using a text editor or, if you do not want to install SQL Server, invoke the setup program normally and on the Installation Options screen select Advanced Options and then select the Record Unattended ISS File option. Continue the setup selecting the options you want to have recorded in the ISS file. In SQL Server 7, you can also invoke the setup program from the command line using the **k=Rc** switch to indicate that you are recording an ISS file (which still works in SQL Server 2000).

ISS files are combined with a corresponding BAT file that invokes the appropriate ISS file to install SQL Server, usually without any screen display or user interaction. Table 2-6 lists the BAT and ISS files provided with SQL Server 7 and 2000.

Examination of each of the BAT files listed will indicate that they invoke the SQLSETUP.EXE file that actually performs the setup. This executable has a number of command-line switches that are worth mentioning and are listed in Table 2-7.

BAT File	ISS File	Version	Purpose
SETUP.BAT		SQL 2000 SQL 7	Used to invoke the interactive/attended setup program.
SQLINS.BAT SQL70INS.BAT	SQLINS.ISS SQL70INS.ISS	SQL2000 SQL 7	Performs a typical installation of SQL Server.
SQLCLI.BAT	SQLCLI.ISS SQL70CLI.SS	SQL 2000 SQL 7	Installs the SQL Server management tools and network connectivity only.
SQLCST.BAT SQL70CST.BAT	SQLCST.ISS SQL70CST.ISS	SQL 2000 SQL 7	Performs a custom installation selecting all components.
SMSSQINS.BAT SMSCLI.BAT	SQLSMS.ISS	SQL 2000	Used in conjunction with SMSSQL.PDF to perform an unattended installation of SQL Server or the management tools using Systems Management Server 1.2 or later.
SQLREM.BAT	SQLREM.ISS	SQL 2000	Removes SQL Server 2000.

Table 2-6. Unattended Installation BAT and ISS Files and Their Uses

Switch	Purpose
-s	Runs in silent mode without any user input or display.
-f1 *<filename>*	Indicates the path and name of the ISS file to use.
-SMS	Used with **start/wait** to indicate that an SMS install is taking place and not to return control to the BAT file until SQLSETUP completes.
k=Rc	Invokes an interactive setup and records actions to create the ISS file specified by **-f1** (officially SQL Server 7 only).

Table 2-7.   SETUPSQL.EXE Command-Line Switches

When performing an unattended installation, it is very important to edit the ISS file to specify the CD key to be used and the organization that the software is registered to. Furthermore, if you created the ISS file yourself using either the **k=Rc** switch or the RECORD Unattended ISS File option during interactive setup, verify that the paths specified in the ISS file exist on the target system.

Remote Installation of SQL Server

SQL Server setup also allows you to install the software on a computer other than the one on which you are running the setup program. Remote installation requires that the user account you are using to run SQL Server setup remotely be a member of the local Administrators group on the target computer and that account have read access to the location of the setup files. The setup files, in this scenario, should be located on a network share or on the CD-ROM drive of the computer from which you are invoking the setup program so that any potential problems accessing them are avoided.

Remote installation of SQL Server is performed by combining the recording of an ISS file with an unattended installation. The actual steps taken by SQL Server setup are as follows:

1. Record the options selected interactively for the remote installation in a SETUP.ISS file.

2. Invoke the remote setup process.

3. The remote setup process starts a remote service as the user specified to perform the installation.

4. The remote setup process copies the necessary setup files to the Admin$ share of the target computer from the source location.

5. The remote setup process runs an unattended installation of SQL Server using the SETUP.ISS file created in step 1.

Remote installation has been a feature of SQL Server for some time. In SQL Server 2000, you have the option to specify the path where SQL Server files are to be installed, whereas in previous releases this was not available. SQL Server remote installation used to always install SQL Server in the default path (typically C:\MSSQL).

Testing the Installation

Determining if SQL Server is up and running after it is installed is relatively straightforward. After ensuring that all SQL Server services have started (especially MSSQLServer service, or the named instance you installed), invoke Query Analyzer from the computer where you installed SQL Server, connect as SA or an Administrator if using Windows Authentication, and issue the following SQL statement:

```
select * from pubs..authors
```

If the number of rows returned is 23 and you do not receive an error, your SQL Server installation is up and running. Repeat the same test from a remote computer to test network connectivity and look for the same result—23 rows.

Upgrading to SQL Server 2000

Between SQL Server 6.5 and SQL Server 7, Microsoft made a fundamental change in the architecture of the product, including changing the size of the minimum storage unit (the data page) from 2K to 8K. This necessitated a rather involved upgrade process that typically required having SQL Server 6.5 and 7 co-exist on the same computer and then running an Upgrade Wizard that exported data from SQL Server 6.5 to temporary files, and then imported them into SQL Server 7. When upgrading from SQL Server 6.5 to SQL Server 2000, the process you use can be the same as when upgrading to SQL Server 7, or you can have SQL Server 6.5 and 2000 co-exist by installing a named instance of SQL Server 2000 and then migrating the databases over. This last method is preferred.

When upgrading from SQL Server 7 to SQL Server 2000, you can also install a named instance and then use the Copy Database Wizard to migrate the SQL Server 7 databases to the SQL Server 2000 named instance in a phased approach. A second option is to upgrade the SQL Server 7 default instance in-place. Since the architecture of SQL Server 7 and 2000 is close, this upgrade is relatively straightforward. However, it is always a good idea before performing any upgrade to protect yourself and your data in case of anomalies by performing the following steps:

1. Back up all system and user databases.

2. Ensure no users are accessing the databases.

3. Disable all jobs and alerts on the server to be upgraded.

4. Document the current configuration of SQL Server.

5. Back up all system and user databases. (Yes, again!!)

Not all versions of SQL Server can be upgraded to SQL Server 2000, nor can they all coexist at the same time. Some things to consider include the following:

- The default instance of SQL Server can be either SQL Server 6.5, SQL Server 7, or SQL Server 2000.

- If SQL Server 7 is the default instance and you elect to install SQL Server 2000 as the default instance on the same server, SQL Server 7 will be automatically upgraded to SQL Server 2000.

- The default instance can only run one version of SQL Server at one time. In other words, if you have SQL Server 6.5 and SQL Server 2000 installed as the default instance, only one version will be active at any given time.

- You can switch between SQL Server 6.5 and 7/2000 by using the SQL Server Switch program.

- A SQL Server 2000 named instance can coexist with either a SQL Server 7 or SQL Server 6.5 (Service Pack 5 or later) default instance.

- If SQL Server 2000 is installed as a named instance with a SQL Server 7 default instance, the client tools on the computer will be upgraded to the SQL Server 2000 version for all instances.

Generally, if you have the option to install a named instance for upgrading, and the hardware will support this, do so. The ability to gradually upgrade and test the upgrade before committing to it is worth it every time.

Troubleshooting SQL Server Installation

As much as Microsoft tries to minimize any pain during installation of SQL Server, they cannot test for every eventuality. Problems may occur, so knowing how to diagnose and fix problems is important. Diagnosing problems can be easy if you follow some simple rules:

1. Read the error messages provided by the SQL Server setup program. Record them if the problem does not appear to be obvious.

2. Verify that SQL Server services are up and running using the Computer Management or Services MMC consoles in Windows 2000, or Control Panel/Services in Windows NT.

3. Review the log files for any further information. Log files used by SQL Server during setup include the following:

   - **SQLSTP.LOG**   Located in C:\WINNT, this file is a record of the actions that took place during installation. The end of the file could indicate what part of the process failed.

   - **Windows Application Log**   SQL Server records important events during operation in this log. Use Event Viewer to review events with a source of MSSQLServer or MSSQL$*instancename.*

   - **SQL Server Error Log**   All errors and warnings that occur while SQL Server and SQL Server Agent are running are placed in the SQL Server error log located in the LOG folder that is in the folder where you installed SQL Server. The most current log is always called ERRORLOG and older logs will have an incremental number appended to the filename (ERRORLOG.1, ERRORLOG.2, the highest number log being the oldest—in this example, ERRORLOG.2 would be the oldest log).

   Messages provided by SQL Server logs are generally to the point indicating exactly where the problem lies. Always review the message and correct the problem that is indicated instead of reinterpreting the message presented. If, after correcting the specific problem indicated in the error message, you still have issues, investigate further to determine the underlying cause. If you have several messages in a row, start with the first error and correct it, since this may correct errors that follow—the domino effect often works on both the fault and resolution.

4. Check with SQL Server's documentation help file, SQL Server Books Online, for information on the error received.

5. Check the Microsoft Support Knowledgebase for any information on the problem. You can search the knowledgebase by navigating to http://support.microsoft.com and selecting the Search Our Database of Support Articles link.

Some of the more common problems that may be encountered while installing SQL Server, as well as their likely solutions, are listed in Table 2-8.

If you still are unable to resolve the problem, search the knowledgebase again (step 5) or consult the Microsoft SQL Server public Usenet newsgroups (microsoft.public.sqlserver*) for peer assistance. If you still cannot resolve the problem, contact Microsoft Product Support Services for your region.

Problem	Likely Cause	Solution
SQL Server services do not start.	SQL Server startup account cannot be authenticated by a domain controller.	Confirm network communications to a domain controller. Configure SQL Server to use the Local System Account.
The following message appears in the event log: Error 1069: The service did not start due to a logon failure.	The password for the SQL Server startup domain account is not valid. The password has expired. The password has been configured to be changed at the next logon. The domain account has not been granted the Logon as a service right. The account may not have permissions to log on to the computer.	Change the password for the service startup account in the Services MMC snap-in or Control Panel/Services. Configure the password to never expire. Clear the User Must Change Password at Next Logon dialog box. Modify the Domain Security Policy or the Local Security Policy to grant the Logon as a service right. Remove any workstation restrictions on the domain account.
SQL Server service does not start.	SQL Server registry entries may be corrupt.	Rerun Setup and select Registry Rebuild under Advanced Options in SQL Server 2000 to rebuild the registry. For SQL Server 7, run the **regrebld** utility.
SQL Server Agent does not start.	The startup domain account for SQL Server Agent does not have permission to access SQL Server.	Add the domain account used to start SQL Server Agent to the local Administrators group. Grant the domain account the **sysadmin** role on SQL Server.
Clients cannot connect to SQL Server.	SQL Server service has not been started. Client and server network libraries do not match. Client and/or server do not have the underlying operating system network protocol installed or configured. The client does not have permissions to access the SQL Server.	Start SQL Server services. Verify the network libraries on the client and server using the Client Network Utility and Server Network Utility, respectively. Install and configure the appropriate network protocols on the client and server. Use an account that has the appropriate permissions or grant the user permissions.

Table 2-8.   Common SQL Server Installation Problems, Causes, and Solutions

Applying SQL Server Service Packs

As we all know, software is developed by humans and, unlike Commander Data in *Star Trek: The Next Generation*, humans make mistakes. This is why we have service packs for software, including SQL Server. Before installing a service pack, you should always take precautions against data loss by backing up all databases at least once. Applying a service pack is akin to running the setup program and will in fact appear similar and allow you to create ISS files for unattended and remote installs. However, service packs may change the behavior of SQL Server to correct problems (for example, a bug that is fixed in a service pack may actually have been a feature your application was relying on) so they should always be tested before being put into production.

One way to test a service pack in SQL Server 2000 is to install a named instance and use the Copy Database Wizard to duplicate your existing environment. You can then apply the service pack on the new named instance and test the results before applying it in production. One important thing to remember is that the application of a service pack to any named instance will automatically update the management and client tools on the server since there is ever only one copy of these installed.

If you want to test a service pack on releases of SQL Server prior to 2000, you will need to install SQL Server on another computer and use a backup and restore to duplicate the databases, install the service pack, and perform the tests.

Completing Installation and Upgrade

The installation and upgrade of SQL Server is typically one of the easier aspects of working with the product and generally is painless. To minimize the likelihood of any problems creeping in, always plan all aspects of your installation and have handy the answers for the questions that the setup program will ask. If you need to install multiple instances of SQL Server, you can create an ISS file for unattended installation or use Systems Management Server 1.2. If you do encounter problems, review the logs and check the Knowledgebase on Microsoft's web site for any information on the problem.

Chapter 3

SQL Server Security

In recent years, the question of secure data and security in general has become more important. With SQL Server potentially being a repository of sensitive information such as financial data, electronic commerce data including credit cards, and other information vital to an organization, it is vitally important that proper security be implemented. A key step in this goal is to understand how security is implemented in SQL Server.

SQL Server Security Model

SQL Server's security model consists of the following four key concepts:

- **Login**   A login is an account created at the SQL Server level to allow an individual user or Windows group to connect to SQL Server. The way a login is authenticated depends upon the authentication mode configured for the SQL Server. SQL Server 7 and 2000 support two authentication modes (Windows Authentication Mode and Mixed Authentication Mode) while SQL Server 6.x supports three authentication modes (Windows/ Trusted Authentication Mode, Mixed Authentication Mode, and SQL Server/Standard Mode). Logins are stored in the **sysxlogins** table of the **master** database in SQL Server 7 and 2000, or the **syslogins** table of the **master** database in SQL Server 6.x.

- **User**   A user is created within a database on a SQL Server to allow a login to access data in the database, provided permissions are granted to allow this. While a login allows an individual to connect to SQL Server, in order for the individual to get access to data in a database, a user is required. Database users are stored in the **sysusers** table of the database in which they are defined.

- **Role**   A role is a container for permissions. Roles can be created at the SQL Server or database level. All permissions that have been granted to the role are granted to the login or user with which the role has been associated. Essentially, a role is a mechanism that can be used to simplify security administration in SQL Server. Roles are stored in the **sysusers** table of the database in which they are defined. Server roles are stored in the **sysusers** table of the **master** database.

- **Permissions**   Permissions are granted to allow a user or role to perform specific actions (statement permissions) or to access database objects (object permissions). They can be granted to a user or a role. SQL Server 7 and SQL Server 2000 let you grant **allow** permissions that let a user

37

perform an action or **deny** permissions that explicitly prevent a user from performing an action or accessing an object. Permissions are stored in the **sysprotects** table of the database where the objects they are controlling access to are created.

In SQL Server 6.*x* and earlier releases, SQL Server did not have support for roles or **deny** permissions. In place of roles, SQL Server 6.*x* supported groups. Unlike roles, users were granted membership in a group and permissions could be granted to the group. All users also belonged to a special group called PUBLIC, which is now called the PUBLIC role. Users could belong to one, and only one, additional group. Furthermore, permissions could only be granted or revoked, but there was no explicit denial of permissions—a somewhat simpler model for managing permissions.

Configuring SQL Server Authentication Modes

The first step in ensuring you have a proper security configuration for your SQL Server is to choose an authentication mode for login processing. Some of this information was covered in the previous chapter, since you need to specify the authentication mode at installation time. Authentication modes include the following:

- **Windows Authentication Mode**   SQL Server uses the security mechanism of the Windows operating system to validate a user attempting to connect to the server. Windows Authentication Mode requires all clients connecting to SQL Server to have a valid Windows account.

- **Mixed Authentication Mode**   When Mixed Authentication Mode is configured, users connecting to SQL Server have the option to be authenticated by Windows (if they have a valid Windows account), or use a SQL Server login and password (if connecting from a non-trusted domain or another operating system such as Linux or Novell NetWare). The DBA will need to create and maintain SQL Server logins.

- **Standard Security Mode**   Available in SQL Server 6.*x* or earlier, it requires that all users have a valid SQL Server login and does not allow the use of Windows Authentication.

Should you need to change the SQL Server authentication mode after you have installed SQL Server, the easiest way is to invoke SQL Enterprise Manager, connect to SQL Server, right-click on the SQL Server and select Properties. On the resulting Properties dialog box, select the Security tab and select the authentication mode you wish to use, as shown in Figure 3-1. You will need to stop and restart the MSSQLServer service or the MSSQL$*instancename* service for which you are changing the authentication mode.

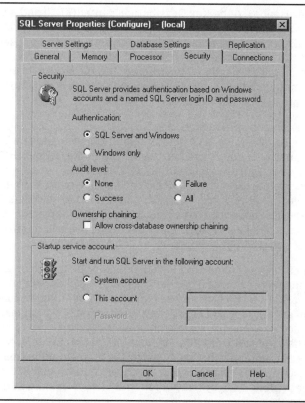

3

Figure 3-1. You can change the authentication mode using Enterprise
Manager by modifying the properties of the SQL Server
instance.

SQL Server 2000 and Kerberos

When SQL Server 2000 is operating in an Active Directory domain
environment, it may be possible for client authentication to make use
of the Kerberos authentication protocol available in Windows 2000 and
later releases. Kerberos provides a number of advantages over the standard
NT LAN Manager (NTLM) authentication mechanism for clients in Windows
Authentication Mode. These include a more secure protocol minimizing the
likelihood of someone impersonating a client to the server, as well as the
ability for mutual authentication, impersonation, and delegation.

Kerberos authentication in Windows 2000 and later releases uses tickets for
authentication. An Active Directory user is issued a ticket granting ticket
(TGT) when he logs on. The TGT includes encrypted information about the
user's identity. When the user wants to gain access to data on a SQL Server,

the TGT is presented to the Key Distribution Center (KDC) and a request for a session ticket for the appropriate service (SQL Server, in this case) is made. The KDC issues a session ticket for the service and the user presents the ticket to the service and is then granted access. The user may also request mutual authentication to guarantee that the service is in fact what he is requesting, in which case the service (SQL Server) responds with encrypted data identifying itself.

In order for Kerberos authentication to be used, both the client and server must be running Windows 2000 or later operating systems. The TCP/IP protocol and network library are also required on both. Also, SQL Server must properly configure a Service Principal Name (SPN) when it starts, which it does automatically when using the Local System Account, to start the SQL Server services. If a domain account is used to start SQL Server, additional settings need to be configured for the SQL Server service startup account and the computer running SQL Server. These will be covered in the following section dealing with impersonation and delegation.

In some cases, clients connecting to SQL Server will execute operating system commands or access other services on the SQL Server computer or on the network. To ensure that these actions are not automatically granted the elevated security level of SQL Server itself, impersonation takes place. SQL Server accesses the file system or another service using the security context of the connected user thereby providing appropriate access permissions neither above nor below what the user would normally have. The only exception to this rule is that any user connected to SQL Server that has been granted the **sysadmin** role will always operate in the security context of the SQL Server service itself.

When Kerberos is used for authentication, SQL Server 2000 also supports delegation—the ability to connect to multiple SQL Servers while always retaining the login credentials of the original Windows user. This ensures that when an individual accesses one SQL Server and from there connects to other linked servers or remote data sources, permissions are always at the level that the user should have—no higher and no lower. In order for delegation to work, the requirements for Kerberos authentication must be met and the following must be true:

- The user's Active Directory account must have the "Account is sensitive and cannot be delegated" option enabled, as shown in Figure 3-2.

- The Active Directory domain account used to start the SQL Server service must have the "Account is trusted for delegation" option enabled, which is on the Account tab of the Properties dialog box of the user in Active Directory Users and Computers. (See Figure 3-2.)

- The Active Directory computer account where SQL Server is running must have the "Trust computer for delegation" option enabled, which is located on the General tab of the Properties dialog box for the computer in Active Directory Users and Computers. (See Figure 3-3.)

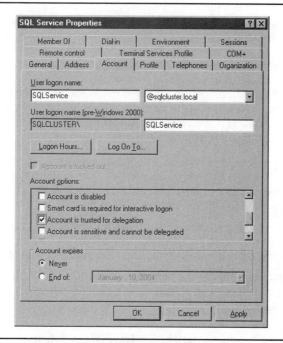

3

Figure 3-2. Use Active Directory Users and Computers to modify user accounts to allow delegation.

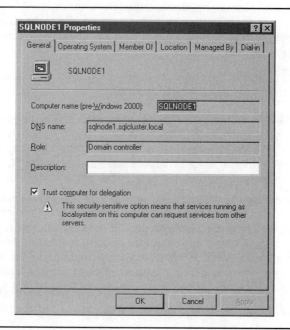

Figure 3-3. Use Active Directory Users and Computers to modify the SQL Server computer account to allow delegation.

Managing SQL Server Logins

Once you have configured an authentication mode, you will need to create logins for individuals or applications connecting to your SQL Server. If using Windows or Mixed Authentication Mode, logins can be mapped to Windows users or groups. If some of these connections will be from non-Windows computers, or if your SQL Server computer is not part of a domain, you will need to create logins for authentication by SQL Server.

When creating a login, it is important to remember the following restrictions:

- Login names cannot exceed 128 characters in SQL Server 7 and 2000, or 30 characters in SQL Server 6.*x*.

- Login names using Windows Authentication Mode cannot be specified using the Active Directory User Principal Name (UPN) format of *user@domain.com* but only using the *DOMAIN\account* format.

- SQL Server authenticated logins cannot contain a backslash, be NULL or an empty string (''), or be a reserved (**SA,** for example) or existing login account.

Managing Logins with Enterprise Manager

The easiest way to add or modify logins is to invoke SQL Enterprise Manager and navigate to the Security folder and then click on Logins. A list of current logins will appear. Right-click anywhere in the details (right-hand) pane, or on Logins itself, to display a dialog box that will allow you to create a login, as shown in Figure 3-4.

When you bring up the dialog box to create a login, you will need to specify a number of things, including the following:

- **Name**   A unique name (not case sensitive) for the login on this SQL Server. If you are using SQL Server 2000, you will be able to click the ... button to get a list of domains and users from which you can add logins. These will be available for Windows authentication. For SQL Server authentication you will need to type in the name of the login manually.

- **Authentication**   Specify whether you will be using Windows Authentication Mode or SQL Server authentication. If you selected a Windows user or group, this will default to Windows Authentication Mode with the name of the computer or domain filled in. For SQL Server authentication you will need to type in an initial password for the login, which will be confirmed before saving the login.

  Windows Authentication Mode also allows you to specify whether to explicitly grant or deny a login for a Windows user or a group—the

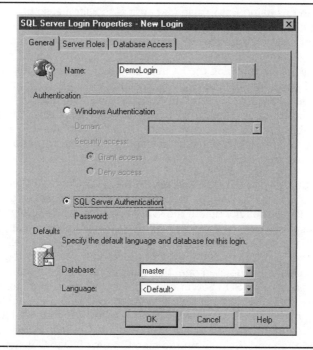

Figure 3-4. Right-click on Logins in Enterprise Manager to create a new login.

default is to grant but you can also explicitly forbid a user or group to connect to SQL Server by denying access. It is generally not a good idea to explicitly deny a Windows user or group login access to SQL Server since the deny privilege always wins. If you grant a Windows account login belonging to a user access to SQL Server and then deny access to a group that user is a member of, the Windows user will not be able to connect to SQL Server since the deny privilege *always* becomes the effective privilege.

- **Default database and language** When a login successfully authenticates with SQL Server and is granted access, it will be connected to the default database unless the connection request specifically indicates a database. This does not mean that the login will be able to access the database or its data—a user or role is needed for that to happen. The default database simply specifies which database it will attempt to connect to, by default. The **master** database is the default database, unless you specify another database.

The default language specifies in which language SQL Server error and other messages will be returned to the client. If none is specified, the default language for the server based upon installation settings is used.

Removing logins using Enterprise Manager is too simple, so be sure it is what you need to do. Click on the login and then press DELETE on your keyboard, or right-click and select Delete to start the deletion process. Enterprise Manager will present a warning that deleting a login will delete any database users to which the login is mapped, which can result in loss of access. If any of the database users to which the login is mapped own objects (tables, views, procedures, and so on), those will need to be dropped before the login can be deleted, or the object ownership changed using the **sp_changeobjectowner** stored procedure. This last safeguard is to prevent a DBA from accidentally causing catastrophic data loss by the touch of a key or mouse click.

An important thing to remember when deleting Windows Authentication Mode logins is that deleting the mapping of a Windows user or group to a SQL Server login does *not* delete the Windows account. Similarly, deleting a Windows user or group in Windows will *not* delete the login mapping—you will need to manually delete it from SQL Server. If you accidentally delete a Windows user or group in Windows and then add a new user or group with the same name as the deleted one, the mapping will not automatically be reestablished because SQL Server keeps track of the Security Identifier (SID) for the Windows account that is mapped. Deleting a Windows account and adding one with the same name creates a new account which changes the SID. The original SID can never be re-created. Therefore, you must remove and then add the mapping to map the new SID to SQL Server.

System Stored Procedures for Managing Logins

Another way to create logins is through the use of system stored procedures. In SQL Server 7 and 2000 there are five system stored procedures that can be used, based upon the type of login. They include **sp_grantlogin, sp_revokelogin, sp_denylogin, sp_addlogin,** and **sp_droplogin**. The first three of these are used with logins using Windows Authentication Mode; the last two are used for logins using SQL Server authentication. There is also the **sp_password** system stored procedure that can be used to change the password of a SQL Server authenticated login.

The syntax for stored procedures used to manage Windows Authentication Mode logins is as follows:

```
sp_grantlogin [ @loginame =] 'login'

sp_revokelogin [ @loginame = ] 'login'

sp_denylogin [ @loginame = ] 'login'
```

In each of the above cases, *login* must be a Windows user or group in a domain accessible via trust relationships to the SQL Server computer, or be a local user or group.

sp_grantlogin and **sp_denylogin** require that the Windows user or group must not already be mapped to a login.

sp_revokelogin requires that the login already exist so that it can be removed.

The syntax for the stored procedure used to create SQL Server authentication logins is as follows:

```
sp_addlogin [ @loginame = ] 'login'
    [ , [ @passwd = ] 'password' ]
    [ , [ @defdb = ] 'database' ]
    [ , [ @deflanguage = ] 'language' ]
    [ , [ @sid = ] sid ]
    [ , [ @encryptopt = ] 'encryption_option' ]
```

As you can see, the password is optional (blank passwords are allowed) but highly recommended for security reasons. If any option is not specified, it will default to whatever the installation settings are, except for **@defdb** which always defaults to **master**. **@sid** indicates that you want to explicitly specify a SID for the login. A SID is assigned by default and should always be used instead of creating one explicitly. **@encryptopt** indicates whether the password shall be encrypted (the default is **NULL**), is already encrypted and should not be re-encrypted (**skip_encryption**), or is being transferred from a previous version of SQL Server and should be left alone to allow the server upgrade to succeed (**skip_encryption_old**).

The syntax for the stored procedure used to drop SQL Server authentication logins is as follows:

```
sp_droplogin [ @loginame = ] 'login'
```

For SQL Server logins, you may also have to change the password for the login. The syntax for the stored procedure to change the password is the following:

```
sp_password [ [ @old = ] 'old_password' , ]
    { [ @new =] 'new_password' }
    [ , [ @loginame = ] 'login' ]
```

If you invoke **sp_password** with only the old and new password as parameters, this will change the password for the current login if it is a SQL Server authenticated login (otherwise it will generate an error). An example of changing the current login's password from password to newpass is as follows:

```
sp_password 'password', 'newpass'
```

All of the stored procedures return a status code of 0 for success and 1 for failure.

Default Logins

When you install SQL Server 7 or 2000, two logins are automatically created and granted full permissions on the SQL Server. They are as follows:

- **BUILTIN\Administrators**   Corresponds to the Administrators local group of the computer on which SQL Server is installed. Anyone that is a member of this special Windows group can manage your SQL Server, though these permissions can be changed or the login deleted.

- **SA**   Corresponds to the special historical SQL Server login with full permissions. **SA** can be used to connect in Mixed Authentication Mode and should always have a password since the full permissions granted to it cannot be removed, nor can the login.

It is generally considered good practice to assign a password to the **SA** login no matter which authentication mode is used. Secondly, if you do not want members of the local Administrators group to have full access to SQL Server, either remove permissions granted to the login or deny the login access. If denying access, make sure you create another login mapping to an appropriate Windows group you create (SQLAdmins, for example) and grant it the same privileges held by **SA** or the **BUILTIN\Administrators** login.

Getting Information on Logins

If you need to get a list of logins or even change the password for an existing SQL Server authenticated login, the best tool to use is Enterprise Manager. A second option is the **sp_helplogins** system stored procedure, which has the following syntax:

```
sp_helplogins [ [ @LoginNamePattern = ] 'login' ]
```

If you do not provide a value for the *@LoginNamePattern* parameter, you will get a listing of all logins on the server, as well as databases they have been granted access to, and the username or role they are mapped to in each database.

A final method is to query the **sysxlogins** (**syslogins** in SQL Server 6.*x*) table of the **master** database directly, though the information here will not be formatted in a particularly useful way and may change between SQL Server versions. For this reason, Microsoft does not recommend querying system tables directly.

Database Access with Users and Roles

Once a login has been created, in order for the login to gain access to data on the SQL Server, it must be assigned to a user or role within a database, or be associated with a server role to create a database or perform other privileged operations. Each login that you want to have access to a database must be assigned to a database user, though not all logins need to be assigned to all databases.

Assigning Logins to Database Users

Assigning a login to a user account can be done through Enterprise Manager on the properties dialog box for the login by selecting the Database Access tab and then enabling the check boxes in the Permit column for the databases you want the user to be able to access, as shown in Figure 3-5. You must also provide a database username to which the login should be mapped, which can be different than the login name itself (though this may create some confusion when managing the login later). The database username must be unique in the database. You can also grant the login a database role, either fixed or user-defined, by selecting the check box next to the role name.

To remove a login from a database using Enterprise Manager, or to remove a role from a login, simply deselect the appropriate check box and click OK to save your changes. Before doing so, ensure that the actions you are taking are the ones you desire, as there is no going back—all changes are immediate.

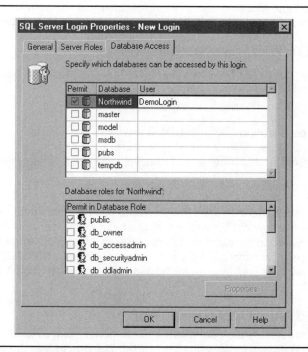

Figure 3-5.   A login can be mapped to database users by modifying its properties.

Another method of assigning logins to database users is to make use of the **sp_grantdbaccess** system stored procedure. The syntax is as follows:

```
sp_grantdbaccess [@loginame =] 'login'
    [,[@name_in_db =] 'name_in_db' [OUTPUT]]
```

This system stored procedure is executed within the context of the database to which the user is currently connected, so be sure that you issue a "use *dbname*" command to change the execution context to the database in which you want to create the login assignment. When executing the procedure, you must specify the name of the login to map to a database user, and may optionally specify a different name by providing a value for the *@name_in_db* parameter, which can also be an OUTPUT parameter returning the value entered. A return code of 0 indicates success and 1 indicates failure when executing the procedure.

Two other system stored procedures exist for managing database users, which must also be executed while connected to the database in which you wish to affect a change. These include **sp_change_users_login** and **sp_revokedbaccess**.

The **sp_change_users_login** system stored procedure allows you to correct any problems with a mapping between a login and a database user when using the **Auto_Fix** action. It also allows you to re-map a database user from an old login to a new one without losing any of the permissions assigned to the user in the database when using the **Update_One** action and to list database users and their corresponding SIDs when using the **Report** action. The syntax is as follows:

```
sp_change_users_login [ @Action = ] 'action'
    [ , [ @UserNamePattern = ] 'user' ]
    [ , [ @LoginName = ] 'login' ]
```

To disassociate a login from a database user, you can use the **sp_revokedbaccess** system stored procedure. You need to pass it the name of the database user to remove, as in the following syntax:

```
sp_revokedbaccess [ @name_in_db = ] 'name'
```

It is not possible to remove the link between a login and a database user if the database user owns objects in the database, unless those objects have first been moved to another owner using the **sp_changeobjectowner** system stored procedure. You cannot remove the **dbo** or **INFORMATION_ SCHEMA** database user from any database or the **guest** user from the **master** and **tempdb** databases.

DBO and Guest Database Users

When you create any new database, that database, as well as all system databases, will have at least one user—**dbo**. The **dbo** user is the owner of the database and cannot be removed. This user is also the granted the **db_owner** fixed database role which provides for all privileges in the database, and this role cannot be revoked from **dbo**. The **dbo** user is special because anyone that is granted the **db_owner** database role will act like **dbo** and any objects that someone granted the **db_owner** role will be owned by **dbo**. In fact, this is the preferred method for ensuring that when permissions are assigned, you do not get any broken ownership chains (discussed in Chapter 5).

Another user that exists in the **master, msdb, pubs, Northwind,** and **tempdb** databases initially, and can be created in any database on the SQL Server, is **guest**. The **guest** user is handy when you want to grant a basic set of permissions in a specific database for any login that is defined on the SQL Server, but do not necessarily want to be troubled with managing too many login assignments on a regular basis. This is useful when the database content is mostly for general consumption and all you want to do is assign permissions to the PUBLIC role that **guest** will automatically be granted. Creating a **guest** user in a database should be done with significant forethought as it may open up data to a large number of individuals, especially if you are mapping SQL Server logins to Windows groups. When a **guest** user is created in a database, anyone with a SQL Server login has access to at least some data in the database.

Getting Information on Database Users

SQL Enterprise Manager provides the easiest interface to view information about users in a database. To display the list of users in a database, navigate in the left pane to the Databases folder of the SQL Server you are managing and expand the name of the database, then click on the Users object, as shown in Figure 3-6. Double-clicking on any user will bring up a dialog box that displays a list of the database roles that can be, or are, assigned to the user, as well as a method to view the permissions assigned to the user.

SQL Server also provides a system stored procedure to list all users in the database, or to provide details on a specific user—**sp_helpuser**. The syntax is as follows:

```
sp_helpuser [ [ @name_in_db = ] 'security_account' ]
```

If you do not provide a security account, a list of all database users in the current database will be returned along with their associated logins and default database information. Providing a username will return the same details about the user specified.

Roles in SQL Server

Roles are a very important mechanism for managing security in SQL Server 7 or later. Roles are best described as containers for permissions. When created, a role has no default permissions, nor is it automatically assigned to users or other roles. Similar to a pop bottle, which is a container for a refreshing beverage, a role is a container for permissions. Only once the bottle has pop, or the role has been assigned permissions, does its true

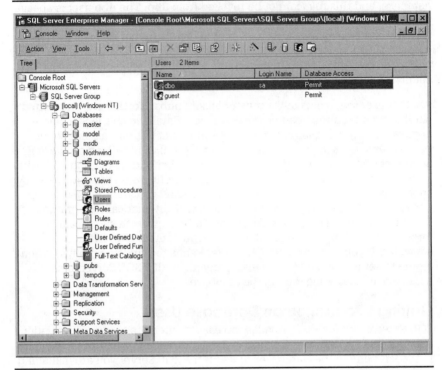

Figure 3-6. Double-click on a user in Enterprise Manager to get additional information.

value begin to be realized. You can give a bottle of pop to a friend to quench her thirst, and you can grant a role to a user (or another role) to provide the user with all of the permissions that have been granted to that role.

SQL Server has four different role types that are either automatically or manually created. These include the following:

- **Fixed server roles** Fixed server roles are created in the **master** database and stored in the **sysxlogins** table of that database. They are used to grant server-wide permissions to logins and have been granted one or more privileges that will affect the server as a whole.

- **Fixed database roles** These roles are automatically created in each database on SQL Server and deal with permissions that apply to the database and/or all objects within the database. They are stored in the **sysusers** table of the database.

- **User-defined database roles** These are roles created by database users and may be assigned permissions on the database as a whole, or on objects within the database. Their definition is also stored in the **sysusers** table. They can be assigned to users or other roles. The user to whom they have been assigned is granted all of the permissions of the role. If a user has been associated with multiple roles, the combination of all permissions granted to (and denied from) all roles is inherited by the user.

- **Application roles** Application roles are similar to user-defined database roles except that the permissions granted them are only available to a user once the role has been activated. Application roles are typically used when you want to give the user a higher set of permissions when connecting to a database using a front-end client application, and a lower set of permissions when using Query Analyzer or another ad-hoc tool. They can also be used to increase the level of functionality for a user while in an application when necessary to perform an extraordinary task.

SQL Server 6.5 and earlier releases used the concept of groups instead of roles for management of permissions for multiple users. Whereas in SQL Server 7 and later in which users can be granted more than one role, in SQL Server 6.x, users can be a member of only one group in addition to the PUBLIC group that all users belonged to.

Fixed Server Roles

Out of the box, SQL Server 7 and later versions have a number of pre-defined fixed server roles. The list of fixed server roles, description of allowed actions, who may grant the role, and default members are listed in Table 3-1.

Role	Allowed Actions	Who Can Grant	Default Members
sysadmin	All actions on SQL Server; all fixed server role privileges.	sysadmin	BUILTIN\ Administrators **SA**
dbcreator	Create, alter, and drop any database.	sysadmin dbcreator	
diskadmin	Manage disk files (database files, log files, and so on).	sysadmin diskadmin	
processadmin	Manage SQL Server processes (for example, kill).	sysadmin processadmin	
serveradmin	Execute sp_configure, RECONFIGURE, and other commands to change server-wide settings.	sysadmin serveradmin	
setupadmin	Install and configure replication.	sysadmin setupadmin	
securityadmin	Create, modify, audit, and drop SQL Server logins.	sysadmin securityadmin	
bulkadmin	Issue BULK INSERT statements.	sysadmin bulkadmin	

Table 3-1. Fixed Server Roles in SQL Server 2000

Once again, using Enterprise Manager you can assign a fixed server role to any login in the database, provided you have been assigned the **sysadmin** role or the role you want to assign to another login. If you display the properties dialog box of an existing login, the Server Roles tab provides a list of fixed server roles and a check mark next to the ones assigned to the login. To add others simply check the appropriate box. A second method is to double-click on the role name in the Roles container of the Security folder in SQL Enterprise Manager and then use the Add button to add the login to which you want to assign the role (see Figure 3-7).

System stored procedures for fixed server role management also exist. They include **sp_addsrvrolemember** and **sp_dropsrvrolemember**. The syntax for each is as follows:

```
sp_addsrvrolemember [ @loginame = ] 'login', [ @rolename = ] 'role'

sp_dropsrvrolemember [ @loginame = ] 'login', [ @rolename = ] 'role'
```

To add the role to another login, you must already have been added to the role you want to add or have the **sysadmin** role. The same holds true for dropping a role from a login. For either stored procedure a status of 0 indicates success and 1 indicates failure.

To determine who has been granted membership in a role or other information about fixed server roles, SQL Enterprise Manager provides the easiest way of getting this information. The **sp_helpsrvrole** and **sp_helpsrvrolemember** system stored procedures can also be used. The first of these lists the fixed server roles and a brief description. Since you cannot add or remove fixed

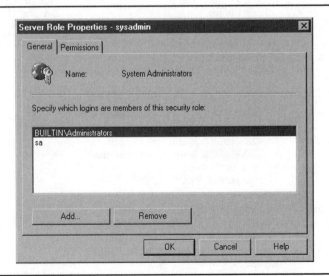

Figure 3-7.   Adding and removing server role members is done in the Properties dialog box of the role in Enterprise Manager.

server roles, this has limited use. The **sp_helpsrvrolemember** procedure is useful in finding out who has been granted membership in a single fixed server role, or in all of them. Syntax for these stored procedures is as follows:

```
sp_helpsrvrole [ [ @srvrolename = ] 'role' ]

sp_helpsrvrolemember [ [ @srvrolename = ] 'role' ]
```

Fixed Database Roles

Within each database a number of fixed database roles are created to allow for easier delegation of administrative functions to users and roles. Like fixed server roles, fixed database roles cannot be deleted. Table 3-2 lists the fixed database roles available.

Role	Allowed Actions	Who Can Grant:	Default Members
db_owner	All permissions in the database, including dropping the database.	db_owner	dbo
db_accessadmin	Manage login access to the database.	db_owner db_accessadmin	
db_ddladmin	Manage database objects (create, alter, or drop).	db_owner db_ddladmin	
db_securityadmin	Manage roles and statement and object permissions.	db_owner db_securityadmin	
db_backupoperator	Perform database backups and issue DBCC and CHECKPOINT commands.	db_owner db_backupoperator	
db_datareader	Can query (SELECT) any table or view in the database.	db_owner db_datareader	
db_datawriter	Can issue DML (INSERT, UPDATE, and DELETE) statements against any table.	db_owner db_datawriter	
db_denydatareader	Cannot SELECT data from any table in the database.	db_owner db_denydatareader	
db_denydatawriter	Cannot perform any DML on any table in the database.	db_owner db_denydatawriter	
PUBLIC	No permissions by default.	**Automatically granted to all users**	All database users

Table 3-2   Fixed Database Roles in SQL Server 2000

While the reason to use a particular fixed database role is usually pretty easily deduced (Bob needs to be able to back up the database, so let's grant him the **db_backupoperator** role, for example), use of the **db_denydatareader** and **db_denydatawriter** roles is something that should be avoided. As mentioned earlier in this chapter, the **deny** permisison always wins no matter what other permisisons are granted. For this reason, and because the deny-based fixed database roles include the **deny** permission, granting them to any user or another role will explicitly forbid anyone holding the role from performing any SELECT or DML statements, respectively, *even if they have been explicitly granted permissions to do so*. Only use the **db_denydatareader** and **db_denydatawriter** roles when the user to whom you wish to grant them should not, under any circumstances, be able to perform SELECT or DML statements.

Assigning fixed database roles to users and other roles is easily done with SQL Enterprise Manager by navigating to the database you are concerned with. Click on the User folder and then double-click the user you wish to assign a role to and check the box next to the role name. When you save your changes, the user will be assigned the role. A second method is to click on the Roles folder in the database and then double-click the role to which you wish to assign users. On the dialog box that appears, click the Add button to add users (see Figure 3-8). To remove a user from the role, click on the user you wish to remove and then click Remove. Changes do not take effect until you click on Apply or OK, at which point the changes are immediately implemented.

Once again, SQL Server also provides system stored procedures that are created in each database to manage roles. The **sp_addrolemember** procedure adds a member to a role and the **sp_droprolemember** procedure removes a member from a role. The syntax for these stored procedures is as follows:

```
sp_addrolemember [ @rolename = ] 'role' ,
    [ @membername = ] 'security_account'

sp_droprolemember [ @rolename = ] 'role' ,
    [ @membername = ] 'security_account'
```

Aside from using SQL Enterprise Manager to get information on roles and their members, SQL Server also allows you to query role information using the **sp_helprole** and **sp_helprolemember** system stored procedures. The **sp_helprole** stored procedure will display a list of roles in the database (or a single role's information if the role name is provided), the internal ID of the role, and whether or not it is an application role. The **sp_helprolemember** stored procedure will list the members of a role (or all roles if a role name is not specified) and their SIDs. These stored procedures also work for user-defined database roles. Syntax for each is as follows:

```
sp_helprole [ [ @rolename = ] 'role' ]

sp_helprolemember [ [ @rolename = ] 'role' ]
```

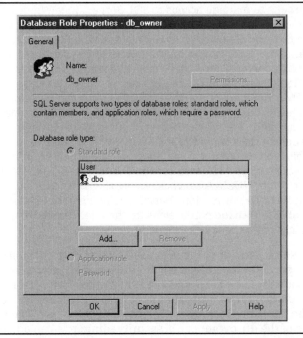

3

Figure 3-8. You can assign roles to users or other roles using Enterprise Manager.

User-Defined Database Roles

Roles provide an easy way to group several permissions under a single name. You can grant membership in the role to a user or another role to have these permissions available to the members. If permission is removed from a role, anyone that has been granted membership in the role also loses the privileges that were removed with the permission.

For example, you have created a database to manage order entry for your company. In the database, you store information about products, customers, orders, shipments, and so on. You want some users to be able to manage customers, others to be able to enter but not modify orders, while some others to be able to perform all actions. If you have a lot of new employees joining the company and you want them to be able to enter orders or manage products, you can grant them these privileges individually. Or, to simplify privilege administration, create roles corresponding to each task that needs to be performed—enter an order, change an order, add a new product, receive shipments, update inventory, and so on. Grant the necessary permissions to database objects for each task-oriented role (for example, SELECT and INSERT on the orders table, SELECT and UPDATE on the inventory table). Create a second set of roles corresponding to the jobs in the organization and then grant the task-oriented roles to the job-related ones. This second layer of roles can be removed if you are using Windows authentication and

Windows groups to manage access to SQL Server since Windows groups
tend to already be job-related. Finally, add the users that need to perform
the tasks to the job-related roles. If you need to change permissions for
a task, making the modification on the role ensures that the change
is inherited by everyone down the chain. The result is very flexible
administration of permissions. To add a user-defined database role in SQL
Enterprise Manager, navigate to the database, right-click the Roles container,
and select New Database Role. You must provide a unique name for the role
in the database and specify whether it is a standard (user-defined database)
role or an application role, as shown in Figure 3-9. For a user-defined
database role, you can also add members by clicking the Add button. The
role name can be up to 128 characters and cannot include a "\", be an
empty string ("), or NULL. After clicking OK, the next time you bring up the
role's dialog box, the Permissions button will no longer be grayed out and
you will be able to manage permissions for the role. To remove role members,
select a member and then click Remove.

System stored procedures to manage user-defined database roles include
sp_addrole, **sp_addrolemember, sp_droprole**, and **sp_droprolemember**.
The user that executes the **sp_addrole** stored procedure must be a member
of the **db_owner** or **db_securityadmin** role and automatically becomes the
owner of the role, although you can specify another owner. The role's owner
or members of the **db_owner** or **db_securityadmin** role can add or remove

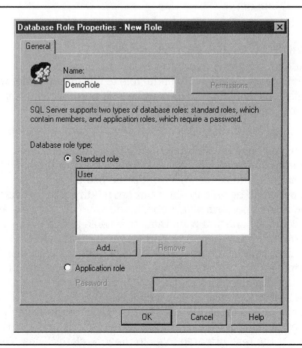

Figure 3-9.   You can create user-defined database and application roles in
Enterprise Manager by specifying the type on this dialog box.

members of a role, or drop the role. The syntax for these system stored procedures is as follows:

```
sp_addrole [ @rolename = ] 'role'   [ , [ @ownername = ] 'owner' ]

sp_addrolemember [ @rolename = ] 'role',
    [ @membername = ] 'security_account'

sp_droprole [ @rolename = ] 'role'

sp_droprolemember [ @rolename = ] 'role' ,
    [ @membername = ] 'security_account'
```

When adding roles to other roles, it is not possible to create a circular reference as in roleA is a member of roleB and roleB is a member of roleA. SQL Server will generate an error if this happens. The error will also be generated if a chain of role memberships (for example, roleA to roleB to roleC to roleD to roleA) will cause a circular reference. It is always a good idea to verify and track the membership of roles in other roles.

If you want to drop a role, you must first drop all role members. The **sp_droprole** procedure will fail unless the role is empty (has no members). Verify role membership before issuing **sp_droprole** by using the **sp_helprolemember** stored procedure. The same is also true of you attempt to drop a role using Enterprise Manager.

Application Roles

A role type that can be assigned permissions but not members is an application role. Application roles are activated from within Transact-SQL code or a query tool and, once activated, provide the user who activated the role with all permissions of the role. To ensure that only users who should activate the role do so, the application role requires a password to be activated. Application roles replace all permissions granted to the user (except those granted to the PUBLIC role), in the database where they exist, with permissions from the application role. In other words, if a user activates an application role, any existing permissions or roles that have been granted to him in the database or server are ignored and permissions of the application role and PUBLIC become the effective permissions. The user may access data in other databases on the SQL Server provided the other databases have a **guest** user. For the user to regain other role or specifically assigned permissions, she needs to disconnect from SQL Server and then reconnect using a login that does not use the application role.

When using SQL Enterprise Manager, you create application roles the same way you create user-defined roles, except you need to provide a password to be used for role activation and you cannot assign members to the role. The Roles container in the database where you want to create or manage the role is the location you go to. The role name must be unique in the database, and you must be a member of the **db_owner** or **db_securityadmin** role to create an application role. All application roles are owned by **dbo**.

You can also use the **sp_addapprole** stored procedure to create an application role, as in the following syntax:

```
sp_addapprole [ @rolename = ] 'role' , [ @password = ] 'password'
```

Once an application role has been created, it can be granted permissions and membership in other roles just like any user-defined role. The only difference is that those permissions only take effect (and replace all existing permissions for the user with the exception of PUBLIC) when the role is activated. To activate an application role, any user can execute the **sp_setapprole** system stored procedure providing the role name and password to activate the role. The application role's permissions now replace any other role or direct-granted permissions, except for those granted to the PUBLIC role, for the user and login activating the role. Once an application role is activated, it cannot be deactivated except by disconnecting from the SQL Server. The syntax for the **sp_setapprole** stored procedure is the following:

```
sp_setapprole [@rolename =] 'role' ,
    [@password =] {Encrypt N 'password'} | 'password'
    [, [@encrypt =] 'encrypt_style']
```

When issuing the **sp_setapprole** procedure, you can specify that the password should be sent to SQL Server encrypted if you are connecting to SQL Server using an ODBC or OLE-DB provider (the default). If your client application is using the older-style DB-Library connection, you cannot encrypt the password. It will be sent across as clear-text (the default). When encrypting the password, the *encrypt_style* value should be set to ODBC (since there are no other encryption options), and you must specify the Encrypt keyword and Unicode encoding string (using N) when providing the password, as in the following example:

```
sp_setapprole 'OrderEntry', {Encrypt N'rolepass'}, 'ODBC'
```

An additional side-effect of using application roles is that connections where they have been activated cannot take advantage of ODBC connection pooling since the activation of a role changes the permissions available to the user. Connection pooling requires that a login's permissions remain static for the life of the session, which activating an application role changes. The net effect of not allowing connection pooling is that application roles create a slight performance hit when connecting to SQL Server because they cannot use already-created pooled connections and must incur the overhead of creating a connection.

If it is necessary to change the password for an application role, a **db_owner** or **db_securityadmin** can always use SQL Enterprise Manager to make the change in the role's dialog box, or execute the **sp_approlepassword** system stored procedure. The password you specify cannot be NULL. Once you have changed the application role password, ensure that all application programs or Transact-SQL procedures that activate the role have been modified and/

or users have been notified of the new password. The syntax of this stored procedure is the following:

```
sp_approlepassword [ @rolename = ] 'role', [ @newpwd = ] 'password'
```

Because an application role does not have members, it can be dropped by a **db_owner** or **db_securityadmin** at any time when it is no longer required. However, because an application role can own objects if the object is created when the role is active (for example, a user activates a role and then creates a table—the table is now owned by the role and not the user), all objects that are owned by the role must be dropped or their owner changed using the **sp_changeobjectowner** system stored procedure. The syntax of the **sp_dropapprole** procedure is as follows:

```
sp_dropapprole [@rolename =] 'role'
```

Controlling Access with Permissions

If a login allows the user to connect to SQL Server, and a username in a database allows the user to access a database, permissions assigned to the user, or roles of which the user is a member, determine specifically what the user is able to do in the database, which object he can manipulate, and how. Permissions are the final piece of the security puzzle for SQL Server.

Permission Management Commands

SQL Server provides three commands for managing permissions—GRANT, REVOKE, and DENY. The GRANT command allows the grantee (the user or role being granted the permission) to perform a specified action and removes any DENY permission applied for the same statement or object for the user. The DENY command explicitly forbids the grantee from issuing a statement or manipulating an object in the method specified and overrides any GRANT permission applied. The REVOKE command removes any GRANT or DENY permission on the statement or object for the specified user and role, and leaves the ability for a user to issue a statement or manipulate an object up to other permissions available to the user or roles of which the user is a member.

If you think of the GRANT, REVOKE, and DENY commands in terms of concepts that most DBAs are familiar with, they correspond to the values of TRUE, NULL, and FALSE, respectively. Issuing a GRANT command sets the availability of the indicated permission to TRUE for the user or role. Issuing a DENY command overrides the TRUE and sets the value to FALSE for the indicated permission. When combining either TRUE or FALSE with NULL, the result is always NULL, so a REVOKE command removes any permission setting and sets things back to the default value, which is nothing. For example, if the following set of statements are issued, the resulting permissions will allow Bob to SELECT (single GRANT) from the Orders table, under no circumstances perform a DELETE (single DENY) on the Orders table, and possibly perform an INSERT (GRANT and then REVOKE) or UPDATE (DENY and then REVOKE) on the orders table, based upon permissions granted to the roles that Bob is a member of.

```
GRANT SELECT, INSERT ON Orders TO Bob

DENY UPDATE, DELETE ON Orders TO Bob

REVOKE INSERT, UPDATE ON Orders FROM Bob
```

An important corollary here is that, by default, users do not have any permission at all and cannot perform any action on an object or issue any statement unless granted permissions to do so directly, or through a role of which they are a member.

SQL Server Permission Categories

SQL Server has two broad categories of permissions—statement permissions and object permissions. As a generalization, statement permissions let you perform an action such as creating a database object or backing up a database, while object permissions allow you to manipulate database objects such as insert data into a table or execute a stored procedure.

Permission information is stored in the **sysprotects** table of the database to which the permission applies. This is also true of membership granted to users in all SQL Server roles—the record of roles granted and to whom they were granted is also in **sysprotects**.

Statement Permissions

Table 3-3 lists the statement permissions that are available in SQL Server as well as who they are granted to by default, can be granted by, and the version in which the permission is available.

All of the statement permissions available in SQL Server, with the exception of CREATE DATABASE, are granted to a user or role within a specific SQL

Permission	Description	Granted To by Default	Who Can Grant	SQL Server Versions
CREATE DATABASE	Allows the grantee to create a database in SQL Server.	**sysadmin** **db_creator**	**sysadmin**	6.x 7.0 2000
BACKUP DATABASE	Allows the grantee to back up a specific SQL Server database.	**sysadmin** **db_owner** **db_backupoperator**	**sysadmin** **db_owner**	7.0 2000

Table 3-3.   Common Statement Permissions Available in SQL Server

3

Permission	Description	Granted To by Default	Who Can Grant	SQL Server Versions
BACKUP LOG	Allows the grantee to back up the transaction log of a SQL Server database.	**sysadmin** **db_owner** **db_backupoperator**	**sysadmin** **db_owner**	7.0 2000
CREATE TABLE	Allows the grantee to create a table in the specified database.	**sysadmin** **db_owner** **db_ddladmin**	**sysadmin** **db_owner**	6.*x* 7.0 2000
CREATE VIEW	Allows the grantee to create a view in the specified database. Must have SELECT or REFERENCES permission on the underlying objects for the view to be created.	**sysadmin** **db_owner** **db_ddladmin**	**sysadmin** **db_owner**	6.*x* 7.0 2000
CREATE PROCEDURE	Allows the grantee to create a stored procedure in the specified database.	**sysadmin** **db_owner** **db_ddladmin**	**sysadmin** **db_owner**	6.*x* 7.0 2000
CREATE RULE	Allows the grantee to create a rule in the specified database.	**sysadmin** **db_owner** **db_ddladmin**	**sysadmin** **db_owner**	6.*x* 7.0 2000
CREATE DEFAULT	Allows the grantee to create a default in the specified database.	**sysadmin** **db_owner** **db_ddladmin**	**sysadmin** **db_owner**	6.*x* 7.0 2000
CREATE FUNCTION	Allows the grantee to create a user-defined function in the specified database.	**sysadmin** **db_owner** **db_ddladmin**	**sysadmin** **db_owner**	2000

Table 3-3. Common Statement Permissions Available in SQL Server *(continued)*

Server database. The CREATE DATABASE permission is granted to a login in the **master** database. Statement permissions are only valid in the database where the user exists and not in any other database on the SQL Server. Once a user has been granted a statement permission, she can perform the actions allowed by the permission but cannot grant the same permission to others.

Statement permissions can be granted to users or roles in SQL Enterprise Manager by right-clicking on the database in which you wish to grant them, selecting Properties and then selecting the Permissions tab. By clicking on the box for the row of the user or role for which you want to manage statement permissions, and the column of the permission you want to manage, you can grant, deny, or revoke the permission, as shown in Figure 3-10. When the check box contains a green checkmark, the GRANT command has been issued; a red X indicates a DENY and a clear check box denotes that the permission has not been explicitly assigned or has been revoked. Clicking OK will save your changes and Cancel will allow you to exit the dialog box without committing changes to the database.

Another method of managing statement permissions is to use the GRANT, REVOKE, and DENY commands. The syntax for each is as follows:

```
GRANT { ALL | statement [ ,...n ] }
    TO security_account [ ,...n ]

REVOKE { ALL | statement [ ,...n ] }
    FROM security_account [ ,...n ]

DENY { ALL | statement [ ,...n ] }
    TO security_account [ ,...n ]
```

Figure 3-10. Statement permissions can be granted by modifying the properties of the database in Enterprise Manager.

As you can see from the syntax, you can manage several permissions at the same time for more than one user or role using any of the above commands. The ALL keyword will GRANT or DENY all permissions to the grantee that the grantor is allowed to manage, or remove any statement permissions from the grantee when the REVOKE command is used.

Object Permissions

In order for users to be able to query or modify data in a database, or execute procedures or functions, they (or roles to which they have been granted membership) need to be assigned the appropriate permissions. Table 3-4 lists the object permissions available in SQL Server, and the object types to which they apply. Anyone who creates an object has full control over the object and may manage the object's permissions. Members of the **sysadmin, db_owner,** and **db_securityadmin** role can also manage permissions for any object in the database (or the SQL Server for **sysadmin**).

Managing object permissions with SQL Enterprise Manager can be done from the properties dialog box of the object itself or of the user or role for which you want to manage permissions. As you can see in Figure 3-11, the appearance and determination of GRANT, DENY, or REVOKE is the same as with statement permissions—a green checkmark, red X, or clear check box, respectively. A nice bonus when using Enterprise Manager is that only the permissions available for an object based on its type will have check boxes to manipulate, thus taking the guesswork out of which permission to assign, as shown in Figure 3-12.

Permission	Objects Applied To
SELECT	Table View Column of a table or a view User defined function
INSERT	Table View
UPDATE	Table View Column of a table or a view
DELETE	Table View
REFERENCES	Table View Column of a table or a view
EXECUTE (also called EXEC)	Stored Procedure User-defined function

Table 3-4. Common Object Permissions and the Objects They Apply To

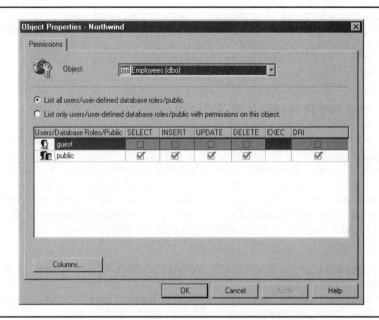

Figure 3-11.   Enterprise Manager allows you to manage permissions for an object by looking at the object's properties.

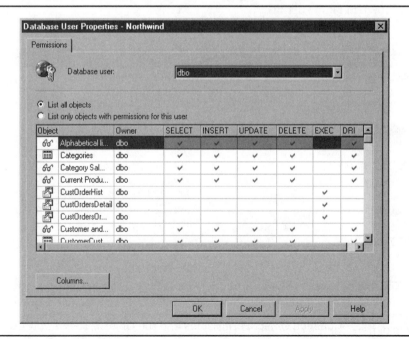

Figure 3-12.   One of the properties pages for a user allows you to view and manage permissions for all objects that the user has access to.

A second way of managing object permissions is using the GRANT, REVOKE, or DENY commands. The syntax for each is as follows:

```
GRANT { ALL [ PRIVILEGES ] | permission [ ,...n ] }
     { [ ( column [ ,...n ] ) ] ON { table | view }
       | ON { table | view } [ ( column [ ,...n ] ) ]
       | ON { stored_procedure | extended_procedure }
       | ON { user_defined_function }        }
     TO security_account [ ,...n ]
     [ WITH GRANT OPTION ] [ AS { group | role } ]

REVOKE [ GRANT OPTION FOR ]
       { ALL [ PRIVILEGES ] | permission [ ,...n ] }
     { [ ( column [ ,...n ] ) ] ON { table | view }
       | ON { table | view } [ ( column [ ,...n ] ) ]
       | ON { stored_procedure | extended_procedure }
       | ON { user_defined_function }        }
     { TO | FROM }  security_account [ ,...n ]
     [ CASCADE ]   [ AS { group | role } ]

DENY { ALL [ PRIVILEGES ] | permission [ ,...n ] }
     { [ ( column [ ,...n ] ) ] ON { table / view }
       | ON { table | view } [ ( column [ ,...n ] ) ]
       | ON { stored_procedure | extended_procedure }
       | ON { user_defined_function } }
     TO security_account [ ,...n ]   [ CASCADE ]
```

When managing object permissions, specifying the keyword ALL will grant, deny, or revoke all available permissions on the object based on its type to the grantee. If the WITH GRANT OPTION is chosen when granting a permission, the grantee will be allowed to also grant the same permissions to other users or roles in the database, which may compromise security on the object. When denying or revoking permissions, using the CASCADE keyword will also revoke or deny the same permissions to anyone that the grantee has granted those permissions to, if the grantee was granted the permission WITH GRANT OPTION. Essentially, CASCADE has a waterfall effect so that the permission is removed from the grantee and anyone he gave the permission to as well.

The AS keyword, which is new in SQL Server 2000, allows a user to grant object permissions to other users that have been granted WITH GRANT OPTION to a role of which the user is a member. For example, Bob has been granted the OrderEntry role. The OrderEntry role has been granted SELECT on the Orders table WITH GRANT OPTION. Bob wants Dave to be able to SELECT on the Orders table. Since the SELECT permission on the Orders table was not granted to Bob directly, but to the OrderEntry role of which Bob is a member, he cannot grant SELECT to Dave unless he takes on the role of the OrderEntry role when issuing the GRANT command, as follows:

```
GRANT SELECT ON Orders TO Dave AS OrderEntry
```

Obtaining Information on Permissions

Using SQL Enterprise Manager, you can review permissions granted
on databases, to users and roles, and on database objects. The method
for viewing them is similar to the method used to manage them. SQL
Server also includes a system stored procedure to query permission
information—**sp_helprotect**. The syntax is as follows:

```
sp_helprotect [ [ @name = ] 'object_statement' ]
    [ , [ @username = ] 'security_account' ]
    [ , [ @grantorname = ] 'grantor' ]
    [ , [ @permissionarea = ] 'type' ]
```

When executing **sp_helprotect** without any parameters, you will get a list
of all permissions assigned to all users and roles in the current database. If
you want to limit the information it returns, the @name parameter allows
you to limit the output to permissions granted on an object or specific
statement permission, the @username parameter lets you specify for which
user or role to report permissions, the @grantorname parameter lets you
limit the results to the user or role who issued the permission statements,
and the @permissionarea parameter lets you specify whether to display
object permissions only (**o**), statement permissions only (**s**), or both (**s o**).
Any combination of parameters that makes sense can be used.

Security Management Recommendations

Ensuring that you have a security configuration for SQL Server that makes
administration manageable and data access controlled but flexible is the
ideal to strive for. Some things that you may want to consider when designing
a security configuration for your SQL Server include the following:

- Use Windows authentication where possible since it allows you to map
  Windows groups to SQL Server logins and provide a single sign-on
  capability for individuals to access a SQL Server and its data.

- Create user-defined database roles and assign permissions to them
  based upon the tasks that need to be performed. Make database users
  or other roles members of roles so that they inherit the appropriate
  permissions.

- Grant or deny permissions to database users directly only as an exception
  when a specific user needs to have greater or lesser access than that of
  the roles available.

- Grant the permissions all users in a database should have to PUBLIC.
  All users are members of PUBLIC and will automatically receive the
  permissions granted.

- Never use DENY unless you really have to. Use REVOKE to remove a granted permission rather than explicitly denying a permission because DENY *always* wins.

- Unless all logins in a SQL Server should have access to data in a database do not create a **guest** user in the database.

- If you want all databases to have a **guest** user, add the user to the **model** database, which will ensure that any new database created will have a **guest** user. You can always remove the user in a specific database if **guest** should not be there.

- Reduce the permissions granted to the BUILTIN\Administrators group if you do not want members of the local Administrators group on the SQL Server computer to be able to have full control over SQL Server. If you decide to do this, create another Windows group and grant it the **sysadmin** role.

- *Always* assign a password to the **SA** login.

- Grant users that will create objects in the database the **db_owner** role. This will ensure that any object created is owned by **dbo** and avoid broken ownership chains.

Now that you have an understanding of how permissions work on SQL Server and databases, it is time to start using some of them to create and manage a database in SQL Server.

Chapter 4

Creating and Managing Databases

Efficient storage and management of data requires that the data files used by any SQL Server database be properly sized and in locations allowing both performance and data protection. The DBA must plan the size and location of data and log files (or device files if using SQL Server 6.*x*) based upon available hardware, as well as anticipated database capacity requirements. A basic understanding of disk fault tolerance technology also helps. Let's start at the beginning—understanding how SQL Server stores data and how that impacts managing database data.

SQL Server Storage Structure

SQL Server stores its databases in a series of data files. Data files are only one component of the storage architecture of SQL Server. Other key concepts include the following:

- **Data page**   A data page, also called a database block, is the smallest unit of allocation in a SQL Server database. Each row in a table cannot be larger than a data page (except for columns of **text** or **image** data types, which are stored in a different manner). In SQL Server 7 and later releases, a data page is 8K, or 8192 bytes, which, taking into account the overhead for managing a page, allows for a maximum row size of 8060 bytes. In SQL Server 6.5 and earlier releases, the size of a data page was 2K or 2048 bytes, with a maximum row size of 2016 bytes.

- **Extent**   An extent is 8 contiguous pages. Whenever SQL Server needs to increase the amount of space for a table or an index, it will allocate an extent of storage space for the object (64K in SQL Server 7 or later, 16K in SQL Server 6.5 or earlier). Small tables can mix data and index information, as well as other data, on a single extent, but in larger tables SQL Server will try and make the data in an extent all of the same type (table, index, and so on) so as to more efficiently manage storage.

- **Data file**   A data file is used to store data for tables, indexes, and other database objects. It has both a logical name (used by SQL Server to reference the file during backups and other operations) and a physical name (the actual name of the file on disk). In SQL Server 7 and later, databases must have one primary data file, typically with an MDF extension, and potentially several secondary data files, typically with an NDF extension.

- **Log file** A log file is a data file used to store transaction log information for a SQL Server database. A log file also has a logical and physical name, with the physical file typically having an LDF extension. A database *must* have one, and may have several, log files.

- **Transaction log** When modifications to the data in a database take place, they are first written to the transaction log before being saved to the database. The transaction log keeps a chronological record of all the changes. It can be used to rollback an unwanted or aborted transaction, or roll-forward changes to the data file. It can also be used to maintain transactional integrity in the event of hard disk failure or some other catastrophe. Transaction logs and their log files should be stored on separate physical disks from data files to protect against disk failure and for improved performance.

Transactions Explained

One term that is often confusing or misunderstood when it comes to the operation of databases in general is *transaction*. A transaction is a single unit of work that must either complete as a whole (no partial changes are allowed) or be rolled back completely. Transaction in SQL Server, as well as other databases such as Oracle, must meet the *ACID* test as outlined by Jim Gray and Andreas Reuter. ACID stands for the following:

- **Atomicity** The entire transaction must commit completely, or not at all. For example, when you deposit $500 cash at an ATM, your account is credited with $500 and the bank is also debited $500 to record the fact that the $500 is yours and not theirs. It would not be nice if the bank was debited $500 and you were not credited that amount—you would be $500 poorer. A transaction ensures that both updates take place or that neither does.

- **Consistency** The transaction must follow some logical rules. Essentially, this means that performing the same task—for example, making a $500 deposit to your account at an ATM—will always result in the same action taking place—$500 credited to your account and $500 debited from the bank. Under no circumstances would the transaction credit $500 to your account and not debit it from the bank's account, or vice versa.

- **Isolation** Isolation means that while one process is performing a transaction, it must have absolute control over all of the elements it is affecting. This means that only one user at one time can be making changes to the same rows of data. Using the banking example above, while you are updating the account balance with the $500 deposit, another user cannot be also updating the same account by removing $200 from it. SQL Server achieves isolation through the use of *locking* so that when one process is changing data it has an exclusive lock on the rows it is changing, not allowing others to change the same data until it is done.

Isolation also extends to reading data. While one process is reading data another cannot be changing it at the same time. Read locks prevent users from modifying the same row while it is being read. Write locks, used when data is being changed, prevent others from changing or reading the data until the transaction commits its changes.

- **Durability** Durability means that after a transaction completes (or *commits*), all its changes will remain and be recoverable should SQL Server, or the computer it is running on, crash. In SQL Server the transaction logs are the mechanism used to ensure durability.

Implicit and Explicit Transactions

Transactions in SQL Server can be initiated by issuing a command that implies a modification to the database (implicit transaction) or by indicating that the next series of commands will be a transaction (explicit transaction).

Explicit transactions are started by issuing the command BEGIN TRANSACTION and terminated by either a COMMIT TRANSACTION (to save the changes) or ROLLBACK TRANSACTION (to back out the changes) statement. When using explicit transactions, you can also define savepoints by issuing the SAVEPOINT *<name>* statement. Savepoints, though not 100 percent kosher in database theory, are markers in the transaction that allow you to rollback all changes that occurred after a savepoint but commit those that occurred before the savepoint. In the ATM example, if you were depositing $500 cash and a $200 check in the same transaction, you could define a savepoint after all the modifications for the $500 deposit had taken place. In this way, if an error occurred while depositing the $200 check, you could rollback the transaction to the defined savepoint and the cash deposit of $500 would be recorded in the database. Anything involving the $200 check would not be recorded.

An implicit transaction will automatically start when using one of the statements in Table 4-1, and commit when the statement has performed its work. It is not possible to rollback an implicit transaction, but SQL Server will automatically roll the changes back if an error occurs that prevents the transaction from completing (disk or system failure, for example). This mode of operation is known as *Autocommit* Mode and is the default transaction mode in SQL Server. SQL Server also supports *ImplicitTransaction* Mode, where SQL Server initiates an implicit transaction when any of the statements in Table 4-1 are executed, but requires a COMMIT TRANSACTION or ROLLBACK TRANSACTION statement to end the transaction.

CREATE	INSERT	OPEN
ALTER	UPDATE	FETCH
DROP	DELETE	TRUNCATE TABLE
GRANT	REVOKE	SELECT

Table 4-1. SQL Server Statements That Initiate an Implicit Transaction

Transaction Processing

The method used to apply changes to the database has a few steps. When an application issues a command to modify the database, data pages containing the data to be changed are brought into the buffer cache, if they are not already there. SQL Server requires all changes to data pages be made in memory to minimize any possibility of disk corruption.

As the statements changing data (INSERT, UPDATE, DELETE, and so on) are issued by the application, SQL Server records each change in the transaction log on disk. In fact, the transaction log is the most write-intensive portion of SQL Server and will incur the most disk I/O in Online Transaction Processing (OLTP)-type databases such as order entry systems, accounting, customer relationship management, and so on. As pages in the buffer cache become full or the buffer cache needs to free pages to bring in additional data, it will write the changed pages to disk when a *checkpoint* occurs.

A checkpoint is a marker that indicates which database modifications have been written to disk. It is also recorded in the transaction log. A DBA can manually imitate a checkpoint by issuing the CHECKPOINT command to force writes at a specific time.

It is important to note that pages written to disk may include committed and uncommitted transactions. However, the transaction log will have a record of all changes (and the checkpoint) to bring the database to a consistent state should a failure occur.

Finally, when the transaction is committed, a commit record is also written to the transaction log indicating that the change should be permanent.

Devices in Previous Releases of SQL Server

If you are using SQL Server 6.5 or earlier, another important term that also needs to be explained is *database device*. A database device is a logical name given to a physical disk file on which you create a database and transaction log. Devices were used in earlier releases of SQL Server to pre-allocate disk space from the operating system before creating a database, so as to minimize the overhead of allocating additional disk space during database operation. The reasons for this dealt primarily with relatively slow hard disk and CPU speed in older computer systems. The majority of these issues have been overcome in the last few years due to the advent of very fast processors and much faster hard disks. Nonetheless, if you are using SQL Server 6.5 or earlier, you will need to create database devices because a database in SQL Server 6.x can only be allocated storage on preexisting devices.

To create database devices issue the DISK INIT command in SQL Server 6.x. Device size is specified in 2K pages and not megabytes or kilobytes, so a bit of math is needed. You must also specify a virtual device number between 0 and 255 that uniquely identifies the disk device in the database. You may need to use Enterprise Manager or query the **sysdevices** table to determine the next available number. Virtual device number 0 is always reserved for the **master** database.

The syntax of the DISK INIT command is:

```
DISK INIT
        NAME = 'logical_device_name',
        PHYSNAME = 'physical_file_name',
        VDEVNO = virtual_device_number,
        SIZE = number_of_2K_blocks
```

4

Creating Databases

Creating a database in SQL Server is done by issuing the CREATE DATABASE command or using Enterprise Manager. Only the **sysadmins** and **dbcreator** roles have the necessary privileges to issue this command by default. The syntax for this command in SQL Server 2000 is the following:

```
CREATE DATABASE database_name
[ ON
    [ PRIMARY ]( [ NAME = logical_file_name , ]
        FILENAME = 'os_file_name'
        [ , SIZE = size ]
        [ , MAXSIZE = { max_size | UNLIMITED } ]
        [ , FILEGROWTH = growth_increment ] ) [ ,...n ]
    [FILEGROUP filegroup_name < filespec >] [,...n ]
]
[ LOG ON { ( [ NAME = logical_file_name , ]
        FILENAME = 'os_file_name'
        [ , SIZE = size ]
        [ , MAXSIZE = { max_size | UNLIMITED } ]
        [ , FILEGROWTH = growth_increment ] ) [ ,...n ]} ]
[ COLLATE collation_name ]
[ FOR LOAD | FOR ATTACH ]
```

When creating a database, you must specify a unique name for the database on the SQL Server where you are creating it, as shown next. You must also specify the logical name and physical location of the first data file in the PRIMARY filegroup, and the logical and physical names of the transaction log file. The database file sizes must be at least as large as the **model** database since the CREATE DATABASE command makes a copy of **model** under the new database name you assigned it, adding empty data pages up to the size of data files specified.

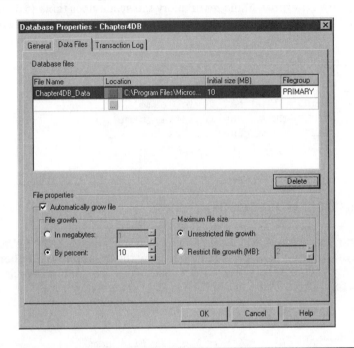

NOTE *Filegroups and their uses will be covered in the "Filegroups in SQL Server" section of this chapter.*

When specifying logical and physical filenames to be used for the database, the first data file must always be part of the PRIMARY filegroup. The logical name for each filegroup and data file must be unique within the database. The initial size (SIZE) for data files is specified in megabytes (MB) by default, but can be specified in gigabytes (GB) or kilobytes (KB), and must have a minimum size of 512KB each for the first data file and transaction log file (1MB total size—the size of **model**). You can also specify what the maximum size of each physical file can be (MAXSIZE) when FILEGROWTH is enabled, allowing the file to automatically grow if additional storage is required. The default for MAXSIZE is UNLIMITED. FILEGROWTH can be specified in megabytes, kilobytes, or as a percentage of the current data file size. If FILEGROWTH is not specified, it will default to 10 percent. If a whole number is provided for FILEGROWTH, it will be assumed to indicate a growth increment in megabytes. FILEGROWTH=0 disables automatic file growth.

In SQL Server 2000 you may also specify the default collation for database objects in the database, which will default to the collation specified when you installed SQL Server 2000. In SQL Server 7, the COLLATE clause is not available and all databases will always use the same collation (character set, sort order, and Unicode collation) specified at installation time.

Finally, you can indicate that you will be performing a database restore (load) by adding the FOR LOAD clause (FOR RESTORE in SQL Server 7). This places the database in *dbo use only* mode so that no users can connect to it, but a restore is allowed.

The FOR ATTACH clause, which is new in SQL Server 2000, lets you create the database using existing physical files. This option should only be used if you have more than 16 files in the database to be attached. When using the FOR ATTACH clause, specify only the name of the existing file of the PRIMARY filegroup—the rest will be read from the system tables. In SQL Server 7 you can perform the same action by executing the **sp_attach_db** or **sp_attach_single_file_db** stored procedure, which is still the recommended method in SQL Server 2000.

The following is an example of the CREATE DATABASE command:

```
CREATE DATABASE OrderEntryDB
        ON PRIMARY (NAME=OEDB_PRIMARY_01,
        FILENAME='D:\OEDATA\OEDBPR01.MDF',
        SIZE=100MB, MAXSIZE=500MB, FILEGROWTH=100MB)
     LOG ON (NAME=OEDB_LOG01.LDF,
        FILENAME='E:\OEDATA\OEDBLG01.LDF',
        SIZE=25MB, MAXSIZE=100MB, FILEGROWTH=25MB)
```

In SQL Server 6.x the CREATE DATABASE command has a slightly different syntax and an additional step—creating disk devices. You must first use the DISK INIT command to create at least one device to hold your database and transaction log, although you should create at least two devices (one for the database and another for the transaction log) to ensure good recoverability. After you have created your devices, issue the CREATE DATABASE command, specifying the size of the database and transaction log on each disk device in megabytes. The syntax is as follows:

```
CREATE DATABASE database_name
        ON device_name = size   [, …]
        LOG ON device_name = size [, …]
```

Planning File Placement

One of the more important considerations when creating and managing databases deals with the placement of data files and transaction log files (or, in SQL Server 6.x, disk devices containing them). While not all databases will require thorough planning, those that your business relies upon need to provide the best combination of performance and recoverability within the budgetary constraints of your enterprise. As a general set of guidelines, the following provide a broad framework of what to consider when designing file placement:

- *Always place data files and transaction log files on separate physical disks.* The ability to recover up to the point of failure hinges on having a backup of the data files and the current transaction log files. In this way, if you lose one or more data files, the transaction log will contain a record of all changes up to the time the data files were lost. On the flip side, if you lose the disk where the transaction log files are located and still have all your data files, you can issue a CHECKPOINT and still have all your data at the point of failure, losing nothing. Placing data and log files on the same disk ensures that some data will be lost when disk failure occurs.

- *Place transaction log files on high-speed disks.* Placing your data files away from log files also will separate the disk I/O associated with very write-intensive log writes from typically less I/O-intensive data file access. Log files are written to as changes to the database occur, and when a transaction is committed. Data file writes only take place when a checkpoint occurs—a less frequent occurrence. Placing transaction log files on high-speed disks, preferably with a separate controller, will minimize any I/O contention that could occur and provide better performance.

- *Never place transaction log files on RAID5 arrays.* The most common type of RAID arrays are RAID level 5, which provides good fault tolerance at the expense of write performance. If you have a very busy OLTP database, placing transaction logs on RAID5 arrays will slow down write performance and cause the whole database to perform poorly.

NOTE   *A discussion on RAID and its pros and cons can be found in the RAID and Storage Technology Overview section of this chapter.*

- *Stripe data across disks.* Use RAID to stripe data across disks so that SQL Server can make use of the improved performance parallel I/O can provide. In all cases, use hardware-based RAID controllers that offload processing of disk striping from the main computer's CPU. This is especially necessary for RAID 5 arrays that incur a significant CPU overhead when calculating parity during a write.

- *Use appropriate technology that fits within your budget.* While Microsoft and most authors/consultants will provide guidelines for an ideal world, the reality is that we all have to live within our means. Generally, buy the equipment and disk technology that you can afford, based on what your data is worth to your organization. If your SQL Server holds your corporate accounting system and all customer records, you should strongly consider spending the money for better disk technology to protect it and provide excellent performance. Purchasing fiber-channel or high-end SCSI disk subsystems makes sense if your company's corporate intelligence resides in the database. On the other hand, if the database is for a small project that goes away in a few weeks, or simply for testing, using IDE hard disks and placing everything on a single disk may make sense. Always consider the value to you of the data that you are storing.

- *Data warehouses are different*   Most guidelines dealing with file placement consider OLTP systems where the data cannot be easily re-created. If you use SQL Server to store data-warehouse data or to perform extract/transform/load (ETL) for a data warehouse, your data file placement considerations will be different because you can more easily repeat the process and not have any data loss. An implementation using fewer larger disks typically make sense for data warehousing because of data volumes, whereas many smaller disks tend to work better for OLTP systems, since they contain less data and spreading the load across many disks will provide better write performance.

- *Use filegroups to further separate data and indexes*   Filegroups allow you to create certain database objects on a specific set of data files placed on separate disks from other data files. This can let you perform very careful tuning and planning of data locations and create better-performing systems. You can also control fault tolerance by placing items easily rebuilt (non-clustered indexes) away from data and transaction logs, or less redundant disk configurations to save cost. While using RAID can alleviate some of the complexities of managing this, SQL Server can take advantage of parallel I/O and multiple CPUs on the host computer to optimize I/O during read and write operations.

- *Place the **tempdb** database on its own high-speed disk*   **tempdb** is written to by users in any database on your server creating temporary tables or performing sorts. Placing **tempdb** on a fast disk device will ensure that you don't encounter bottlenecks that slow down all users of the SQL Server when performing sorting or creating temporary objects.

RAID and Storage Technology Overview

RAID stands for Redundant Array of Inexpensive Disks and is a standards-based way to group from 2 to 32 hard disks for improved performance and/or greater fault tolerance. There are six standard RAID levels called RAID0, RAID1, all the way to RAID5. Other RAID levels also exist, but are combinations of the existing six standard levels or manufacturers' derivates. The RAID levels most in use today include the following:

- **RAID0**   Using a minimum of 2 and a maximum of 32 disks, RAID0 allows you to stripe data across multiple disks. Called a Striped Set in Windows NT or Striped Volume in Windows 2000/2003, RAID0 provides great read and write performance because multiple disks can have I/O performed on them at the same time, but provides zero–fault tolerance (which some say is the reason for it being called RAID0). If you lose a single disk in a RAID0 stripe set, all of the data on the stripe set is lost in much the same way removing a single card from a pyramid of cards can cause the whole pyramid to fall. RAID0 by itself is not recommended for database environments.

- **RAID1**   Also referred to as disk mirroring, RAID1 uses two disks to copy everything written on one disk to another disk on the same (mirroring) or different (duplexing) hard disk controller. RAID1 has very low overheard and provides about the same level of performance as writing to a single disk, although some, not all, implementations allow both disks to be used for read operations, thereby providing better read performance. Windows NT and Windows 2000/2003 support mirroring in the operating system, which works fine and does not necessarily require a hardware-based controller, although they are available.

- **RAID5**   Known as striping with parity, RAID5 uses a minimum of 3 and a maximum of 32 disks to stripe data across drives while also calculating parity information that allows for a single drive to be lost while still retaining all of the data. Some implementations (HP/Compaq, for example) allow for the loss of a second disk though this is not the norm. RAID5 incurs significant CPU overhead for write operations since every time you write to the RAID5 stripe set, parity information needs to be calculated and written to one of the disks. Because of the need to write parity information, RAID5 stripe sets always lose the capacity of one (and only one) hard disk. For example, if you have a RAID5 array with 5 20GB hard disks, you would only have 80GB of actual storage, since the capacity of one of the 5 disks would be used for parity, leaving 4X20GB of available storage for data.

  Parity information is written to a different disk for each write so that no one disk contains all data or all parity—it is all striped. In defining parity, think of it as storing the result of an addition (2+7=9) with each piece (2, 7, and 9) on a different disk. If one of the disks is lost (7), you can calculate what the value was by taking the parity information (9) and subtracting the remaining data (2) to come up with the missing data (9−2=7). Although this is an over-simplification, it is essentially what happens on a much larger size piece of data (64K, typically) using a mathematical XOR algorithm.

  Because of the necessity to calculate parity for writes, RAID5 should not be implemented in the operating system, although Windows NT (Stripe Set with Parity) and Windows 2000/2003 (RAID-5 Volume) allow you to do so. You should always use a hardware-based RAID controller with its own CPU for parity processing and sufficient cache to provide good write performance. Also purchase a battery backup option for the cache if you have enabled write-behind caching (the ability of the controller to notify the OS that a write has taken place to disk while the data is still in cache), in case of power loss. For better fault tolerance, disable the write-behind caching, but be aware that this will slow down write performance (you can't have both unless you pay extra).

- **RAID 10 / 1+0**   Over the years, several combinations of RAID have been introduced to deal with the performance problems of RAID5. One of the best implementations involves combining mirroring (RAID1) with disk striping (RAID0). The names RAID 10 and RAID 1+0 are often used to refer to this.

The idea here is simple—mirror several sets of hard disks and then take all the mirror sets and create a RAID0 stripe set. In this configuration you do not incur any parity calculation overhead but you do have fault tolerance through mirroring. Performance for reads and writes is great since data is written to, or read from, several sets of disks simultaneously. In fact, you can lose one disk from each mirror pair and still get good performance, although losing both disks in any mirror pair will lose all of the data, as in RAID0.

The major problem with this implementation is cost—you need double the disks since everything is mirrored. If you have a busy OLTP system that holds your critical corporate information, the investment may be worth it.

- **RAID 0+1**   RAID 0+1 is similar to RAID 10 / 1+0 but instead of creating mirrors and then striping them, you create one stripe set and then mirror it to another stripe set on a different set of disks. The drawback here is that even though you need the same number of disks as RAID 10, if you lose one disk in each mirrored stripe set, all of your data is lost. RAID 10 provides greater fault tolerance, the same performance, and is the preferred choice.

RAID is also the foundation for many Storage Area Network (SAN) technologies available from third-party storage vendors such as EMC, HP, Dell, and others. These vendors also offer other technologies (three-way mirroring, for example) that can provide additional benefits, such as snapshot backups. Use technology that fits your business requirements and is appropriate given the value of your data to you. Be frugal but wise.

Managing Database Files

Once you have created your database, chances are you will need to monitor space usage, resize existing data and log files, add additional files, create filegroups to better manage placement of database objects, and perform other tasks related to database storage. While most data file management tasks can be performed using the properties dialog box for a database, understanding the commands issued by SQL Server is important. These commands will be discussed in the remainder of the chapter.

Managing File Growth and Numbers of Data Files

As indicated earlier, one of the options available when creating a database is to specify whether or not data and log files should automatically grow when the data within them requires more space. SQL Server will default to enabling automatic file growth at 10 percent of the current size up to an unlimited size (or the use of all available disk space on the drive the file resides on). The default settings of SQL Server may be fine for a development and testing environment, but production systems typically require more control from the DBA. You can control file growth, as well as add and remove data files using the ALTER DATABASE command in SQL Server 7 and 2000. The partial syntax for the command is as follows:

```
ALTER DATABASE database
{ ADD FILE < filespec > [ ,...n ] [ TO FILEGROUP filegroup_name ]
| ADD LOG FILE < filespec > [ ,...n ]
| REMOVE FILE logical_file_name
| ADD FILEGROUP filegroup_name
| REMOVE FILEGROUP filegroup_name
| MODIFY FILE < filespec >
| MODIFY FILEGROUP filegroup_name {filegroup_property | NAME =
new_filegroup_name }
}
< filespec > :=
( NAME = logical_file_name
    [ , NEWNAME = new_logical_name ]
    [ , FILENAME = 'os_file_name' ]
    [ , SIZE = size ]
    [ , MAXSIZE = { max_size | UNLIMITED } ]
    [ , FILEGROWTH = growth_increment ] )
```

To change the characteristics of an existing file, you would use the MODIFY FILE clause and only need to specify the logical name of the data file. You can use this option to resize an existing data file, enable or disable automatic file growth characteristics, or change the logical filename. However, the ALTER DATABASE command cannot be used to change the physical location of a data file—to do this you must detach and re-attach the database (covered in Chapter 8), or back up and restore the database (covered in Chapter 7).

To add a data file to a database and resize an existing file, you would issue the following commands:

```
ALTER DATABASE Northwind ADD FILE
        (NAME='Northwind_Data02',
         PHYSNAME='D:\MSSQLDATA\NWDATA02.NDF'
         SIZE=50MB, FILEGROWTH=50MB, MAXSIZE=200MB)
GO
ALTER DATABASE Northwind MODIFY FILE
        (NAME='Northwind_data', SIZE=50MB)
GO
```

In a similar fashion, you can also add a second or third log file to a database by using the ADD LOGFILE clause, or change the size of an existing log file using MODIFY FILE. Most ALTER DATABASE commands cannot be combined and must be issued sequentially, as shown in the previous example. You cannot, for example, add a data file and log file to the database in a single statement, or drop and add a file in the same command.

Filegroups in SQL Server

One of the best ways available to a DBA to control storage for database objects is to create and use filegroups. Each SQL Server database always has one filegroup to store database objects—PRIMARY. The PRIMARY filegroup is required and should contain the data dictionary (system tables) for the database. Ideally, all other objects should be created on DBA-defined filegroups for specific objects. Using filegroups, you can separate a big busy table from other big busy tables, or those with different access patterns or fragmentation tendencies from others with different behaviors. Filegroups provide great control over storage and I/O performance for a DBA. Filegroups are similar in functionality to tablespaces in Oracle and DB2 and can be useful in tuning complex databases.

The creation of filegroups and placement of objects on them involves a three-step process. You first create a filegroup in the database using the ALTER DATABASE command and specifying a unique filegroup name within the database At this point, you have a name for a potential collection of data files. The next step is to add one or more data files to the filegroup. Finally, you can specify on which filegroup to allocate storage for an object when you create the segment (an object requiring storage—table, index, and so on). You cannot specify in which data file belonging to the filegroup the data will be stored—you can only specify the filegroup itself. SQL Server manages all storage in a filegroup. An example of these tasks is as follows:

```
ALTER DATABASE Northwind CREATE FILEGROUP ArchiveData
GO
ALTER DATABASE ADD FILE
        (NAME='Northwind_Archive01',
         PHYSNAME='E:\ArchiveData\NWARCH01.NDF',
         SIZE=200MB, FILEGROWTH=0) TO FILEGROUP ArchiveData
GO
```

Before using filegroups, it is very important to have a thorough understanding of your database and its access patterns. You need to apply the KYD factor (*Know Your Data*) to ensure that you are not creating more work in managing filegroups and thereby countering the improved performance that you may be gaining. It is possible to over-engineer a database, so only use filegroups when circumstances call for a separation of data due to volume or for performance reasons, or to take advantage of multiple disks and CPUs to parallelize I/O.

One important task that each DBA should perform is changing the default filegroup for all new database objects to a filegroup other than PRIMARY. This is accomplished by using the MODIFY FILEGROUP clause of the ALTER DATABASE command as follows:

```
ALTER DATABASE MODIFY FILEGROUP filegroup_name
{READWRITE | READONLY | DEFAULT | NAME = new_filegroup_name }
```

Using the ALTER DATABASE command, you can make one (and only one) filegroup in the database the default, change a filegroup to contain READONLY data (useful for storing lookup tables, or tables in data warehouses), READWRITE (the default) for normal operation, or change the name of the filegroup using the NAME option.

Filegroups can be very useful in a large data-warehousing environment, and they do allow you to back up a filegroup instead of the entire database, thereby allowing for a more granular backup strategy in very large database (VLDB) environments. Though it may seem obvious, you cannot create transaction log files on filegroups—only data files used for storing segments (tables, indexes, or any database object requiring storage).

Shrinking Databases and Database Files

SQL Server allows you to shrink the size of either your entire database or individual data files. Both are accomplished using a DBCC command. DBCC, which stands for Database Consistency Checker, is an advanced system stored procedure with many options (covered throughout the rest of this book).

Shrinking the Entire Database

The syntax for shrinking a database is as follows:
```
DBCC SHRINKDATABASE
    ( database_name [ , target_percent ]
        [ , { NOTRUNCATE | TRUNCATEONLY } ]
    )
```

The DBCC SHRINKDATABASE command (which replaced the SHRINKDB command used in SQL Server 6.*x* or earlier) will shrink all data files individually down to the space occupied by the data. DBCC will first reorganize the data to densely pack it so that data completely fills the leading portion of the data file. If you specify a *target_percent*, DBCC SHRINKDATABASE command will leave that percentage of free space in the file for future growth. If the percentage specified is more than is currently available, or if that would shrink the file below the SIZE specified when the file was originally created, the file will not be shrunk. A file cannot shrink below the space used by objects in the file or its original size.

DBCC SHRINKDATABASE will also shrink the size of log files by placing them all in a pool and determining the size of the entire log by the value provided for *target_percent*. It will then shrink each file down to the size required. If a log file contains data beyond the target size, DBCC SHRINKDATABASE will shrink the log file as much as it can, and notify you to back up the log to reduce its size further, or any other action you need to take.

An important element regarding log files is that each is internally divided into *virtual log files*, which are an allocation of storage within the log file of at least 256KB, although SQL Server will try and keep the size of a virtual log larger for efficiency. As transactions get written, they fill up virtual logs that combine to make a *logical log*—the collection of all virtual logs in all log files holding log data. When you back up a transaction log, you are emptying out virtual logs that are full and contain data. If all virtual log files in all log files become full before being backed up, log files will grow, if you have enabled that option, and create additional virtual logs.

When trying to shrink log files, the size of virtual logs and their location within a log file may result in log file shrinkage below what was anticipated. Because the size of a virtual log determines increments by which the log file can be shrunk, if you create a log file of 500MB in size, that file may contain 5 virtual logs of 100MB each. If you attempt to shrink the log file to 50MB, the operation will not succeed and you will be left with a log file of at least 100MB—the size of the virtual log. Furthermore, if the virtual log that is currently active is towards the end of the file, SQL Server will add dummy virtual log entries to fill up the log forcing the next log write to start at the beginning of the log file (log files operate in a circular fashion), which will cause the shrinkage operation to fail. This forces you to perform a log backup to allow the overwriting of information at the beginning of the log file with new transactions. In general terms, do a backup before shrinking log files. If a log file shrinkage fails, back up the transaction log and then try to shrink the log file again.

DBCC SHRINKDATABASE will not delete any data or log files. If you wanted to only reorganize the data (without reducing the file size), you can specify the NOTRUNCATE option. To simply reduce the size of the data files without performing any reorganization, use the TRUNCATEONLY option.

SQL Server 2000 also provides an AUTO_SHRINK option allowing you to force SQL Server to reorganize a database back to a smaller size whenever free space is available in the database, such as when a large table is dropped. SQL Server will shrink a file when it is more than 25 percent empty. It can shrink the database based on a schedule, or shrink only specific files configurable through the AUTO_SHRINK option.

While the AUTO_SHRINK option can free the DBA from the need to reorganize the database manually, it can have an impact on performance as it may be triggered at inopportune times. For this reason, it is recommended that you shrink databases manually instead.

Shrinking Database Files

The DBCC SHRINKFILE command will reorganize and shrink a single data file, as in the following syntax:

```
DBCC SHRINKFILE
    ( { file_name | file_id }
        { [ , target_size ]
            | [ , { EMPTYFILE | NOTRUNCATE | TRUNCATEONLY } ] 
        }
    )
```

The DBCC SHRINKFILE command works similarly to DBCC SHRINKDATABASE except that instead of a target free space percentage, you specify the *target_size* (in megabytes) you want the file shrunk to. If you do not specify a *target_size*, SQL Server shrinks the file as much as possible after reorganizing the data in it. If you use the EMPTYFILE option, SQL Server attempts to move all data from the file to other files in the same filegroup. It does not allow new data to be stored in the file, so you can drop the file using the ALTER DATABASE command later.

Shrinking Takes Time

DBCC SHRINKDATABASE and SHRINKFILE commands work on a deferred basis. This means that the shrinkage task may not start immediately and will most certainly take time to complete. Be patient, especially if you have a large database.

Retrieving File Information

Aside from using Enterprise Manager to get information about your data files, SQL Server also includes a couple of stored procedures to help you, as follows:

```
sp_helpfile [ [ @filename = ] 'name' ]
sp_helpfilegroup [ [ @filegroupname = ] 'name' ]
sp_helpdb [ [ @dbname= ] 'name' ]
DBCC SQLPERF (LOGSPACE)
```

To get a listing of all filegroups in the database and the number of data files within each filegroup, use the **sp_helpfilegroup** stored procedure. For a list of datafiles (or details on a single datafile) including logical and physical name, size, space used, and filegrowth characteristics, run the **sp_helpfile** stored procedure. To get a listing of all data and log files for a database, use the **sp_helpdb** stored procedure and supply the database name (otherwise, you simply get a list of databases on the server). The DBCC SQLPERF (LOGSPACE) command will return the amount of space used in the transaction log files of all databases.

Setting Database Options

Not all databases require the same characteristics. For this reason, SQL Server includes a number of database options that can be set. In SQL Server 2000, you use the ALTER DATABASE command to change database options. In previous releases, you execute the **sp_dboption** system stored procedure to change database options. The syntax for **sp_dboption** is the following:

```
sp_dboption [ [ @dbname = ] 'database' ]
    [ , [ @optname = ] 'option_name' ] [ , [ @optvalue = ] 'value' ]
```

Database options can be broken down into five broad categories: auto, cursor, recovery, SQL, and state. Table 4-2 outlines the category, available options, versions supported, and a brief description of the options that can be set using the ALTER DATABASE command in SQL Server 2000. All options can only be set by members of the **sysadmin** or **dbcreator** role. Options outlined in Table 4-3 can be set using the **sp_dboption** stored procedure. These options have similar meaning to those listed in Table 4-2. The syntax for ALTER DATABASE is as follows:

```
ALTER DATABASE database
    SET < optionspec > [ ,...n ] [ WITH < termination > ]
```

4

The *<termination>* option determines how users are handled when a state change takes place in the database. The *<termination>* option can be either ROLLBACK AFTER *integer* [SECONDS] (wait the requisite number of seconds and then perform a rollback of all transactions), or ROLLBACK IMMEDIATE (rollback all transactions immediately). Optionally, specifying NO_WAIT will return an error if the state change cannot be completed without waiting for transactions to commit or rollback. This means that users are working with the database.

Category	Option	Description	SQL Server Version
AUTO	AUTO_CLOSE ON | OFF	When ON, instructs SQL Server to take the database offline when the last user disconnects. Default is OFF.	7.0 2000
	AUTO_CREATE_STATISTICS ON | OFF	Instructs SQL Server to create statistics needed to optimize a query if they are not available. Default is ON.	7.0 2000
	AUTO_SHRINK ON | OFF	Enables (ON) or disables (OFF—the default) automatic periodic shrinking of files in the database.	7.0 2000
	AUTO_UPDATE_STATISTICS ON | OFF	Instructs SQL Server to automatically update any out-of-date statistics required by a query for optimization. If this feature is turned off, the UPDATE STATISTICS command reenables automatic statistic updates unless the NORECOMPUTE parameter is specified. The default is ON.	7.0 2000
CURSOR	CURSOR_CLOSE_ON_COMMIT ON | OFF	When ON, any cursors open when a transaction is committed or rolled back are closed. If set to OFF (the default), cursors remain open when a commit takes place but a rollback closes any cursors except INSENSITIVE or STATIC cursors.	6.x 7.0 2000

Table 4-2. SQL Server Database Options Settable Using ALTER DATABASE

Category	Option	Description	SQL Server Version
	CURSOR_DEFAULT LOCAL | GLOBAL	Determines if a cursor will be GLOBAL (referanceable in any stored procedure or batch for the session) or LOCAL to the procedure or batch. GLOBAL is the default.	6.*x* 7.0 2000
RECOVERY	RECOVERY FULL | BULK_LOGGED | SIMPLE	RECOVERY determines how transaction logs and certain operations are handled. When FULL is specified, transaction logs are not cleared out until they are backed up. Recovery can be up to the point of failure. When BULK_LOGGED is specified, certain operations (SELECT INTO, bcp, BULK INSERT, CREATE INDEX, WRITETEXT and UPDATETEXT) will not generate transaction log entries. Backups will need to be made after any operation of this type occurs to prevent data loss. When SIMPLE is specified, transaction logs are cleared whenever a checkpoint occurs, thereby reducing log space. Requires greater backup vigilance. The default model is inherited from the model database when you create a new database.	2000
	trunc. log on ckpt. true | false	Truncates the transaction log when a checkpoint occurs. Similar to the SIMPLE recovery model of SQL Server 2000. (Requires **sp_dboption**.)	6.*x* 7.0
	select into/bulk copy true | false	Enables performing non-logged operations such as a SELECT ... INTO and bcp on a database. Similar to the BULK_LOGGED recovery model of SQL Server 2000. (Requires **sp_dboption**.)	6.*x* 7.0
	TORN_PAGE_DETECTION ON | OFF	When ON (the default) is specified, SQL Server can detect pages with incomplete or damaged structures and prevent further corruption.	2000
SQL	ANSI_NULL_DEFAULT ON | OFF	Specifies whether the database follows SQL-92 rules to determine whether a column allows null values when a CREATE TABLE command is issued. The default is OFF.	6.*x* 7.0 2000

Table 4-2. SQL Server Database Options Settable Using ALTER DATABASE *(continued)*

Category	Option	Description	SQL Server Version
	ANSI_NULLS ON | OFF	If ON is specified, all comparisons to NULL evaluate to NULL. If OFF is specified, comparisons to NULL evaluate to TRUE, if both values are NULL. The default is OFF.	6.x 7.0 2000
	ANSI_PADDING ON | OFF	Strings are padded to the same length before comparison or an INSERT when set to ON. OFF specifies that strings are not padded. ON is the default and recommended setting.	6.x 7.0 2000
	ANSI_WARNINGS ON | OFF	When ON, errors or warnings are issued when conditions such as divide-by-zero occur. OFF, the default, ignores these errors and returns NULL instead.	6.x 7.0 2000
	ARITHABORT ON | OFF	When ON, a query is aborted when an overflow or divide-by-zero error occurs. If a transaction was active at the time, the transaction is rolled back. OFF simply generates an error and does not abort the transaction or batch. Default is OFF.	6.x 7.0 2000
	CONCAT_NULL_YIELDS_NULL ON | OFF	When ON, the result of a concatenation operation with NULL on either side yields NULL. When OFF, the null value is treated as an empty character string. The default is OFF.	6.x 7.0 2000
	QUOTED_IDENTIFIER ON | OFF	When ON, double quotation marks (" ") can be used to enclose delimited identifiers. Square brackets [ ] are always valid delimiters in SQL Server 7 and 2000. The default is OFF.	6.x 7.0 2000
	NUMERIC_ROUNDABORT ON | OFF	When ON, if a loss of precision occurs in an expression, an error is returned.	2000
	RECURSIVE_TRIGGERS ON | OFF	When ON, recursive firing of triggers is allowed. OFF, the default, prevents direct recursion only. Disabling indirect recursion can be accomplished by setting the nested triggers server option to 0 using **sp_configure**.	2000

Table 4-2. SQL Server Database Options Settable Using ALTER DATABASE *(continued)*

Category	Option	Description	SQL Server Version
STATE	SINGLE_USER | RESTRICTED_USER | MULTI_USER	Determines which users may access the database. SINGLE_USER only allows one user at a time to access the database. This user can be anyone and need not be one of the special roles defined for RESTRICTED_USER. RESTRICTED_USER allows only members of the **db_owner**, **dbcreator**, or **sysadmin** roles access to the database. MULTI_USER (the default) allows any users with privileges to connect to the database.	2000
	dbo use only true | false	Similar to RESTRICTED_USER in previous releases of SQL Server. (Requires **sp_dboption**.)	6.x 7.0
	OFFLINE | ONLINE	Determines database availability. When ONLINE (the default), users may access the database. When OFFLINE, the database is closed and cannot be used.	6.x 7.0 2000
	READ_ONLY | READ_WRITE	Determines if changes to the database can be made (READ_WRITE, the default) or if the database can be read only, with changes allowed (READ_ONLY). Changing this state requires all users to be disconnected from the database.	7.0 2000

Table 4-2. SQL Server Database Options Settable Using ALTER DATABASE *(continued)*

auto create statistics	auto update statistics	autoclose
autoshrink	ANSI null default	ANSI nulls
ANSI warning	arithabort	concat null yields null
cursor close on commit	db chaining	dbo use only
default to local cursor	merge publish	numeric roundabort
offline	published	quoted identifier
read only	recursive triggers	select into/bulkcopy
single user	subscribed	torn page detection
trunc. log on ckpt.		

Table 4-3. Database Options Settable Using sp_dboption

When using **sp_dboption** to set database options, the option value you provide can be one of **true** or **false**. Some options are set when you enable or disable publishing (published, subscribed, merge publish) and you do not normally set them manually. The db chaining option determines if an object in a database (view or stored procedure, for example) can include objects from other databases in its definition. This can be difficult to manage and is not recommend because if a dependent object is not available, users cannot reference the object relying on it.

Some, but not all, database options can also be set using Enterprise Manager and the properties screen of the database, as shown next. The ALTER DATABASE command or **sp_dboption** provide more functionality here.

4

To determine which options are currently set for a database, you can execute the **sp_dboption** stored procedure passing it the database name whose options you want to see. The **sp_helpdb** stored procedure, syntax shown here, will also display a list of options and their values, as well as other database information.

```
sp_helpdb [ [ @dbname= ] 'name' ]
```

Dropping Databases

Anyone who is a member of the **sysadmin** or **dbcreator,** and **db_owner** role for the database can drop it. This can be done with Enterprise Manager or using the DROP DATABASE command, with the following syntax:

```
DROP DATABASE database_name [ ,...n ]
```

Dropping a database removes all the data files in SQL Server 7.0 and later. In SQL Server 6.5 or earlier, you need to use the **sp_dropdevice <*devicename*>** system stored procedure to drop the devices associated with the database, but the disk files would remain and need to be cleaned up manually. Or, you could specify the **,delfile** parameter for **sp_dropdevice** to remove the device files at the same time.

In order for the command to succeed, the database cannot be in use (no user connections are allowed), be a publisher or distributor in replication, have a backup taking place, or in any way have any activity taking place on it. You cannot drop the **master, model, tempdb,** or **msdb** databases. Once dropped, a database and its data are gone unless a backup has been made. Before dropping a database, take a backup because the only way to get it back is to restore it from a backup.

The DBA Responsibility Truly Begins

Creating databases and managing data files, transaction logs, and database options is the starting point for much DBA activity. You will no doubt spend a lot of time ensuring that your databases have the proper number and placement of files, filegroups to support proper separation of database objects and increase performance, and the appropriate recovery and other options set to ensure proper disaster recovery and behavior. Understanding how to manage data files, how disk subsystems and RAID work, and what transaction logs really do, is basic knowledge all DBAs should have. DBAs also need to know which database objects are available, what they are used for, and how to manage them so as to be able to assist database designers and developers when they get bogged down.

Chapter 5

Creating and Managing Database Objects

In order to make databases useful after they have been created, you need to create tables, indexes, stored procedures, views, and other objects that will be used to store and manipulate data. Programming SQL Server and efficiently using Transact-SQL is a topic that requires a book or two of its own. In this chapter, you will find out what database objects are available in SQL Server and how to manage them.

For more information on programming SQL Server you may want to look at a couple of titles from McGraw-Hill/Osborne: *SQL Server 2000 Developer's Guide,* by Michael Otey and Paul Conte (2001), and *SQL Server 2000 Stored Procedure & XML Programming,* Second Edition, by Dejan Sunderic (2003).

SQL Server Database Objects

SQL Server allows for the creation and management of many objects in addition to tables. While tables are the most basic database object used to store data, other objects are also available to help manage that data and ensure that no business rules are broken, enforce security, maintain data integrity, and so on. Table 5-1 lists the database objects available in SQL Server, most of which are in versions of SQL Server 6.*x* to 2000. Only user-defined functions are new in SQL Server 2000.

Object	Description
Table	A collection of columns and rows representing a single entity (students, courses, instructors, and so on).
Column	A single attribute of an entity stored in a table. A column has a name and a data type. A table may have, and typically does have, more than one column as part of its definition.

Table 5-1. Database Objects in SQL Server

Object	Description
Row	A single instance of an entity in a table including all columns. For example, a student row will store all information about a single student such as his id, name, address, and so on.
Constraints	Database objects that are used to enforce simple business rules and database integrity. Examples of constraints are PRIMARY KEY, FOREIGN KEY, NOT NULL, CHECK, and others.
Views	A logical projection of data from one or more tables as represented by a SQL statement stored in the database. Views are used to simplify complex and repetitive SQL statements by assigning those statements a name in the database.
Indexes	Database objects that help speed up retrieval of data by storing logical pointers to specific key values. By scanning the index, which is organized in either ascending or descending order according to the key value, you are able to retrieve a row quicker than by scanning all rows in a table.
Stored Procedures	A collection of Transact-SQL statements that perform a specific task such as insert a row into a table, update data, and so on. They are one of the programming aspects of SQL Server.
Triggers	A special kind of stored procedure that cannot be invoked manually, but rather is automatically invoked whenever an action is performed on a table. Triggers are associated with a table or view and a corresponding action such as INSERT, UPDATE, or DELETE.
User-Defined Functions (UDF)	New in SQL Server 2000, user-defined functions are similar to stored procedures except that they must return a value. The function can return a single value or a rowset of data.
User-Defined Data Types	Database objects that can be used in any table definition within a SQL Server database and help to ensure consistency between tables.

Table 5-1. Database Objects in SQL Server *(continued)*

Object	Description
Rules	Similar to constraints in that rules apply a condition to ensure data meets certain criteria. Rules can be used in tables, or be applied against a user-defined data type.
Defaults	Defaults allow you to specify a default value for a column or user-defined data type when no other value is provided during an insert. Defaults are created at a database level.

Table 5-1. Database Objects in SQL Server *(continued)*

Managing Tables and Data Types

A database primarily stores data. Data has certain characteristics, so understanding how to manage tables and data types available to store data is an important aspect of any DBA responsibility.

SQL Server Scalar and User-Defined Data Types

Every column in every table in a SQL Server database has three important characteristics—name, data type, and size. SQL Server supports a number of different data types, as listed in Table 5-2. These include numeric, character, date and time, monetary, and other special data types.

Character data types include fixed-length types (**char**, **nchar**) and variable-length types (**varchar**, **nvarchar**). Fixed-length character data is stored in the database according to the size specified for the column. This means that if you define a column as **char(50),** data for that column will always occupy 50 bytes of disk space even if you only store the value "ABC" in the column. This is different from a column defined as a **varchar(50)** whose data will only occupy as much space in the database as is required to store the data, plus a couple of bytes of overhead. For example, the value "ABC" will only occupy 3 bytes for the data plus 2 bytes of overhead for a total of 5 bytes, instead of 50 bytes for the same data stored in a column of **char(50)**.

Character types **nchar** and **nvarchar** are Unicode data types and store data according to the Unicode collation of the SQL Server 7 or 2000 database, whereas **char** and **varchar** types store data according to the character set of the database, and are available in all SQL Server versions.

Data Type	Size	SQL Server Version	Description
char *[(n)]*	0–8000 bytes 0–2000 bytes	7.0, 2000 6.x	Fixed-length character data.
nchar *[(n)]*	0–8000 bytes	7.0, 2000	Fixed-length Unicode character data.
varchar *[(n)]*	0–8000 bytes 0–2000 bytes	7.0, 2000 6.x	Variable-length character data.
nvarchar [(n)]	0–8000 bytes	7.0, 2000	Variable-length Unicode character data.
text	0–2GB	6.x, 7.0, 2000	Variable-length character data stored as a large object.
ntext	0–2GB	7.0, 2000	Variable-length Unicode character data stored as a large object.
bigint	8 bytes	7.0, 2000	Integer data from -2^{63} to $2^{63}-1$.
int	4 bytes	6.x, 7.0, 2000	Integer data from -2^{31} to $2^{31}-1$.
smallint	2 bytes	6.x, 7.0, 2000	Integer data from $-32{,}768$ to $32{,}767$.
tinyint	1 byte	6.x, 7.0, 2000	Integer data from 0 to 255.
decimal [(p,s)] **numeric** [(p,s)]	2–17 bytes 2–17 bytes	6.x, 7.0, 2000 6.x, 7.0, 2000	Exact numeric data of precision (p) and scale (s). Precision is the total number of digits to store to the left and right of the decimal point and can be from 1 to 38 with a default of 18. Scale can be from 0 to the value of precision and is the number of digits to the right of the decimal point.
float [(n)] **real**	4 bytes if n is 1–24; 8 bytes if n is 25–53 4 bytes	6.x, 7.0, 2000 6.x, 7.0, 2000	Approximate numeric data where n is the number of bits to store the mantissa of the number and can be any range from 1 to 53 with a default of 53. Specifying the real data type is the same as float(24).
money	8 bytes	6.x, 7.0, 2000	A numerical value with a maximum of 19 digits of which 4 can be to the right of the decimal.
smallmoney	4 bytes	7.0, 2000	A numerical value with a maximum of 10 digits of which 4 can be to the right of the decimal.

Table 5-2. SQL Server Built-In Data Types

Data Type	Size	SQL Server Version	Description
datetime	8 bytes	6.x, 7.0, 2000	Date and time data from January 1, 1753 to December 31, 9999, with accuracy to 3/100th of a second.
smalldatetime	4 bytes	7.0, 2000	Date and time data from January 1, 1900 to June 6, 2079, with an accuracy of 1 minute.
binary [(n)]	0–8000 bytes	7.0, 2000	Fixed- (binary) or variable-length (varbinary) binary data.
varbinary [(n)]	0–2000 bytes	6.x	
Image	0–GB	6.x, 7.0, 2000	Variable-length binary data stored as a large object.
uniqueidentifier	6 bytes	7.0, 2000	A globally unique identifier (GUID) generated using the NEWID function.
Bit	1 byte	6.x, 7.0, 2000	Integer data with either 0 or 1 as the data value.
cursor	0–8 bytes	7.0, 2000	A data type that stores a reference to a cursor. Useful in storing cursor references returned from stored procedures.
timestamp	8 bytes	6.x, 7.0, 2000	A database-wide unique number (not actual date and time) that is updated when a row is changed. It most closely resembles the ANSI **rowversion** type.
sysname	256 bytes	7.0, 2000	Data type used to store system name values. Useful in storing parameters to pass to stored procedures or returned from them.
sql_variant	0–8016 bytes	2000	Data type similar to the Visual Basic 6.0 and earlier **variant** variable type. Can be used to store values for any SQL Server data types except **text**, **ntext**, **image**, and **timestamp** types.

Table 5-2. SQL Server Built-In Data Types *(continued)*

User-Defined Data Types

In many situations it may be worthwhile to create additional data types for use in a database to enforce consistency and assist in readability. For example, if you store a telephone number in several tables (Customers, Employees,

Suppliers, Contacts, and so on), creating a user-defined Telephone data type is useful to ensure that all tables will store telephone numbers in the same amount of storage. It also makes it easier to determine the contents of a column when the data type name also helps to describe its content. SQL Server allows the creation of user-defined data types based upon existing SQL Server scalar data types. To add or drop a user-defined data type, you can use Enterprise Manager and navigate to the database in which you want to create the user-defined data type, expand the database node, and then right-click on the database name and select New User-Defined Data Type, or right-click on User-Defined Data Types and select New User-Defined Data Type. The dialog box presented, shown in Figure 5-1, will allow you to specify a name for the data type, which must be unique in the database, as well as its base type, size, and whether or not to allow NULLs. You can also attach an existing Rule or Default to the data type.

NOTE *Rules and Defaults will be covered later in this chapter in the section called "Enforcing Integrity."*

To drop a user-defined data type using Enterprise Manager, select it in the details pane of User-Defined Data Types and press DELETE, confirming the delete on the dialog box that appears.

The other way to manage user-defined data types is to use the **sp_addtype** and **sp_droptype** stored procedures, which have the following syntax:

```
sp_addtype typename, 'system_data_type' [, NULL | NOT NULL] [, owner]

sp_droptype typename
```

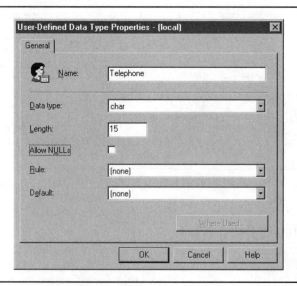

Figure 5-1.   Specify a name and base type/size for a user-defined data type.

For example, to create the **telephone** data type you would issue the following command:

```
sp_addtype telephone, 'char(15)', NULL
```

User-defined data types reside in a single database on the SQL Server. If you want to include one or more user-defined data types in all future databases, define them in the **model** database. They will then be included in any new databases that are created. If you want to add them to existing databases, you will need to add each user-defined data type to each database individually.

To retrieve a list of current user-define data types in a database, execute the **sp_help** stored procedure. It is also important to remember that, in order to change the definition of a user-defined data type, you must first make sure it is not being used in any table definition, and then drop the data type and re-create it with the new characteristics. Enterprise Manager will allow you to see a list of dependent objects before dropping a user-defined data type.

Data Type Usage Guidelines

To ensure that your databases are as efficient as possible, these guidelines regarding data type usage should be followed:

- Use the smallest data type possible to store the data you need to store. For example, if you only need to store date information that includes the day, month, and year, consider using the **smalldatetime** data type instead of **datetime**, since it only occupies 4 bytes of storage instead of 8.
- If data in character columns will vary widely, use a **varchar** data type instead of **char**. This will reduce the storage space used for the data while still allowing it to grow.
- If the size of character or binary data will be greater than the size of a SQL Server page (2K in SQL Server 6.*x* and 8K in SQL Server 7 and 2000), use the **text**, **ntext**, or **image** data types to store the data.
- For numerical data, use **decimal** or **numeric** instead of **real** or **float**, since these provide greater precision.
- Do not use **real** or **float** in the definition of PRIMARY KEY columns of a table as their values are not precise and should not be used in exact comparisons such as in joins between tables.
- For storage of currency values, generally use the **money** data type to allow for storage of larger values.
- Be careful when using **tinyint** as it can only store 256 differing values.
- The size of all columns of a table, with the exception of columns defined as **text**, **ntext**, or **image**, cannot exceed the SQL Server page size, so use appropriate data types.

Creating and Managing Tables

A table is a collection of columns and rows. Each column in a table must have three attributes: name, data type, and size. A row is a single instance of the data, across all columns. In relational database theory a row is sometimes referred to as an entity, and a table is an entity set—that is, a collection of all rows.

Tables are created in a schema, which is the collection of all database objects owned by a database user. As a general guideline, each database should consist of a single schema—the **dbo** schema—since the user **dbo** should own all database objects to avoid broken ownership chains. The table name must be unique in the schema and a column name must be unique in a table. For example, it is perfectly fine to have a column called CustomerID in a table called Customers as well as in a table called Orders—a common occurrence, since this allows you to easily relate the data between the two tables using a join condition. However, you cannot have two tables called Customers, both created in the **dbo** schema in the same database. But you can have a table called Customers in the **dbo** schema and another schema in the same database (AR, for example). As a corollary, schema names must be unique in the database since user names must be unique within the database.

To create a table, you must have been granted the CREATE TABLE system permission, or have been assigned the **db_owner** or **db_ddladmin** role that allows object creation. You can use Enterprise Manager to complete a grid of the table's columns and then save the results. To do so, right-click on the database and select New | Table, or right-click on Tables in the navigation pane for the database where you want to create the table and select New Table. Just fill in the names of columns and their attributes in the grid presented, as shown in Figure 5-2, and then save the results (you will be prompted for the table name).

The other way to create a table is to use the CREATE TABLE Transact-SQL command, whose partial syntax in SQL Server 2000 is as follows:

```
CREATE TABLE tablename
( column_name data_type | column_name AS expression
    [NULL | NOT NULL] [COLLATE collation]
    [IDENTITY [(seed, increment) [NOT FOR REPLICATION]]]
    [DEFAULT expression] [CONSTRAINT constraint_name constraint_definition],
    [ROWGUIDCOL]
[...] )
[ON {filegroup_name | DEFAULT}]
[TEXTIMAGE ON {filegroup_name | DEFAULT}]
```

Most of the syntax for creating a table is the same as with any other database—specify the columns including column name, data type, and size. A few of the table creation options are designed to provide the DBA with ways to manage storage in an effort to optimize performance. These include the following:

- **ON *filegroup_name*** Allows you to specify the filegroup that the table will be created on. By default, the table will be created on the default filegroup for the database. This is easy, but can also cause tables with differing storage requirements or access patterns to be stored on the same disk drives, and potentially cause performance problems. By specifying a filegroup on which to create the table, you can separate two tables that are frequently accessed onto two filegroups with data files on separate physical drives, thereby making the I/O more even and not causing a bottleneck on any one drive.

- **TEXTIMAGE ON *filegroup_name*** Allows you to specify the location for storing data in **text**, **ntext**, and **image** columns. In many cases, users will access the **text**, **ntext**, or **image** data less frequently from other columns of the table. By separating storage of these columns from other columns in the table, you can make I/O for the table more efficient and also reduce disk contention.

NOTE   *In SQL Server 6.x a little-used database object called a segment is available that allows you to place tables and indexes on specific devices. You create a segment on a device and then create the table on the segment. In this way you have functionality similar to filegroups for object placement only, but you cannot independently back up segments like you can filegroups.*

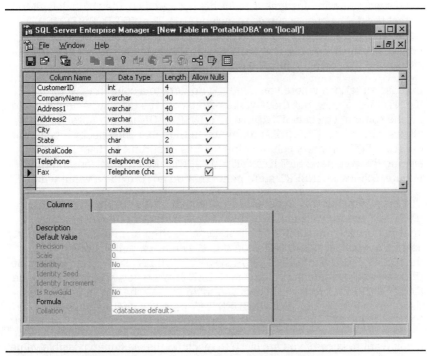

Figure 5-2.   Enterprise Manager allows easy definition of tables and columns.

Automatically Generating Column Values

In many applications it may become necessary to generate unique values for a column. This can be a numerical value such as a check or invoice number, or it can be an identifier that must be unique throughout the database, such as a confirmation code for an electronic order. SQL Server supports two ways to automatically generate unique values for a column—the IDENTITY property and the NEWID function with a DEFAULT.

The IDENTITY Property   The IDENTITY property is available in SQL Server 6.*x* to 2000. It can automatically generate a numeric value in a column of **integer** (**tinyint**, **smallint**, **int**, **bigint**), **numeric**, or **decimal** data type, with **decimal** and **numeric** data types requiring a scale of 0—typically an integer data type is used. Only one IDENTITY property column is allowed per table and is usually, though not always, associated with a PRIMARY KEY or UNIQUE constraint. You cannot update a column that is defined with the IDENTITY property and the column cannot support NULL since a value must always exist for the IDENTITY property.

To define a column with the IDENTITY property, the syntax is as follows:

```
CREATE TABLE table_name
 (column_name data_type
 [IDENTITY [(seed_value, increment_value)] [NOT FOR REPLICATION]])
```

If the *seed_value* and *increment_value* are not specified, they both default to 1 so that the definition is assumed to include (1,1). The NOT FOR REPLICATION clause states that when data is inserted into the table through SQL Server replication, the IDENTITY property should not be enforced and data should be allowed to be entered into the column as is.

In those situations where you need to add data to a column with the IDENTITY property, but these values are below the next incremental value for the column, you can SET IDENTITY_INSERT ON in your session. This allows you to issue INSERT statements on the table and specify a value for the IDENTITY property column directly. It is important to disable this by issuing the command SET IDENTITY_INSERT OFF after performing the update, otherwise INSERT statements that do not provide a value will fail.

The most common way to determine what value was inserted into an IDENTITY property column is to query the @@**identity** system variable after performing an INSERT. The last value inserted in an IDENTITY property column in your session will be stored in @@**identity**. In SQL Server 2000, the IDENT_SEED and IDENT_INCR system functions allow you to determine the seed and incremental value for an IDENTITY property column, while the IDENT_CURRENT function allows you to determine the last value used in the table in any session. SCOPE_IDENTITY provides information similar to IDENT_CURRENT, but only for your session.

If you want to know if you are close to reaching the maximum possible value for the data type by which the IDENTITY property column was defined, you can execute the **DBCC CHECKIDENT** stored procedure. This will allow you to see what the current and maximum values for the column are.

The NEWID Function and GUIDs   In SQL Server 7, Microsoft introduced the **uniqueidentifier** data type in conjunction with the NEWID function. These two features work together to allow you to store a Globally Unique Identifier (GUID), a 16-byte binary string whose value is guaranteed to be unique in the database at the time that it is inserted.

Because the **uniqueidentifier** data type does not automatically generate new GUIDs when an INSERT takes place, if you want SQL Server to automatically create a GUID for the column when an INSERT statement is issued, you define a DEFAULT on the column and specify the NEWID function for the DEFAULT, as follows:

```
CREATE TABLE GuidExample
    (TestGUIDColumn uniqueidentifier NOT NULL DEFAULT NEWID())
```

If you do not want the GUID to be created automatically, you can use the NEWID function in the INSERT statement to generate the value at that time. Either way, the value placed in the column will be globally unique.

In SQL Server 2000 you can also designate a column of **uniqueidentifier** data type as a ROWGUIDCOL, which will make it the column that can be used to enforce uniqueness in the table through a PRIMARY KEY or UNIQUE constraint. Only one designated ROWGUIDCOL is allowed per table, though more than one column of **uniqueidentifier** data type can be in the same table. Designating a column as a ROWGUIDCOL is most useful for documentation as this property is not enforced by SQL Server in any way, except for not allowing another column in the same table to also hold the property.

Adding, Modifying, and Dropping Columns

As your databases evolve and tables are used, you may need to add or remove columns to deal with new requirements. SQL Server's ALTER TABLE command can be used to add new columns to a table, change some elements of existing columns (but not the column name), or drop existing columns.

To add a new column to an existing table, the syntax is as follows:

```
ALTER TABLE tablename ADD column_name data_type { NULL | NOT NULL}
```

Adding a column uses basically the same syntax as defining a column in a table. You can specify an IDENTITY property (assuming another column in the table does not already have it defined), a DEFAULT, other constraints, or anything else that is valid. In SQL Server 2000 you can also specify that the column is a calculated column whose data is calculated when it is referenced (which can also be done when defining a table), as in this example:

```
ALTER TABLE Orders ADD Margin AS (Price-Cost)
```

To modify certain elements of a column, use the ALTER COLUMN clause of
the ALTER TABLE command, as shown here:

```
ALTER TABLE tablename
   ALTER COLUMN column_name  { new_data_type [(precision [,scale])]
          [ COLLATE <collation> ]
          [ NULL | NOT NULL ]
          | {ADD | DROP } ROWGUIDCOL }
```

When changing the column's data type, you need to ensure that the new
data type is compatible. For example, you can go from a **char** to a **varchar**
but not from a **char** to an **int**. Generally, you want to make sure that you are
in the same category of data types—string, numeric, date. The same also
holds true for a collation, so that it is not possible to modify the column to
accept an 8-bit collation when column data is based on a 16-bit collation
originally.

To drop an existing column on a table, the syntax is similar to the following:

```
ALTER TABLE tablename DROP COLUMN column_name
```

When you drop a column, any data that existed in it is gone. Furthermore, if
you attempt to drop a column that is referenced in a FOREIGN KEY constraint
in a table, you will get an error and the column will not be dropped. Any
constraints depending on the column being dropped must be dropped first.
The same also holds true for indexes since dropping a column will **not**
automatically drop the index—the index must be dropped manually.

To change the name of a column, you need to add a new column with the
appropriate name, update its values with the old column's data, and then
drop the old column. Or use the Table Designer in Enterprise Manager,
which does exactly that.

Dropping Tables

Dropping a table is a simple process, though with dire consequences if not
intended—all the data is lost and there is no easy way to get it back. The
syntax for dropping a table is as follows:

```
DROP TABLE table_name
```

It is impossible to drop more than one table at the same time. Any table
being dropped cannot be currently referenced by a FOREIGN KEY constraint
in another table—the constraint or child table must be dropped first. Once
the table is dropped, all indexes defined on the table are also dropped. Any
user-defined data types or rules are also unbound from the table.

In order to drop a table you must be the table owner or have been granted
the **sysadmin, ddl_admin**, or **db_owner** role. If you are not the owner of the
table, you must specify the ownername as part of the DROP TABLE statement.

Managing Indexes

Storing your data in a table is only half the battle—now you have to retrieve it. If the amount of data is small, retrieval speed can be quite quick. As the volume of data grows, however, query speed decreases and you need to provide other means to speed up the process. Using indexes is the method most frequently cited as the way to increase query speed, but having too many can also cause writes (INSERT, UPDATE, DELETE) to slow down.

Why (Not to) Create Indexes?

Creating and managing indexes is always walking a fine line between query speed and data-modification speed. The right number of indexes should always be decided by the following maxim: As many as you need, and as few as you can get away with. That in itself is like a statement made by a politician during elections—technically accurate, but not terribly useful. The right answer, in terms of how many indexes to create, depends upon your database and its intended purpose.

Databases are frequently categorized into the three following groups:

- **Online Transaction Processing (OTLP)** OLTP databases are primarily modification-intensive. For these databases, the typical access pattern is to query a single or small number of rows at a time from a table, or insert and update data in these tables. For OLTP systems you want to create indexes on only those columns frequently queried or those used to enforce uniqueness. A smaller number of indexes is the norm here. Typical examples of an OLTP database are order entry and banking systems.

- **Decision Support Systems (DSS)** DSS systems and their corollaries, such as data warehouses or data marts, are primarily reporting-oriented systems that are updated in large bulk–load operations, and then queried for large amounts of data until the next load. For DSS databases you typically will create more indexes because the fields being queried can be anything, since ad-hoc queries are the norm here. You need to determine the types of queries being executed against the database to determine on which columns to create indexes. The Index Tuning Wizard in SQL Enterprise Manager can be useful here.

- **Hybrid** It's hardest to properly decide on the correct number of indexes and columns to index for hybrid databases. These databases are used both for inserting and updating data, and also for reporting, at the same time. In these cases you will have to create indexes that are the best compromise between query speed and data-modification speed. Furthermore, as data access and modification patterns change, you will have to reevaluate the indexes. Hybrid systems require the most work on the part of the DBA.

Up to this point, we've really only talked about using indexes to speed up queries, but another important reason to use indexes is to enforce uniqueness. You can create unique indexes on tables that will ensure that data in the indexed columns is unique within the table.

In SQL Server 2000 you can also create indexes on computed columns (also referred to as function-based indexes) that will index the result of an expression, further allowing for faster query retrieval. Many restrictions exist on index creation on computed columns, but the key one to remember is that the result of the computed column's expression must be deterministic (consistent and predictable) in order for it to be indexed. This means that you cannot index an expression that calculates age (today's date minus the customer's birth date, for example), because every time the date changes, you will get a different value. However, something like margin (sales price minus cost) is deterministic and can be indexed.

In deciding which columns to index, general guidelines state that PRIMARY and FOREIGN KEY columns should always be indexed. Columns frequently searched in ranges (using =, BETWEEN, >, >=, <, <= in the WHERE clause), accessed in sorted order (ORDER BY), or specified in a GROUP BY are good candidates for an index. On the flip side, columns infrequently queried by, those with a small number of distinct values (gender or country, for example), or those defined using the **text**, **ntext**, or **image** data type should not be indexed.

While indexes speed up data retrieval, they also slow down data modifications and occupy disk space. These are the two main reasons to create just as many indexes as you need and not too many. Another important thing to keep in mind is that if your queries will, in general, retrieve more than 25 percent of the data in a table, creating indexes on the table may not actually help speed up queries. Instead of using the indexes, the SQL Server Query Optimizer may decide that a full table scan may cause less I/O. Again, the Index Tuning Wizard can help you determine if indexes are actually being used.

SQL Server Data Retrieval Overview

To understand why indexes are useful in making queries faster, you need to understand how SQL Server retrieves data. There are two possible ways to retrieve and index data—using a heap or an index.

When you create a table and add rows to it, data is stored in a heap, which is a collection of all pages belonging to that table. Pages are 8K in size in SQL Server 7 through 2000, and 2K in previous releases. A set of eight pages is an extent, which is the amount of space allocated whenever SQL Server needs to add more space to a table or an index.

When you issue a query against a table (SELECT * FROM Customers WHERE Lastname = 'Smith'), SQL Server performs a full table scan of a table, which is a read of all pages in all extents of the table that contain data until the last page indicated in the header page (page 0 of the table). When there is a small amount of data to be retrieved, this scan and checking whether or not data satisfies the condition (Lastname='Smith') can be quite quick, but as data grows each time the query is executed, the entire table must be read. You can see the problem with this in a large database that is accessed by 50, 100, or 500 users.

When you create an index, additional pages are created holding the index key value and a row identifier (for a non-clustered index) or cluster key (for a clustered index) for each row in the table. The key values are organized in a logical sequence (alphabetic, numeric, date) and in a binary tree (B*Tree) format with a root, branch level, and leaf pages (holding the key and identifier/ cluster key). When you query the Customers table for LastName BETWEEN 'Martin' and 'Ristow' and an index is created on the Lastname column, SQL Server scans the root page to determine the branch(es) holding the location of the leaf pages that hold the values between Martin and Ristow. It then retrieves the row identifiers, which contain the file ID, page, and row ID of a row (its physical location) for all matching rows. SQL Server then only reads those pages containing matching data, as shown in Figure 5-3. In this way, indexes allow you to retrieve specific sets of rows instead of scanning all the data in a table.

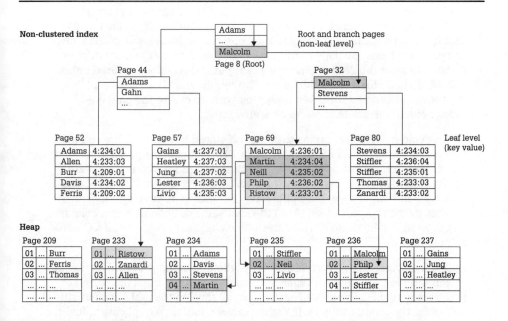

Figure 5-3. Traversing a non-clustered index to get row identifiers for values matching the query.

Creating and Dropping Indexes

To create an index on one or more columns of a table, you can use SQL
Enterprise Manager or the CREATE INDEX command, whose syntax in
SQL Server 2000 is as follows:

```
CREATE [ UNIQUE] [CLUSTERED | NONCLUSTERED] INDEX index_name
  ON { table_name | view_name } ( column_name [ ASC | DESC] [ …n ] )
  [ WITH [PAD_INDEX ] [[,]] FILLFACTOR = fillfactor_value ]
  [[,] IGNORE_DUP_KEY ] [[,] DROP_EXISTING ] [[,] STATISTICS_NORECOMPUTE ]
  [[,] SORT_IN_TEMPDB ]] [ ON filegroup ]
```

When you create an index, you have the option to create either a clustered
or non-clustered index. Non-clustered is the default. This option determines
how indexes will be organized and what they will contain.

A non-clustered index is similar to the index you find at the end of many
books. The data in the non-clustered index includes the key value and a row
identifier indicating the location of the rest of the row data. Just as you can
organize an index in the back of a book in many different ways (an index of
key terms, keyword index, and so on), so it is also possible to have many
non-clustered indexes on a table (up to 249 per table in SQL Server 2000).

A clustered index is organized similarly to a dictionary, with each index
entry containing the key column value and all the other column values as
well. When you create a clustered index, SQL Server physically reorganizes
the table data and stores it at the leaf level of the index. This also means
that it is not possible to have more than one clustered index in a table since
you can only have one copy of the data per table. Another important point
is that, because the data is physically reorganized when a clustered index
is built, all non-clustered indexes are also rebuilt when you create a
clustered index on a table. Generally, you want to create the clustered
index before you create any non-clustered ones.

When deciding which columns to create clustered indexes on, the common
perception is to use the PRIMARY KEY or UNIQUE constraint columns,
which may not always be the best. The clustered index should be created
on the column(s) most frequently queried. This may be the PRIMARY KEY
column(s) in many cases, but not always. For example, customer lookups
may most often be performed using the LastName or PhoneNumber columns,
which would make these the best candidates for clustering, even if a CustID
column exists.

During index creation you can also specify whether an index should be unique
or non-unique (the default). When you create a unique index (clustered or
non-clustered), SQL Server will ensure that all rows in the table have unique
values for the index columns. If, during index creation, a duplicate value is
encountered, the unique index is not created and the operation is rolled
back. If no duplicate values are found, the index is created and all future
INSERT and UPDATE operations will be required to maintain the uniqueness
or be rolled back. You can define more than one unique index on a table,

and a PRIMARY KEY or UNIQUE constraint will also automatically create a unique index to enforce the uniqueness it requires.

When you create unique indexes, you can specify the IGNORE_DUP_KEY option, which ignores any INSERT or UPDATE statement that results in duplicates and generates a warning. This can result in INSERT and UPDATE statements not being applied to the database and cause other problems. Generally, using IGNORE_DUP_KEY is not recommended. If you do not specify this option, a duplicate INSERT or UPDATE will result in an error and the transaction rolling back, which may also roll back other changes, a reason that IGNORE_DUP_KEY was added in SQL Server 2000.

Indexes are typically created on table columns. You can define an index on one or more columns of a table and, in SQL Server 2000, you can also define an index on a view. For each column being indexed, you can specify whether to sort the data in ascending (ASC) or descending (DESC) order, with ascending being the default. Columns can be of different data types and SQL Server will convert each column to a character data type for concatenation in order to index the data. Columns of **text, ntext,** and **image** data types cannot be indexed. The total size of all columns being indexed cannot exceed 900 bytes; otherwise the index creation will fail. Generally, keep index key columns as small as possible. This reduces storage space required and increases speed by storing more index entries per page.

When defining an index on a view in SQL Server 2000, the first index you create must be a unique clustered index. The view on which the index is created can reference base tables in its definition but cannot reference other views. Also, several SET options must be set to specific values. ARITHABORT, CONCAT_NULL_YIELDS_NULL, QUOTED_IDENTIFIER, ANSI_NULLS, ANSI_PADDING, and ANSI_WARNINGS must be set to ON and NUMERIC_ROUNDABORT must be set to OFF. If this is not the case, the creation of the index will succeed, but the SQL Server Query Optimizer may not use the indexes to evaluate a query, or DML operations on the view will result in an error stating that these SET options need to be configured. Other restrictions on querying indexed views also exist and may result in the indexes not being used or the query not executing.

The FILLFACTOR and PAD_INDEX columns deal with what percentage of a page to fill with index entries. The default for FILLFACTOR is 0 and instructs SQL Server to leave room for one additional index entry on each leaf page of the index (but fill all pages at the branch levels unless PAD_INDEX is specified). A value of 100 tells SQL Server not to leave any space for additional index entries at the leaf level, while any other value will instruct SQL Server to fill the page only to that percentage of space, rounded up to the next multiple of entries that can be supported on the page. Leaving space for additional index entries reduces dynamic splits at the leaf level of the index and allows entries with similar key values to be stored on the page more quickly (and also prolongs the time between index rebuilds). If your data is not updated, setting a FILLFACTOR of 100 will fill all pages and make the index smaller—common in data warehouses.

Other options when creating an index in SQL Server 2000 include DROP_EXISTING, SORT_IN_TEMPDB, and STATISTICS_NORECOMPUTE. DROP_EXISTING is used to re-create an existing index if it already exists on the key columns and prevent duplication of indexes, or simply to reorganize an index that has become inefficient over time (and this will happen in any database where indexes are updated). STATISTICS_NORECOMPUTE disables SQL Server's ability to keep statistics for the index up-to-date dynamically. This can be useful when queries are expecting a specific execution plan that can be modified if statistics are updated, but generally is not recommended as it will require manually issuing the UPDATE STATISTICS command to get current statistics information. SORT_IN_TEMPDB tells SQL Server to store the intermediate sort results of key columns values in TEMPDB instead of the filegroup of the index (specified with the ON *filegroup* option of the CREATE INDEX command). This can be useful only if the data files for TEMPDB are on separate physical disks from those of the index.

To drop an index, you can issue the DROP INDEX command as follows:

```
DROP INDEX table.index | view.index [, …]
```

Dropping indexes has some restrictions including the following: you cannot use the DROP INDEX command to drop indexes created as a result of a PRIMARY KEY or UNIQUE constraint definition; you cannot drop indexes on system tables; dropping a clustered index will automatically rebuild all non-clustered indexes. If you drop a table or view on which the index is defined, associated indexes will also dropped.

To rebuild an index you can issue the DROP INDEX command followed by a CREATE INDEX command, but the best method is to use the CREATE INDEX command with the DROP_EXISTING clause since this requires less I/O and makes the old index available while the new one is being built. You can also change a non-clustered index to clustered, make the index unique or not, add or remove columns, and change the filegroup when using DROP_EXISTING, all of which makes using the DROP and CREATE INDEX combination far less attractive.

To get information on indexes in the database, you can use SQL Enterprise Manager to query the information of a table or view, or the **sp_helpindex** *table* | *view* or the **sp_help** *table* | *view* system stored procedures.

Managing Views

In many large databases, the number of tables used to store data can be quite large. Furthermore, determining the series of columns from several tables that need to be joined in a SELECT statement to present data to answer a specific query can be quite daunting for many users and even programmers. A view is a method that can be used to mask database complexity and provide a consistent view of data, even if underlying base table definitions change. Views can also be used to simplify granting permissions by allowing you to define a view on the columns that users need to see, and by granting select permissions on the view, without granting any permissions on the tables that the view depends upon. Users will be able to see the data through the view without problems, provided the same database user owns the base tables and view (more to come in the section "Broken Ownerhsip Chains").

Creating, Altering, and Dropping Views

A view can best be defined as a SELECT statement that has been given a name and whose definition is stored in the data dictionary. To create a view in SQL Server, issue the CREATE VIEW statement as follows:

```
CREATE VIEW [database.][owner.]view_name [(column [,…])]
   [WITH {ENCRYPTION | SCHEMABINDING | VIEW_METADATA} [,…]]
AS select_statement
[WITH CHECK OPTION]
```

The heart of any view definition is the SELECT statement that outlines what data will be returned by the view. The SELECT statement used to define a view can be any simple or complex SELECT statement with a few restrictions. Views cannot reference more than 1,024 columns and cannot contain a COMPUTE or COMPUTE BY clause or the INTO keyword. An ORDER BY clause is allowed in the view definition provided the TOP keyword is used in the column list of the SELECT statement. The SELECT statement can include any type of join, aggregate and scalar functions, complex expressions, the GROUP BY and HAVING clauses, subqueries, and other advanced SQL capabilities. However, views taking advantage of these features will not be updateable (an INSERT, UPDATE or DELETE will not work, for example) unless an INSTEAD OF trigger is defined to decompose the update and populate the appropriate base tables. If the view will be indexed, the SELECT statement can only reference base tables and not other views.

If the SELECT statement for the view contains expressions in place of a column name (SalePrice-Cost, for example), the column name must be aliased either in the SELECT statement (SalePrice-Cost AS Margin) or in the column list in the CREATE VIEW statement. If using the column list in the CREATE VIEW statement, all columns in the SELECT statement must be outlined in the column list. Either way will work, but aliasing the column name in the SELECT statement is the preferred method because if you add or remove columns, you don't have to update the column list in the CREATE VIEW statement each time.

When creating a view, you can specify certain view attributes, as follows:

- **ENCRYPTION** Encrypts the source code used to define the view so that others cannot read it. This is useful when you are developing a

SQL Server database and don't want your view definition code to be easily copied. When creating a view with ENCRYPTION, it is important to keep a copy of the original view source code in a text file since you cannot reverse engineer encrypted view definitions.

- **SCHEMABINDING**   Prevents objects (tables, views, and user-defined functions) on which this view depends from being dropped or altered in a way that would affect the view. SCHEMABINDING requires that two-part (owner.object) notation be used for any referenced elements.

- **VIEW_METADATA**   Changes the way metadata is returned when queried. By default, when metadata about the view is queried, the base table names and columns on which the view is defined are returned. With VIEW_METADATA, information about the view itself is presented to OLE-DB, ODBC, and DBLIB API clients.

A final option that can be specified when creating a view is WITH CHECK OPTION. The WITH CHECK OPTION is used when you want to be sure that any DML on the view will result in data always visible through the view. For example, let's say you create a view called NYClients whose definition is "SELECT * FROM Clients WHERE State='NY'". If you issue a command to change the State of ABC Company from 'NY' to 'CA', the WITH CHECK OPTION, when set, will not allow the update and will return an error indicating that a constraint has been violated. This prevents users from making changes to the data that would not make the data selectable through the view, after the change completes. If the WITH CHECK OPTION was not set, the change of State from 'NY' to 'CA' would succeed and the company would now be in New York, CA (as an example).

If you want to change the definition of a view, issue the ALTER VIEW command, as follows:

```
ALTER VIEW [database.][owner.]view_name [(column [,…])]
    [WITH {ENCRYPTION | SCHEMABINDING | VIEW_METADATA} [,…]]
AS select_statement
[WITH CHECK OPTION]
```

As you can see, modifying a view has the same options as creating one, and these can be changed as needed (encrypt a view after it has been refined, turn on schema binding when the definition is finalized, and so on). If you specify SCHEMABINDING, ENCRYPTION, VIEW_METADATA, or WITH CHECK OPTION during creation, you must also specify them when using ALTER VIEW; otherwise, they will be removed (view settings from creation are not retained). Using the ALTER VIEW command still requires that the entire SELECT statement for the view be provided, but does preserve any permissions that have been granted on the view.

To drop a view, issue a DROP VIEW statement whose only parameter is the name of the view to drop. Any views that depend on the view being dropped will be marked as invalid and will need to be re-created or altered to remove the reference. If dependent views were created using the SCHEMABINDING attribute, the DROP VIEW statement will fail and you will need to alter the dependent view to remove the SCHEMABINDING attribute.

To get information on views, you can query the INFORMATION_SCHEMA .TABLES view for the name of the view, and the INFORMATION_ SCHEMA.VIEWS view for the view definition. The INFORMATION_ SCHEMA.VIEW_TABLE_USAGE view will provide information on dependent objects while the INFORMATION_SCHEMA.VIEW_COLUMN_USAGE view will display the columns that are defined in the view. You can get similar information by querying the **sysobjects, sysdepends, syscomments,** and **syscolumns** system views, respectively, but this is not recommended because their definitions may change between SQL Server versions.

Two system stored procedures are also helpful when searching for view information: **sp_helptext** and **sp_depends.** They provide information on the view definition and dependent objects, respectively.

Broken Ownership Chains

In situations where views are defined on other views, which themselves are defined on other views, and so on, it is important to keep in mind that SQL Server evaluates permissions on each dependent object whenever the object owner changes. For example, if Wendy creates a view called Wendy.View1 that is dependent on a view called Nancy.View2 whose SELECT statement references Steve.Table3, then when Damir issues the statement "SELECT * FROM Wendy.View1" and Wendy has granted Damir SELECT permissions on her view, SQL Server will also need to check that Damir has permissions to query Nancy.View2 and Steve.Table3 because the owner of these objects is not Wendy. This situation is known as a broken ownership chain.

Broken ownership chains can cause many sleepless nights and eat up time trying to figure out permissions within the database to make them work. The best way to avoid them is to make sure that a single user owns all objects. The best way to accomplish this is to grant any user that needs to create objects in the database the **db_owner** fixed database role. Any user granted the **db_owner** role will always create objects whose owner is the **dbo** database user, regardless of his username. If this is not practical because of security or other reasons, be aware of the potential problems associated with broken ownership chains.

Programming in Transact-SQL

In many applications the same commands are executed over and over. Think about the process of entering data for an order—look up customer record, add new order header with ship to and other information, add line items, check customer credit, decrement inventory, and so on. For every order, you perform the exact same set of commands. In encapsulating these repetitive steps, you can write a front-end application in Visual C# .NET to encapsulate all of the code logic and execute the correct SQL statements, or you can write stored procedures in Transact-SQL to perform the tasks.

One of the advantages of using stored procedures and other Transact-SQL programming elements, such as user-defined functions and triggers, is that they execute on the SQL Server. This makes sharing powerful server resources easy and also allows you to change the logic of the stored procedure, if needed, without affecting any client applications that rely upon it. This makes maintenance easier.

Transact-SQL Programming Language Elements

Before getting into creating stored procedures and other Transact-SQL programming elements, it is worthwhile to understand the language components that are available. As a first step, remember that SQL, as a language, does not deal with conditional logic or flow of control in any way. SQL is designed to retrieve and manipulate data, database objects, and database permissions. Outside of those three areas, SQL is not very useful.

Because SQL does not have any support for programming language constructs (for example, there is no IF statement in SQL, but there is one in Transact-SQL), Sybase (the original developer of Transact-SQL), Microsoft, Oracle, IBM, and others have extended SQL to include these programming elements. This allows you to create stored procedures, triggers, and other database objects that have conditional logic and SQL statement execution. Furthermore, in order to make the programming easier, they have also added support for variables, parameters, and other constructs expected by developers. The SQL Server variant of this is Transact-SQL. Table 5-3 lists the various programming language constructs in Transact-SQL.

If you have a programming background, you may look at Table 5-3 and ask, "Is that it?" You may wonder about the FOR..NEXT loop or CASE statement (although there is a CASE function for SELECT statements), or many other programming elements that are available in Visual Basic .NET or even COBOL. They are not available in Transact-SQL. However, don't assume that you cannot do a lot with Transact-SQL—you can. You just have to remember that Transact-SQL is designed to allow you to program database functionality in SQL Server, and not to write device drivers or games.

Stored Procedures

A stored procedure is a named set of Transact-SQL statements whose definition is stored on a database on the SQL Server. Stored procedures allow you to write all the code to perform one (preferably) or more tasks and are often used to validate data before it is inserted into the database. Stored procedures in SQL Server can also pass and return parameters, and even the results of SQL statement execution, to the user, as well as status codes to indicate execution success or failure.

Transact-SQL Construct	Description
Variable	Used to store results of calculations or processing. A variable name must begin with an @ and follows other SQL Server naming conventions. SQL Server also has a number of system variables that can be queried whose names begin with @@.
IF <expression>... ELSE	Allows for conditional logic processing. Note that there is no ENDIF as part of the syntax. If more than one Transact-SQL statements follows the IF or ELSE, it must be enclosed within a BEGIN..END block.
BEGIN...END	Language elements indicating that the Transact-SQL statements within the BEGIN...END are a single logical unit of execution.
GO	Indicates that the server should execute the previous batch of Transact-SQL statements. The GO tells SQL Server to run all the statements since the last GO and perform their actions.
Batch	A batch is one or more Transact-SQL statements between two GO statements. It is possible to have more than one Transact-SQL statement in a single batch, but some statements need to be their own batch (CREATE VIEW, for example).
WHILE <expression>...	WHILE provides for looping within Transact-SQL so that a Transact-SQL block will continue to execute while the expression is true. The BREAK statement within a WHILE will break out of the loop and continue to execute after the END in which the WHILE is enclosed, whereas a CONTINUE can be used to go back to the top of the loop for another iteration.
GOTO <label>	Allows you to jump to a label within the procedure, function, or trigger. A label is indicated by a colon following the label name (*label:*). The use of labels is frowned upon as it can create spaghetti code that is very hard to debug.
Cursors	Used to perform row-by-row processing of data when using a SELECT statement, or other SQL language elements, cannot provide the desired results.

Table 5-3. Transact-SQL Programming Language Constructs

If a user is granted EXECUTE permission on a stored procedure, the user can perform the tasks that are programmed in the stored procedure even if he has no permissions on the objects that the stored procedure references, provided the ownership chain is not broken (remember this from our discussion of views in the section "Managing Views"?). In this way, you can control what actions a user can perform on an object. For example, you can grant SELECT on the table. But, in order to update it, the user would need to have EXECUTE permission on the appropriate stored procedures.

The following four distinct types of stored procedures are available in SQL Server:

- **System Stored Procedures**   System stored procedures allow a database administrator to update and query system tables, create and manage database objects, and perform other tasks without the need to modify system tables directly. They have names beginning with sp_ and are defined in the **master** database.

- **Extended Stored Procedures**   Also created in the **master** database, extended stored procedures, whose names begin with xp_, are written in Visual C++, Visual C# .NET, or other programming languages. They are compiled to include SQL Server APIs so that they may be executed from within SQL Server. They are typically dynamic link libraries (DLLs) and allow SQL Server functionality to be extended to other applications. Some examples include **xp_sendmail,** used to send e-mail from SQL Server, and **xp_readmail**, which is used to retrieve mail.

- **Local Stored Procedures**   Plain, everyday stored procedures created in a specific database (local to that database) containing Transact-SQL statements that encapsulate business logic and perform a specific task.

- **Temporary Stored Procedures**   Stored procedures whose names begin with a single number sign (#) and are local to the session, or those whose names begin with a double number sign (##) and are global to all sessions. Both are temporary stored procedures. The session that creates a temporary stored procedure must remain connected in order for that stored procedure to be available to others, and the stored procedure must be global (##).

A variant of stored procedures sometimes included as a fifth type is a remote stored procedure, which is really a local stored procedure on one SQL Server called from another SQL Server.

Creating and Managing Stored Procedures

The CREATE PROCEDURE command is used to define a stored procedure in SQL Server. The syntax is consistent from SQL Server 6.x through 2000 and is as follows:

```
CREATE PROC[EDURE] procedure_name [;number]
    [{@parameter datatype} [VARYING][=default] [OUTPUT]] [,...n]
    [WITH {RECOMPILE|ENCRYPTION|RECOMPILE , ENCRYPTION}]
    [FOR REPLICATION]
    AS Transact-SQL_statement [ ...n ]
```

The hardest part of creating a stored procedure is writing the code that makes up the Transact-SQL statements providing the logic and work of the stored procedure. As the syntax indicates, you can pass parameters (whose names must begin with the @ sign) to the stored procedure. Parameters can have default values assigned to them in case the calling program does not provide a parameter value, and parameters can also be of an OUTPUT type, which means that they return data to the calling program. OUTPUT parameters can also be of a **cursor** data type, which means that they contain a SQL result set (a set of data returned by a SELECT statement) that will be passed to the calling program.

Stored procedures are checked for syntactical accuracy when created to make sure no keywords are misspelled. If no errors are found, the stored procedure name is added to the **sysobjects** system table and the code is stored in the **syscomments** table, unless the ENCRYPTION attribute has been specified.

The code within a stored procedure can reference any table, view, user-defined function, or other language element that the owner has access to. Those objects do not need to exist yet, but only when the stored procedure is executed (this is known as delayed name resolution). Users executing stored procedures will also need to be granted access to any dependent objects to avoid broken ownership chains (stored procedures execute within the security context of the invoker).

When creating stored procedures, the CREATE PROCEDURE statement must be the only statement in the batch, and Transact-SQL code in the procedure cannot include the CREATE PROCEDURE, CREATE RULE, CREATE DEFAULT, CREATE TRIGGER, or CREATE VIEW statements. Stored procedures can include any other Transact-SQL statements including a SELECT statement. A stored procedure cannot be larger than 128MB in SQL Server 2000, or 64K in SQL Server 6.x and 7. In order to issue the CREATE PROCEDURE command, you must have been granted the CREATE PROCEDURE privilege or the **sysadmin, db_owner,** or **db_ddladmin** roles.

To execute a stored procedure, you can simply specify the procedure name in your code or on the Query Analyzer command line, or issue the EXECUTE statement as follows:

```
[EXEC[UTE]] {[@return_status=] {procedure_name[;number] | @proc_name_var}
  [[@parameter=] {value|@var_name [OUTPUT]|[DEFAULT] [, …]
  [WITH RECOMPILE]
```

When a stored procedure is executed for the first time, SQL Server compiles the stored procedure and stores the execution plan in the procedure cache of the SQL Server. Compilation involves three stages—resolution (to resolve object references in the procedure code), optimization by the Query Analyzer (to determine the optimal method with which to execute each statement in the stored procedure), and compilation (to actually build the execution plan and store it in the procedure cache). If any dependent object's definition changes, the stored procedure will need to be recompiled the next time it is called. If the RECOMPILE attribute was set at create time, or if the stored procedure was executed WITH RECOMPILE explicitly, recompilation will take place when the stored procedure is executed. RECOMPILE substitutes variable values for object names and is, therefore, not recommended because of the high CPU cost, unless the stored procedure will reference different database objects each time.

You can also execute a stored procedure within an INSERT statement when the procedure will return values that can be used to populate a table, as in the following example:

```
INSERT INTO Orders EXEC NewOrderHeader
```

To change the definition of a stored procedure without changing permissions assigned to it, use the ALTER PROCEDURE command as follows:

```
ALTER PROC[EDURE] procedure_name [;number]
    [{@parameter datatype} [VARYING][=default] [OUTPUT]] [,...n]
    [WITH {RECOMPILE|ENCRYPTION|RECOMPILE , ENCRYPTION}]
    [FOR REPLICATION]
    AS Transact-SQL_statement [ ...n ]
```

When using ALTER PROCEDURE, any options that were used during creation (ENCRYPTION, FOR REPLICATION, and so on) must also be specified at the time the procedure is altered.

To drop a stored procedure, issue the DROP PROCEDURE command and pass it the names of the procedures you want to drop.

Information on stored procedures is most easily retrieved using SQL Enterprise Manager. Query the **sysobjects** and **syscomments** tables directly (not recommended) or use the following system stored procedures:

- **sp_stored_procedures**   Returns a list of stored procedures and their owners in the database
- **sp_help**   Provides information on the procedure and create/alter time parameters
- **sp_helptext**   Returns the source code for the stored procedure, unless encrypted
- **sp_depends**   Provides information on which objects the procedure depends on or which objects depend on the procedure

User-Defined Functions

SQL Server 2000 introduced a new database object that had been requested for a long time—user-defined function (UDF). The main difference between a UDF and a stored procedure is that a UDF must return a value. You can also use a UDF anywhere you can use a built-in Transact-SQL function, thus allowing for very flexible database code.

UDFs can be scalar (returns one result for each value passed to it), multi-statement table-valued (returns a table or result set based upon more than one Transact-SQL statement in the function code), which is similar to a stored procedure. Or, it can be in-line table-valued (returns a table or result set based upon only one SELECT statement in the function code), which is similar to a view, but allows parameters to be passed to change the result each time the function is called.

The syntax to create a UDF is similar to that of a stored procedure, except that a UDF must include one RETURN statement somewhere in the Transact-SQL source code. Slight differences in syntax dealing with the return type and code requirements exist for the CREATE FUNCTION command based upon the type of function being created. For a scalar UDF, the syntax is as follows:

```
CREATE FUNCTION [owner.]function_name
 ([{@parameter_name [AS] scalar_data_type [=default]} [,...n]])
 RETURNS scalar_data_type
 [WITH {ENCRYPTION|SCHEMABINDING} [[,]...n]]
 [AS]
BEGIN
    function_body
    RETURN scalar_expression
END
```

For a multi-statement table-valued function, slight changes exist in the way return values are handled, as follows:

```
CREATE FUNCTION [owner.]function_name
 ([{@parameter_name [AS] scalar_data_type [=default]} [,...n]])
 RETURNS @return_var TABLE ({column_def | table_constraint} [,…])
 [WITH {ENCRYPTION|SCHEMABINDING} [[,]...n]]
 [AS]
BEGIN
    function_body
    RETURN
END
```

An in-line table-valued function yet again has slight differences, as shown here:

```
CREATE FUNCTION [owner.]function_name
 ([{@parameter_name [AS] scalar_data_type [=default]} [,...n]])
 RETURNS TABLE
 [WITH {ENCRYPTION|SCHEMABINDING} [[,]...n]]
 [AS]
 RETURN [(] select_statement [)]
```

For scalar and multi-statement table-valued functions, any non-deterministic built-in functions cannot be used within the function body since they would cause the UDF to return different values for the same set of data when run two different times. Examples of non-deterministic built-in functions include GETDATE(), SYSTEM_USER, and CURRENT_TIMESTAMP, as well as system global variables such as @@TRANCOUNT, @@ROWCOUNT, and others. The Transact-SQL Reference Manual can provide a complete list of non-deterministic elements that cannot be included in the definition of a UDF.

In order to create a UDF, you must have been granted the CREATE FUNCTION permissions (or be the **sysadmin, db_owner,** or **db_ddladmin**) and have necessary permissions on dependent objects (since the function always executes in the security context of the user who created it). If the function is created with SCHEMABINDING, the owner must have REFERENCES permissions on any dependent tables, views, and functions within the function body. If you reference a UDF within a CHECK constraint or DEFAULT of a table column definition, the same user must own both the UDF and the table.

The ALTER FUNCTION command, with all the same options available in the CREATE FUNCTION command, can be used to change a function definition without removing any assigned permissions. The DROP FUNCTION statement is used to remove a function from the database.

Enforcing Integrity

A database where the data does not make sense, or that can be modified without regard to its impact on other data in the database, is, at best, useless. The whole point of the relational model of databases is to allow you to define relationships between data elements within the database. This means that data integrity must be enforced by some means. Prior to the introduction of the relational model (and still in use in some databases today), application code was used to verify the integrity of the data before it was added to the database, changed, or deleted. This method works but consumes a fair amount of overhead where the verification application code is run and can be quite slow. SQL Server, and most other relational databases available today, provide for two key mechanisms to enforcing data integrity, constraints and triggers, and a couple of older methods, DEFAULTs and RULEs.

Constraints

The most efficient way to enforce data integrity in SQL Server is through the use of constraints. Constraints are defined on a table when the CREATE TABLE command is issued and are always enforced, unless they have been explicitly disabled or if specific operations (BULK LOAD) are being performed. Because constraints are so closely tied to the table, they have low overhead but also limited functionality. They can be used to enforce entity integrity (uniqueness of rows in a table), domain integrity (validity of data in columns), and referential integrity (ensuring that data between tables is valid). The available constraints in SQL Server 2000 (and every version since 6.*x*) are listed in Table 5-4.

Constraint	Description
NOT NULL	This constraint can be defined only at the column level and states that NULL is not allowed as data in the column.
UNIQUE	A UNIQUE constraint ensures that the value for a column, or combination of columns in a table, is unique or NULL for the entire table. This can be used to prevent the duplication of data. UNIQUE constraints either create or use an existing index to enforce this uniqueness. A table may have multiple UNIQUE constraints.
PRIMARY KEY	A PRIMARY KEY constraint states that data in the column or columns on which the PRIMARY KEY is defined must be unique in the table, and NOT NULL. Like a UNIQUE constraint, a PRIMARY KEY constraint will also either create or use an existing index to enforce the constraint. A table may only have one PRIMARY KEY constraint.
FOREIGN KEY	A FOREIGN KEY constraint states that data in the column or columns of a table will reference a PRIMARY KEY or UNIQUE constraint of another, or the same, table to ensure that the value entered is valid.
CHECK	CHECK constraints are an expression used to enforce simple business rules. CHECK constraints can only reference data in the same row of the table, and cannot perform any kind of lookups in other tables to verify the condition.
DEFAULT	Though not technically a constraint, a DEFAULT can be specified at the column level to assign a value when no other value for the column is specified during an INSERT. A DEFAULT can include a simple expression and use built-in functions such as GETDATE and NEWID.

Table 5-4. Constraints Available in SQL Server 2000

Defining Constraints

Constraints are part of the syntax to create a table. A constraint can be defined at the column level, in which case it can only enforce values for that column. Or, it can be defined at the table level after all the columns have been defined, in which case it can reference other columns (in the case of CHECK constraints) or include more than one column in the constraint definition (PRIMARY KEY, UNIQUE, FOREIGN KEY). DEFAULT and NOT NULL constraints can only be specified at the column level. An example

of a table definition from the **northwind** database of SQL Server 2000 that
includes both column and table level constraints is as follows:

```
CREATE TABLE dbo.Products (
   ProductID      int   IDENTITY (1000,1) NOT NULL,
   ProductName    nvarchar(40)            NOT NULL,
   SupplierID     int                     NULL,
   CategoryID     int                     NULL,
   QuantityPerUnit nvarchar(20)           NULL,
   UnitPrice      money                   NULL
      CONSTRAINT DF_Products_UnitPrice DEFAULT(0)
      CONSTRAINT CK_Products_UnitPrice CHECK (UnitPrice>=0),
   UnitsInStock   smallint                NULL
      CONSTRAINT DF_Products_UnitsInStock DEFAULT(0)
      CONSTRAINT CK_Products_UnitsInStock CHECK (UnitsInStock>=0),
   UnitsOnOrder   smallint                NULL
      CONSTRAINT DF_Products_UnitsOnOrder DEFAULT(0)
      CONSTRAINT CK_Products_UnitsOnOrder CHECK (UnitsOnOrder>=0),
   ReOrderLevel   smallint                NULL
      CONSTRAINT DF_Products_ReOrderLevel DEFAULT(0)
      CONSTRAINT CK_Products_ReOrderLevel CHECK (ReOrderLevel>=0),
   Discontinued   bit                     NULL
      CONSTRAINT DF_Products_Discontinued DEFAULT(0),
   CONSTRAINT PK_Products PRIMARY KEY CLUSTERED (ProductID),
   CONSTRAINT FK_Products_Categories FOREIGN KEY (CategoryID)
      REFERENCES dbo.Categories (CategoryID) ON UPDATE CASCADE,
   CONSTRAINT FK_Products_Suppliers FOREIGN KEY (SupplierID)
      REFERENCES dbo.Suppliers (SupplierID) ON DELETE CASCADE
)
```

Some important things to note from this example are as follows:

- Constraints should be named. Use a naming convention that makes
  sense to you and describes what the constraint is on. A naming
  convention using constraint type, table, and column name is a good
  idea, as in the above example.

- SQL Server 2000 supports cascading deletes and cascading updates for
  FOREIGN KEY constraints, as well as the ability to not allow changes
  that would violate the constraint (the default NO ACTION option).
  Cascading updates means that if data in the parent table changes,
  the child table's rows with the old values in the columns on which the
  FOREIGN KEY is defined will also be automatically changed. For a
  cascading delete, if the parent row is deleted, the child row will also
  be automatically deleted.

- For PRIMARY KEY and UNIQUE constraints you can specify index
  characteristics when defining the constraint. The index created will
  have the same name as the constraint.

When defining a column-level constraint, the available syntax options are
as follows:

```
... [CONSTRAINT constraint_name]
   [{PRIMARY KEY|UNIQUE} [CLUSTERED | NONCLUSTERED]]
       [WITH FILLFACTOR=fillfactor] [ON {filegroup|DEFAULT}] ] |
   [[FOREIGN KEY] REFERENCES parent_table[(column_name)]
       [ON DELETE {CASCADE|NO ACTION}]
       [ON UPDATE {CASCADE|NO ACTION}]] |
   CHECK (expression)
```

For a table-level constraint, defined after all columns have been specified, the syntax is quite similar, with a few more details needed, as shown here:

```
... [CONSTRAINT constraint_name]
   [{PRIMARY KEY|UNIQUE} [CLUSTERED | NONCLUSTERED]]
       {(column_name [ASC|DESC] [, ...]}
       [WITH FILLFACTOR=fillfactor] [ON {filegroup|DEFAULT}] ] |
   [[FOREIGN KEY] [(column_name [, ...])]
       REFERENCES table[(column, [, ...])]
       [ON DELETE {CASCADE|NO ACTION}]
       [ON UPDATE {CASCADE|NO ACTION}]] |
   CHECK (expression)
```

Altering and Dropping Constraints

Constraints are great for enforcing business rules during normal database operations, but if you need to load or transform large amounts of data, they can cause errors in processing that are problematic. For this reason, as well as to allow flexibility in the application of constraints, SQL Server allows a DBA to dynamically disable or enable constraints, and add new constraints to a table or drop existing ones. This is done using the ALTER TABLE command. To add a constraint to an existing table, the syntax is as follows:

```
ALTER TABLE tablename
   [WITH {CHECK|NOCHECK}]
   ADD CONSTRAINT constraint_name
   {[{PRIMARY KEY|UNIQUE} [CLUSTERED|NONCLUSTERED]
       {(column [ASC|DESC] [ ,...])}
       [WITH FILLFACTOR=fillfactor] [ON {filegroup|DEFAULT}] ]
   |FOREIGN KEY [(column[ ,...])] REFERENCES table [(column[ ,...])]
       [ON DELETE {CASCADE|NO ACTION}]
       [ON UPDATE {CASCADE|NO ACTION}] [NOT FOR REPLICATION]
   |DEFAULT expression [FOR column] [WITH VALUES]
   |CHECK [NOT FOR REPLICATION] (condition)
   }
```

When you want to add a constraint to an existing table without adding any new columns, it is always assumed you are adding a table-level constraint, in which case the above syntax applies. If you want to add a new column to a table and also specify a constraint on the column, the syntax is only slightly different, as shown here:

```
ALTER TABLE tablename
   ADD ({column_name, datatype|computed_column AS expression}
       [[DEFAULT expression] [WITH VALUES] |
       [IDENTITY [(seed, increment) [NOT FOR REPLICATION]]]
```

```
    [ROWGUIDCOL]  [COLLATE collation_name] [,…])
[WITH {CHECK|NOCHECK}]
  CONSTRAINT constraint_name
   {[{PRIMARY KEY|UNIQUE} [CLUSTERED|NONCLUSTERED]
       [WITH FILLFACTOR=fillfactor] [ON {filegroup|DEFAULT}] ]
   |FOREIGN KEY REFERENCES table [(column)]
       [ON DELETE {CASCADE|NO ACTION}]
       [ON UPDATE {CASCADE|NO ACTION}] [NOT FOR REPLICATION]
   |DEFAULT expression [FOR column] [WITH VALUES]
   |CHECK [NOT FOR REPLICATION] (condition)
   }
```

There are a few important points to remember when adding constraints to an existing table or adding a column with a constraint. First, all data in the table must satisfy constraint conditions, otherwise the constraint cannot be added. This is controlled by the WITH CHECK | NOCHECK option available when defining constraints or adding columns. If in doubt, specify WITH NOCHECK to bypass checking of existing data. New rows inserted, or any updates to the constraint columns, will enforce the constraint from that point on. The NOCHECK option only works on existing data when the constraint is first created or enabled.

If you are adding a column with a DEFAULT or adding a new DEFAULT constraint to a table, specifying WITH VALUES for the DEFAULT will populate existing data with the result of the DEFAULT expression only if the column has been defined with NULL. If WITH VALUES is not used, existing data is assigned NULL, unless the column has been added with NOT NULL, in which case the result of the DEFAULT expression is assigned.

Although it may be evident from the syntax, it is good to remember that when adding PRIMARY or UNIQUE constraints to a table, you can also specify the filegroup and FILLFACTOR for the index, as well as whether to create a clustered or non-clustered index. This allows better control over storage and prevents all segments from being stored on the same set of disks, which could create contention.

Aside from being able to add new constraints to a table, you can also dynamically disable and enable CHECK and FOREIGN KEY constraints using ALTER TABLE. You can disable one or more constraints for a table, or all constraints using the NOCHECK keyword. Or, you can enable one or more constraints with the CHECK keyword. When a constraint is enabled, all data in the table must satisfy constraint conditions, otherwise the constraint remains disabled and the offending rows will need to be corrected before the constraint can be enabled. The syntax of the ALTER TABLE command to enable or disable constraints is as follows:

```
ALTER TABLE tablename
  {CHECK|NOCHECK} CONSTRAINT
  {ALL|constraint_name [,…]}
```

When a constraint is no longer needed, it can be dropped from the table. If you drop a PRIMARY KEY or UNIQUE constraint, the index that was created when the constraint was defined is also dropped. The syntax to drop one or more constraints is as follows:

```
ALTER TABLE tablename
  DROP constraint_name [,...]
```

To get information on the constraints within a table, you can use the **sp_help** system stored procedure and pass it a table name. The **sp_helpconstraint** system stored procedure can also be used to get information on all tables with constraints of a specific type, or all constraints on a table. As always, SQL Enterprise Manager provides this information in a graphical way.

Triggers

While constraints are efficient and best used for enforcing simple business rules (for example, BirthDate <= GETDATE()), when it comes to more complex rules, such as shipment of goods cannot take place if the customer is over their credit limit, code must be written to ensure these more sophisticated rules are followed. For this purpose, SQL Server allows you to define triggers on a table or, in SQL Server 2000, on a view.

Triggers appear quite similar to stored procedures in that they are a collection of Transact-SQL statements that use control of flow, SQL, and other programming constructs. However, triggers differ from stored procedures in that they are always associated with an action occurring on a table (or view) and cannot be invoked dynamically. Triggers cannot start transactions but are always part of the same transaction that caused them to be fired. Triggers can include a ROLLBACK TRANSACTION statement, but this is not recommended since this may disturb logic if the application code needs to deal with the fact that a trigger has failed.

Triggers are useful when enforcing complex business rules, but can also be used to cascade changes across several tables, get around the inability to update complex views (views defined on more than one table or containing aggregate functions), compare the before and after state of data or log that information to provide a comprehensive audit trail, and much more. The flexibility triggers offer is one of their main strengths. But because they are procedural code and must be executed, their performance is one of their biggest drawbacks—triggers are much more expensive than constraints. Furthermore, triggers do not fire until all constraints have been satisfied, so it is important to plan the combination of triggers and constraints and how they will work. There is no limit to the number of triggers that can be defined for a specific action on a table. You do not have control over the order in which triggers will fire except for setting the first and last trigger to fire on a table with the **sp_settriggerorder** system stored procedure.

Triggers in SQL Server are statement-level and fire only once for each SQL statement, so updating 10,000 rows will only fire the trigger once. You can process all rows together, or use the @@ROWCOUNT global variable to determine the number of rows to be processed. You can then use a cursor to step through the **inserted** or **deleted** (or both) pseudo tables created automatically when the trigger is fired to hold the new and old values, respectively, for the rows that the trigger will process. Triggers can return results of SELECT statements, but their data will not be displayed to the user since trigger code is attached to a table or view, and not to a specific process or session.

Creating and Managing Triggers

SQL Server supports two types of triggers—AFTER triggers, defined on tables, and INSTEAD OF triggers, defined on views. AFTER triggers fire after an INSERT, UPDATE, or DELETE action is performed against the table that the trigger is defined on, and can be used to modify the data being added, modified, or removed from the table. INSTEAD OF triggers, available in SQL Server 2000, fire instead of the INSERT, UPDATE, or DELETE action on the view. In other words, INSTEAD OF triggers cause their code to execute in place of the action taking place on the view. An ironic twist in the SQL Server world is that you can define INSTEAD OF triggers on tables, though this is generally not supported by other databases (Oracle, for example).

The syntax to create a trigger in SQL Server 2000 is shown here:

```
CREATE TRIGGER trigger_name ON {table|view} [WITH ENCRYPTION]
    {{{[FOR|AFTER]|INSTEAD OF} {[INSERT] [,] [UPDATE] [,] [DELETE]}
        [WITH APPEND] [NOT FOR REPLICATION]
        AS
        [{IF UPDATE (column)
            [{AND|OR} UPDATE (column)] [...] }]
    Transact-SQL Code
    }}
```

In order to create a trigger, you must be the owner of the table or view on which the trigger is being created, or be granted the **sysadmin** or **db_owner** role. Furthermore, if other objects are referenced in the trigger code, the user creating the trigger must have permissions on all referenced objects, or the trigger will generate errors during execution and roll back the transaction of which the trigger is a part. Ensuring the **dbo** user owns all objects alleviates these issues.

The WITH APPEND clause is not required in SQL Server 7 or 2000, but is used in SQL Server 6.5 and earlier versions to indicate that an additional trigger is being created on an existing table. Prior to SQL Server 7, only one trigger for each action could be created on a table.

Triggers cannot perform all of the same actions as a stored procedure or user interactively executing commands against the database. Table 5-5 lists Transact-SQL statements not allowed in trigger code.

ALTER DATABASE	CREATE DATABASE	DISK INIT
DISK RESIZE	DROP DATABASE	LOAD DATABASE
LOAD LOG	RECONFIGURE	RESTORE DATABASE
RESTORE LOG		

Table 5-5. Transact-SQL Statements Not Allowed in Trigger Code

If you need to modify the trigger code, you can issue the ALTER TRIGGER command with the new source code. This is similar to the CREATE TRIGGER syntax, as follows:

```
ALTER TRIGGER trigger_name ON {table|view} [WITH ENCRYPTION]
    {{{[FOR|AFTER]|INSTEAD OF} {[INSERT] [,] [UPDATE] [,] [DELETE]}
        [NOT FOR REPLICATION]
        AS
        [{IF UPDATE (column)
            [{AND|OR} UPDATE (column)] […] }]
    Transact-SQL Code
    }}
```

You can also dynamically enable and disable triggers on a table, just like you can with constraints. Once disabled, the trigger will not fire and its actions will not be enforced. This should not be done during normal operation, but is useful when performing large bulk data loads or changes. The ALTER TABLE command is used to do this, as follows:

```
ALTER TABLE tablename
    {ENABLE|DISABLE} TRIGGER
    {ALL|trigger_name [,…]}
```

Dropping a trigger is done using the DROP TRIGGER command. You must be the owner of the trigger to drop it, or have been granted the **sysadmin** or **db_owner** role.

```
DROP TRIGGER trigger_name
```

To get information on triggers defined in the database, you can use the **sp_help** or **sp_helptrigger** system stored procedures, or SQL Enterprise Manager.

Trigger Nesting and Recursion

One of the hardest things to predict accurately in large applications is the flow of application and procedure code. It is possible to have a procedure modify a table, fire a trigger that calls another procedure that inserts into a table that calls a trigger that inserts into the same table as the first trigger, which then fires the first trigger again. This is recursion and is disallowed by default. Any series of actions that cause a second trigger to fire as a result of a previous trigger firing is nesting. SQL Server allows nesting by default but disallows recursion, although both can be allowed or disallowed individually.

Nesting is a powerful ability within SQL Server and generally should not be disabled because it may break the application. However, SQL Server does not allow nesting beyond 32 levels, so any operation that attempts to do so will generate an error and roll back the transaction. If you allow nesting and expect it to happen in your application (and it will happen), remember to always check to see how deeply you are nested before calling another procedure from a trigger. The @@NESTLEVEL system global variable can be used to test the depth of nesting.

Recursion, a trigger firing itself either directly or indirectly, is more problematic as it can more easily exceed the maximum level of nesting if a trigger continues to populate its own table or view. For this reason, recursion is disabled, which means that any subsequent operation that would fire the same trigger again, as a result of it firing originally, will not fire the trigger. For example, if you insert data into Customers which fires the CustomersInsert trigger, and that triggers inserts data into Contacts, which fires a trigger that then inserts new data in Customers, the second INSERT into Customers will not fire the CustomersInsert trigger again since this is a recursive call. You typically would leave recursion disabled unless you needed it to support complex, self-referencing situations such as bill of material explosions.

To enable or disable nesting, use the **sp_configure** stored procedure and pass it a value of 0 for disable and 1 for enable, as shown here. Nesting triggers are enabled or disabled at the server level and apply to all databases on the server.

```
sp_configure 'nested triggers' {0|1}
```

To enable or disable recursion, you can use the ALTER DATABASE command (in SQL Server 2000) or the **sp_dboption** stored procedure. Recursion can be enabled or disabled at the database level, but only if nested triggers are enabled at the server level. If nested triggers are disabled, recursion is also disabled for all databases on the server.

```
ALTER DATABASE database_name SET RECURSIVE TRIGGERS {ON|OFF}

sp_dboption database_name 'recursive triggers', {true|false}
```

SQL Server Defaults

An older SQL Server object that can be created to assign values to columns in tables when these are not specified during an INSERT is a SQL Server Default. Defaults work similar to a DEFAULT constraint except that they can be bound to either a column in a table or a user-defined data type, in which case they apply to all columns using the user-defined data type. SQL Server Defaults are specific to SQL Server and are not ANSI-compliant, meaning that using them is no longer preferred since you can use a DEFAULT constraint to accomplish the same thing. Their main advantage is the ability to be bound to a data type.

To create a SQL Server Default, issue the following command:

```
CREATE DEFAULT default_name AS default_expression
```

The expression used to create a Default must always evaluate to a constant. In other words, the expression cannot result in a value that will change each time it is queried, such as Age (current date minus birth date).

Once you have created the default, you need to bind it to either a table column or user-defined data type using the **sp_binddefault** system stored procedure, which has the following syntax:

```
sp_bindefault [ @defname = ] 'default' ,
    [ @objname = ] 'datatype'|'table.column'
    [ , [ @futureonly = ] 'futureonly' ]
```

Once you bind the Default to a user-defined data type or table column, the Default will apply to all current instances of the user-defined data type or will apply to the column immediately. The *futureonly* parameter indicates that the binding will apply to all future instances of the user-defined data type and will not be bound to existing instances of the data type used in tables. The future only flag does not apply to columns. If a Default is already bound to a column or user-defined data type, executing **sp_bindefault** will unbind any existing Default and replace it with the one currently being bound.

Once a Default is bound to a user-defined data type, you cannot define a DEFAULT constraint on any column based on the user-defined data type. Similarly, if you bind a Default to a table column, you cannot create a DEFAULT constraint on the column. Any CHECK constraints on columns that have a Default bound to them must be made to validate the value of the Default. Any SQL Server Rules on columns or data types to which a Default has been bound will also validate the Default.

To unbind a default from a user-defined data type or column, you execute the **sp_unbindefault** system stored procedure:

```
sp_unbindefault [@objname =] 'datatype'|'table.column'
    [, [@futureonly =] 'futureonly']
```

Executing **sp_unbindefault** will immediately unbind the Default from the table column or user-defined data type (and all instances of the user-defined data type). If the future only flag is specified when unbinding from a user-defined data type, existing bindings of the Default will not be unbound, but the default will not be bound to any future instances of the data type used in tables. In other words, existing tables will function as expected, but new ones will not have the Default applied.

To remove a Default from the database, issue the DROP DEFAULT command whose syntax is as follows:

```
DROP DEFAULT { default_name } [ ,...n ]
```

Before you drop a Default be sure that you have unbound it from any user-defined data types or table columns to which it was bound. You will not be able to drop a Default if it is still bound to a database object. As the syntax indicates, you can drop more than one default at a time.

SQL Server Rules

Like SQL Server Defaults, SQL Server Rules are a non-standard feature that is only implemented in SQL Server and should not be used in favor of CHECK constraints, which Rules most closely resemble. The way you use Rules is similar to the way you use Defaults—you CREATE them first, bind them to a user-defined data type or table column, unbind them if you no longer want them to apply to the table column or user-defined data type, and DROP them when they are no longer needed.

To create a Rule, execute the CREATE RULE command, as follows:

```
CREATE RULE rule_name AS conditional_expression
```

Like a CHECK constraint, the conditional expression can be any valid expression that results in a value; however, Rules cannot reference other table columns or other tables or database objects. For comparison of values, the Rule can include a local variable of any name, as long as it begins with @, as in the following example which tests to ensure that an insurance policy type is within a valid list of values:

```
CREATE RULE PolicyRule AS
  @policy_type IN ('FIRE','AUTO','LIFE')
```

Once you have created the Rule you bind it to a user-defined data type or table column using the **sp_bindrule** system stored procedure, which has the following syntax:

```
sp_bindrule [ @rulename = ] 'rule' ,
    [ @objname = ] 'datatype'|'table.column'
    [ , [ @futureonly = ] 'futureonly' ]
```

The terms for binding Rules are the same as for binding Defaults, with future only applying to any new columns created with the bound data type. As well, binding a rule to an existing column will replace a rule bound to the column, if any. Binding a rule to a user-defined data type will replace any Rule bound to the data type but not any Rule bound explicitly to a column of that data type. In other words, if you bind a Rule to user-defined data type UDF1, and have a column in a table with UDF1 as the data type but with a different Rule bound to the column explicitly, binding the Rule to the data type will not replace the rule bound explicitly to the column of UDF1 data type.

To unbind a Rule from a user-defined data type or table column, execute the **sp_unbindrule** system stored procedure:

```
sp_unbindrule [@objname =] 'datatype'|'table.column'
    [, [@futureonly =] 'futureonly']
```

The same sets of conditions for unbinding Defaults also apply to unbinding Rules.

To drop a Rule, issue the DROP RULE command, which requires that the Rule be unbound from all objects, as in the following syntax:

```
DROP RULE { rule_name } [ ,...n ]
```

5

Chapter 6

Database Backups

Performing effective backups is one of the most important functions that an administrator must perform. The purpose of a database server is to store information—information that is often critical to your company and to your customers. If the system fails (and it will), it is important to be able to quickly and effectively restore your data. The source of failure can be catastrophic like fire or server theft, or can be as simple as a user accidentally deleting important records. In either case, a good backup is needed to recover the data. This chapter will discuss the SQL backup process and provide insight into how to use this tool effectively to protect your data.

Understanding the SQL Server Recovery Models

How you back up the databases on your server will depend on which recovery model you have chosen for each database. Recovery models determine how transactions are stored in the transaction log. This is important, because a good backup strategy should strive to minimize data loss, and this means backing up the transaction log as well as the data files. SQL Server has three recovery models:

- **Full recovery**   Under the Full recovery model, all transactions are written to and maintained in the transaction log. This model should be implemented when you are concerned with minimizing data loss. When you back up a database that is configured to run under the Full recovery model, you can also back up the transaction log. This means that during recovery, you can minimize data loss, ideally, up to the point where the server failed, by restoring both the database and transaction log backups. Also, because you are saving all transactions, it is possible to do a point-in-time restore of a database. For example, if you know that at 9:35 A.M. one of your users accidentally deleted all records from the customer table, you can restore all data up to 9:34:59, and choose to not restore the transactions generated by the erroneous deletion.

- **Simple recovery**   The Simple recovery model reduces the need to manage the transaction log. As checkpoints occur in the database, transactions are slowly written from the cache to the physical data file. These transactions then become part of the inactive portion of the log (inactive because they don't need to be recovered if the system fails). In the Full recovery model this inactive portion is retained. In the Simple recovery model, the inactive portion is removed whenever a checkpoint occurs. This means that, except in rare cases, there is no need to worry about the transaction log filling up. The disadvantage of the Simple

131

recovery model is that there is no complete transaction log from which you can recover so, in the event of a failure, you would lose all changes since the last backup.

- **The Bulk Logged recovery model**   The Bulk Logged recovery model is a middle point between the Full and Simple recovery models. In the Bulk Logged model all logged transactions are written to the transaction log, but the log is not truncated when a checkpoint occurs. The difference between the Full and Bulk Logged recovery models is that non-logged operations are not stored in the transaction log in Bulk Logged recovery; only the fact that the operation took place and the outcome are recorded to the transaction log. In the Full recovery model, however, each step involved in processing non-logged operations is written to the transaction log. Non-logged operations include:

    - The CREATE INDEX statement
    - Bulk load operators through bcp.exe
    - BULK INSERT statements
    - The SELECT INTO statement
    - Using the WRITETEXT or UPDATETEXT functions

NOTE   *Recovery models exist in SQL Server 7 and 6.5 but are not identified as such in these versions of SQL Server. To switch to Simple recovery, you need to enable the Truncate Log on Checkpoint database option, and to implement the Bulk Import model, you must enable the Select Into/Bulk Copy database option. Full recovery is the default model.*

Factors Affecting Your Choice of Recovery Model

The recovery model you choose will directly impact your backup strategy. You'll notice that the common thread between all three models is that they control how and when SQL Server stores and retains transactions in the transaction log. As you will see later in this chapter, you can back up both data files and transaction log files. The ability to maintain a transaction log backup is, of course, contingent on having a transaction log to back up. When running under the Full recovery model, the transaction log is never automatically truncated between backups. This means that you can back up and restore the full transaction log. If you have effective backups of the transaction log, you can restore a database to the actual point of failure and incur minimum data loss. You can also roll the database back to the state it was in prior to an accidental or malicious update using point-in-time restores. The Full recovery model should be used on all databases where you need to reduce the amount of data loss to the absolute minimum. It should also be used on databases that change frequently, such as any production online transaction-processing (OLTP) database.

NOTE   *Point-in-time recovery is covered in detail in the section "Restoring the Transaction Logs" in Chapter 7.*

The Simple recovery model is the one that has the greatest possibility of data loss. Because the transaction log is truncated without being first backed up, you cannot use the transaction log to recover any changes since the last database backup. It is also not possible to perform a point-in-time recovery when using the Simple recovery model. This model is most suited to databases that change infrequently (such as a reporting database), or in situations where there is a higher tolerance of data loss (such as on a test server). You should avoid using the Simple recovery model on a production database that experiences a high number of changes or contains data that is critical to your organization.

The Bulk Logged model is best suited to databases that experience changes throughout the day, but also receive periodic bulk inserts. Because it is not recording each step or a non-logged operation as it happens, and bulk operations are not fully recorded, the transaction logs in this recovery model tend to be smaller, but still useful for recovery (because they store the results of the bulk insert). With this model, it is best to schedule your backups after bulk operations occur. You cannot perform point-in-time restores with this model so you don't have the same protection against data loss that you have in the Full recovery model, but it is still more secure than the Simple recovery model.

Setting the Recovery Model

To set the recovery model, you can use either the Enterprise Manager or Transact-SQL. In all versions of SQL Server, you can specify the recovery model by right-clicking a database and selecting Properties (or Edit on SQL Server 6.5). On the Options tab there is a list box midway through the form that allows you to choose your recovery model. In SQL Server 7 or 6.5 you will need to enable the Truncate Log on Checkpoint option to enable Simple recovery, or the Select Into/Bulk copy option for Bulk Logged recovery. There are different ways to set the recovery model option depending on the version of SQL Server that you are running. In SQL Server 2000, you can also set the recovery model using the ALTER DATABASE statement. This statement has the following syntax:

```
ALTER DATABASE myDB
SET RECOVERY {FULL | SIMPLE | BULK_LOGGED}
```

The SET clause of the ALTER DATABASE statement is not supported in earlier versions of SQL Server. SQL Server versions 7.0 and 6.5 use the **sp_dboption** stored procedure (that also works on SQL Server 2000). The syntax for this stored procedure is as follows:

```
sp_dboption @dbname = 'database name',
 @optname = 'option_name',
 @optvalue = {{true | false} | {on |off}
```

This stored procedure is actually used to set a number of database options. In order to use this procedure to set the database recovery model, you need to specify the name of the option. To enable the Truncate Log on Checkpoint option (and therefore set the database to use the Simple recovery model), the option name is **trunc. log on chkpt**. To enable the Bulk Logged recovery model, the option name is **select into/bulkcopy**. You will set these options to True to enable them or False to turn them off. When you specify either of these options, you must enter them exactly as they are listed above, including punctuation, or the command will not execute.

Understanding and Planning SQL Server Backups

SQL Server has its own backup utility. The advantage of this tool is that it is able to perform a "hot" backup; that is, to back up databases while the server is still running. Users are able to access the database normally (with a few restrictions) while the backup runs. The only adverse effect for users when a backup is running is that it can impact performance on the server. When the backup runs, it backs up both database files and transaction log files. This captures the schema of, and the data in, the database. If the server is damaged or lost, you can use the backup to completely restore the database onto another machine. The backup utility also keeps track of the location from which files were backed up. It also backs up the portion of the transaction log that contains all active transactions since the backup started.

The SQL Server backup tool will allow you to back up to different media. These include the following:

- **Tape backup**   The SQL Server backup utility can back up directly to a tape drive. The backup language even has special commands that are specific to tape backups and restores. There is, however, one restriction. In order to back up to tape, the tape drive must be locally installed. If SQL Server does not detect a local tape drive, it will disable the option to back up to tape. This means that you cannot back up a SQL Server database to a remote tape library (at least not with the native tools).

- **Disk file**   The SQL Server backup utility can back up directly to a file on a disk. The location does not need to be local. Although SQL Server will not allow you to back up to a remote tape drive, it will allow you to back up to a remote file share.

- **Named pipe**   The backup utility also allows you to stream a backup across a Named Pipe connection. Using this functionality you can configure SQL Server to send the backup to a third-party backup utility such as Backup Exec or Arc Server. This allows you to perform hot backups using third-party tools and therefore leverage the third-party utility to send backups to a remote tape drive.

In order to perform backups you must be a member of the following three roles:

- The **sysadmin** fixed server role
- The **db_owner** fixed database role
- The **db_backupoperator** fixed database role

You could create a new database user account and grant that user the permission to back up the database. However, since SQL Server provides these fixed roles, there is really no reason to create users for this purpose.

NOTE   *These roles do not exist in SQL 6.5. If you want to back up a SQL 6.5 database, you must either use the **SA** login or create a new user account and give them Dump DB and Dump Trans permissions.*

Backup Types

SQL Server has four backup types: full, transaction log, differential, and file or filegroup. An effective backup strategy will use a mixture of all four types. This section will describe the backup types and then look at how they can be combined to form an effective backup scenario.

NOTE   *All of the information in this section relates to SQL Server 7 and 2000. SQL Server 6.5 had a different process known as the Dump process.*

Full Backups

As a baseline for all other types of backups, all backup strategies must include at least one full backup. When a full backup starts, it calls a checkpoint and places a mark in the transaction log with a specific Log Sequence Number (LSN), indicating that the backup is beginning. The backup process then goes directly to the file system and backs up all data files in the database. Once the file backup is complete, the backup process places another LSN marker in the transaction log indicating that the backup is complete. Finally, the backup process backs up the transaction log between the two LSNs and appends that log backup to the data file backup. As a result, you can use a full backup to completely restore a database to the point at which the full backup ended.

Because of their write-intensive nature, full backups will have an effect on system performance. Depending on the length of the backup, users may experience degradation in performance on the server while the backup is running. For this reason you should plan to run full backups during periods of lower activity. Remember that many databases run automated processes, such as batch processing jobs or data imports. Therefore, you cannot assume that any time outside of normal business hours is a period of low activity. As a DBA, you will need to perform baseline testing to determine your periods of lowest activity. However, because the full backup can run while users are connected, you can still back up a database that needs to be available 24 hours a day.

There are, however, certain activities that are not permitted while a full backup is running. The backup process places a schema lock on the entire database. The operations that are not permitted include the following:

- Adding or modifying indexes in the database
- Shrinking database and log files
- Increasing the size of the database (including growth triggered by the automatically grow file property)
- Issuing a CREATE or ALTER DATABASE statement
- Performing non-logged operations (such as a Bulk Insert or using the WRITETEXT or UPDATETEXT functions)

These operations are prohibited because they change the underlying data and log files. Schema locks do not affect changes to the data itself. Users can issue SELECT, INSERT, UPDATE, and DELETE operations and execute (nonsystem) stored procedures against the database while a backup is running. These operations are recorded in the transaction log and will be included in the backup when the transaction log backup is appended to the database backup. None of the prohibited operations in the previous list are written to the transaction log.

Transaction Log Backups

As the name suggests, this type of backup backs up the entire transaction log (that is, both the active and inactive portions of the log) and saves it to whatever medium you choose for your backup. The transaction log backup requires that a full backup has already taken place. If the backup process does not detect an existing full database backup, it will not allow you to perform a transaction log backup. Transaction log backups are important because the backup process also removes the inactive portion of the transaction log when it runs. If you are using the Full recovery model, you must include transaction log backups as part of your backup strategy in order to control the size of the transaction log.

Transaction log backups tend to be much smaller and have a lighter impact on server performance. As a result, you can perform transaction log backups more frequently and throughout the day. More frequent transaction log backups serve two purposes: They will control the log size (which can be critical on very active OLTP databases), and they will minimize the amount of data loss because they can be used with a full database backup to restore the database up to the point when the last transaction log backup occurred. You must also use transaction log backups if you need to perform a point-in-time restore. Note that you cannot perform transaction log backups if you are using the Simple recovery model (or if the Truncate Log on Checkpoint option as been enabled).

Special Considerations Regarding Transaction Logging   Even if your database uses the Full recovery model, it is possible for logging to stop. SQL Server only maintains the inactive portion of the log if there is a full database backup against which the transaction log can be restored. When a SQL Server does not have a valid full backup against which to restore the transaction logs, it will not maintain the log. As the transaction log fills up, the log writer will turn back on itself and begin overwriting the existing inactive transactions starting from the beginning of the log. This is different than Simple recovery, which even though it removes all transactions in the inactive portion of the transaction log, the log size will not decrease. However, the net result is the same. The transaction log will never become full provided the log writer never attempts to overwrite the active portion of the transaction log. If, for example, a stalled transaction prevented the checkpoint from marking transactions as inactive, eventually the entire log would be marked as active and the file would become full. When this situation exists, SQL Server is no longer able to perform transaction log backups.

There are ways to avoid this from happening. First, if you are running your database in Full recovery mode, always perform a full backup of the database when it is first created (and populated with tables). Even though there is most likely no data in the database, the full backup creates a baseline that allows SQL Server to log all subsequent inserts. From this point on the database will preserve all transactions in the log. This is only true, however, as long as the full backup remains valid. If you perform non-logged operations against a database that is using the Full recovery model, it will again cease to maintain the logs. If you are working on a new database, remember that any schema change (such as adding or modify a table) is also a non-logged operation. If the log fills before the next full backup, it will again wrap around and overwrite the oldest transactions in the transaction log. Non-logged operations include the following:

- Creating or altering indexes or tables
- Manually clearing the transaction log
- Creating a permanent table with the SELECT … INTO statement
- Using the WRITETEXT or UPDATETEXT statements to modify data in a text column

After each of these operations, you should immediately perform a full backup if you plan to include transaction backups as part of your backup strategy.

The Differential Backup

The differential backup also requires at least one full backup. When a differential backup is run, it stores all changes since the last full backup. It does this by reading a bit flag in the header of each database page. When a full backup is run, the backup process resets all of these bits to 0. As activity occurs after the backup completes, this header flag is set to 1 whenever a row on a page is modified. The differential backup scans the data file and only saves those pages that have been changed. As a result,

6

the differential backup is a much faster and smaller backup than a full backup. The differential backup does not store information from the transaction log and does not truncate the inactive portion of the log. The differential backup stores the changes in the state they were in when the backup ran. For this reason you cannot perform point-in-time restores with a differential backup. For example, a particular value in a table may have changed several times between when the full backup and differential backups ran. However, the differential backup will be unaware of the change history and will only save the current state of the table at the point when the backup process starts. You can perform differential backups while users are accessing the system.

File or Filegroup Backups

In SQL Server 7 Microsoft introduced the concept of the filegroups. As you saw in Chapter 4, SQL Server 7 and 2000 databases can exist in multiple physical files. Furthermore, these files can be grouped together logically into filegroups. To help manage very large databases, the SQL Server backup process allows you to back up individual files and filegroups. You can also restore individual files and filegroups. Using file and filegroup backups allows you to back up and restore parts of a large database without having to back up and restore the whole database. As the name implies, you can back up individual data files, or all of the files in a particular filegroup.

File or filegroup backups allow you to spread a backup of a very large database across multiple days. Suppose that you have a 1TB database that spans 5 filegroups of 200GB each. Suppose as well that the full backup of the database takes 24 hours. Clearly you are not going to perform a daily full backup. Instead, you can back up one filegroup per day. One important thing to remember with filegroup backups is that you must also maintain all transaction log backups. Under this scenario, it is possible to have a failure on Thursday on a filegroup that was last backed up on Monday. When you restore the Monday backup, you will need current transaction log backups to allow SQL Server to bring the filegroup restore to the point of the failure. Otherwise, you could have some tables out of sync with others. Herein lies madness (and a corrupt database). This is a self-defense mechanism on the part of SQL Server. In fact, if SQL Server does not detect that all transaction logs have been backed up, it will not allow you to restore the filegroup.

There is another limitation on backing up and restoring files and filegroups. When you back up files or filegroups, all dependent objects must be backed up together. This is particularly relevant with indexes. For performance reasons it is sometimes advisable to place tables and their indexes on separate filegroups. However, if you do this, both filegroups must be backed up together. SQL Server imposes this restriction because it wants to avoid the possibility of the tables and their indexes getting out of sync if an older filegroup backup is applied to an existing database. Therefore, it you plan to use filegroup backups, make sure that all dependent objects are in the same filegroup.

Creating a Backup Strategy

An effective backup strategy must consider the following four factors:

- How often data changes
- What your tolerance for data loss is
- How long the system can be offline
- How much data must be backed up

Each backup type has its strengths and weaknesses and an effective backup strategy will blend the four backup types together to get the best mix for your particular environment. Full backups are essential, but you don't want them running during peak periods of production on your database. Full backups, by themselves, don't control the size of a transaction log and don't store any information after the backup completes. Also, for very large databases, the time needed to execute the backup will increase (when your database size gets into the tens of Gigabytes, full backups can take hours, depending on your backup media). Transaction log backups can reduce the risk of data loss and take much less time to run than a full backup. However, if you have multiple transaction log backups, it can take a long time to restore the database. Differential backups take a longer time to run than transaction log backups and don't control the size of the transaction log. However, they take much less time to restore than a series of transaction log backups and are still much faster than a full backup. Obviously, file and filegroup backups are only relevant to large databases that are spread across multiple files and filegroups. They are most useful when the size of the database makes a full backup impractical. For example, if you had a database that was so large that the full backup took 20 hours, it would be hard to find a time to back up this database on a regular basis. By designing the database using multiple files or filegroups, you can leverage this backup type to reduce backup times.

To best understand which backup type to use, consider the following three scenarios. If your database is used for reporting and is only updated once during a scheduled file dump through DTS, you would only need to do a full backup. Because the database doesn't change, you could simply run a full backup each night after the import. This solution will allow you to rebuild the reporting database in the event of failure with a minimum of down time (because restoring a full backup is a single operation and tends to be the fastest type of restore).

If you have a production database, however, the requirements change. Suppose that you have a point-of-sale system for a medium-size company. The database exceeds 250GB in size in one file created on a RAID-5 array. Currently with your backup device, the full backup takes 9 hours. Telephone order takers who enter orders into the system use the system. Warehouse staff and the shipping staff also use it to process orders and track shipments. The system is in use 24 hours a day, but activity is lightest between 10 P.M.

and midnight. Data changes frequently and lost data means lost revenue, so data loss must be kept to a minimum. You also have a low tolerance for down time since none of your employees can work without the database. Clearly you don't want to perform a full backup daily because of the continuous activity. The best plan would be to perform a full backup at least once a week. You would perform transaction log backups regularly throughout the day to control the size of the transaction log and to minimize data loss. You should also consider performing a Differential backup each night at 10 P.M. This will speed up the restore process by saving you the time it would take to restore multiple transaction log backups.

Finally, if you had a large enterprise database that exceeded 1GB in size and took 20 or more hours to back up, you would want to divide the database into multiple filegroups and back up one filegroup each day. You would also want to perform regular transaction log backups so you could apply the logs to the filegroup when you restore it. The transaction log backup would need to be maintained for the same length of time as the older filegroup backup.

The Backup Process

The SQL backup tool ships and installs with SQL Server. There are no special utilities that need to be installed. As with most SQL Server functionality, backups can be conducted using Transact-SQL or using the Enterprise Manager.

Creating Backup Devices

SQL Server also includes the ability to create backup devices. A device is simply a named path to the backup media location. Devices are stored in a table called **sysdevices** in the **master** database. Once created, a backup device can store the backups from any database on the server. It can also store multiple backups from different databases. There are several advantages to using permanent backup devices. They are reusable. When you back up to a device, you can specify whether to append to or overwrite the device. This allows you to, for example, have a single device for each day where the first backup of the day overwrote the device and all subsequent backups for that day appended to the first. The second advantage is that these details of the device are stored in the **master** database. This means that SQL Server is aware of their existence. This simplifies automation because the SQL Server Agent is able to retrieve the media location through the device definition.

To create a backup device in Enterprise Manager, follow these steps:

1. Expand the Management folder.

2. Right-click the backup icon and select New Backup Device.

3. Give the device a unique name.

4. Point to the tape or file location where the device will physically reside.

5. Click OK to create the device.

If SQL Server does not detect a local tape drive, the option to set a tape location will be grayed out. It is not possible to create a backup device on a remote tape drive. If you are using SQL Server 6.5, the process is similar; however, you need to right-click the Backup Devices folder and select New Backup Device. Creating the device will not automatically create the file. The physical file will not be created until the first time the device is used in a backup. Be careful with where you place the device. You will notice that you don't set a size for the device. These devices are simply pointers to a particular location. Once created, SQL Server will auto size the backup device file. This means that if you send a 150GB database to a backup device, it will create a 150GB device file.

The syntax for creating a device in Transact-SQL is as follows:

```
sp_addumpdevice @devtype = {'disk' | 'tape' | 'pipe'},
@logicalname ='logical name for backup',
@physicalname = 'physical path to backup location'
```

If your device is pointing to a tape drive, you can also set two additional parameters: @devstatus {skip | noskip}. This parameter indicates whether or not to read the ANSI tape labels on tape media. The default is noskip.

Performing Full Backups

Full backups can be performed at any time and can be created with or without a permanent device. To perform a full backup to a backup device using Transact-SQL, use the BACKUP DATABASE statement with the following syntax:

```
BACKUP DATABASE databaseName TO backupDevice
[WITH option1,[option2 … option n]]
```

Obviously the database device must exist before you execute this statement. When you back up to a device, you have three options that dictate how the backup will treat any existing backups in the device. The options are as follows:

- **WITH INIT** This option overwrites the current contents of any backup device with the current backup. When you back up WITH INIT, the existing backups are deleted permanently. There is no way to recover preexisting backups after the device has been overwritten.

- **WITH NOINIT** This is the default option. When you use the NOINIT option, the current backup is appended to any existing backup in the device. If a device contains multiple backups, you can specify which one you want to restore. You cannot delete individual backups. You will simply attach new backups to the existing set until a WITH INIT or WITH FORMAT statement overwrites it.

- **WITH FORMAT**   In many ways, WITH FORMAT works the same as WITH INIT. It causes the contents of the device to be overwritten. WITH FORMAT, however, turns off some safety checks that exist in SQL Server (such as not backing up to a device that is part of a media set). WITH FORMAT ignores all these checks and overwrites the device.

It is possible to back up a database to a specific tape or file location without creating a backup device. To perform such a backup, you must specify the media type and include the full path to the backup file in the BACKUP DATABASE statement. This is useful if you are performing a one-time only backup. You cannot append to a file when it was not created as a device. The syntax to back up a database without a backup device is as follows:

```
BACKUP DATABASE databaseName TO {DISK | TAPE | PIPE} = 'Full file path'
```

For example, if you wanted to back up the SalesData database to a file called salesdata.bak in the dataarchive folder on your D drive, you would use the following statement:

```
BACKUP DATABASE SalesData TO DISK = 'd:\dataarchive\salesdata.bak'
```

This code will create the backup file and SQL Server will record the fact that a backup was made to this location. But it will not store any information about the contents of the salesdata.bak file. Therefore, it is not possible to append subsequent backups to this file. Each time it is referenced in a BACKUP statement, the file will be overwritten.

Backing Up to Tape

The backup statement has some specific options that deal specifically with backing up to tape. These options are included in the WITH clause of the backup statement and are listed in Table 6-1.

Backing Up to Multiple Devices

The SQL Server backup process also allows you to back up a database to multiple devices at the same time. When you specify multiple devices, SQL Server stripes the backup across all of the devices. When this happens, the devices become a *media set*. The media set must be treated as a single unit. That is, you would be unable to back up a file to one member of the set. The only way to break the set is to back up to each of its members using the WITH FORMAT option.

The purpose of backing up to a media set is to speed up the backup by spreading the write IO across multiple devices. For this reason, you should avoid putting members of the same media set on the same disk or tape drive. This actually defeats the purpose of a media set because each disk will be in contention with each other as the write IO is generated. To

Option	Description
RESTART	If there is an interruption in the backup process to tape, this option allows you to restart at the point where the interruption occurred. This is useful, particularly when a backup spans multiple tapes, because it prevents you from having to restart the entire backup.
FORMAT	This option is similar to the disk FORMAT option. When you include this option, it will overwrite the tape header. This option implies the effect of the INIT and SKIP options.
UNLOAD	When you issue this option, the SQL backup process will rewind and dismount the tape from the drive when the backup is complete. This is a default option.
NOUNLOAD	If you issue this command, SQL Server will not rewind the tape. Use this option if you plan to make subsequent backups to the same tape.
SKIP	Causes the backup process to ignore the ANSI label on a tape.
NOSKIP	Instructs SQL Server to read the tape label. This is default behavior.
BLOCKSIZE	SQL Server dynamically chooses a block size for a tape. However, you can override this using the BLOCKSIZE command. This option cannot be used when appending backups to an existing tape device. It must be used in conjunction with FORMAT, INIT, or SKIP.

Table 6-1. Tape Options for the BACKUP Command

perform this type of backup, you simply list the multiple devices and separate them with commas, as in the following example:

```
BACKUP DATABASE databaseName TO {DISK | TAPE | PIPE}
= 'backupdevice1', 'backupdevice2' … 'backupdeviceN'
```

When you back up to a media set, you can also set two additional parameters, as follows:

```
WITH MEDIANAME = 'unique name for media set',
MEDIADESCRIPTION = 'description of media set'
```

Performing Differential Backups

The process for performing a differential backup is almost identical to that of a full backup. You can back up to a database device or specify a location path when you run the backup. The only difference is that you must include the WITH DIFFERENTIAL option as part of the statement. Since a BACKUP

DATABASE statement can have multiple options, you can mix this with other options. For example, the following statement will perform a differential backup and initialize the SalesBKdevice backup device:

```
BACKUP DATABASE SalesData TO 'SalesBKdevice'
WITH DIFFERENTIAL, INIT
```

Because the order of restore is important, it is a good idea to have a naming convention that easily allows you to recognize the backup type of a backup file (particularly if you append the full and differential backups to the same backup device). You can use the WITH NAME = and WITH DESCRIPTION = to assign a name and description to backup. This has no effect other than to make it easier to identify the contents of the backup.

Backing Up the Transaction Log

You can only back up the transaction log of databases running in Full or Bulk Logged recovery mode that have had at least one full backup. You cannot restore the log backups without first restoring the full backup. When you perform the log backup, it calls a checkpoint and writes unwritten changes back to the data file. This makes sure that only the active transactions will remain in the log after the back up is completed. It then records all transactions before deleting the inactive portion of the log. When you restore log files you must restore them in order, so it is a good idea to have a naming convention that helps identify when a backup was made.

To back up a transaction log, you follow syntax very similar to that of the full backup except, rather than BACKUP DATABASE, you use the BACKUP LOG statement. The syntax is as follows:

```
BACKUP LOG database name TO device [,device2 ...deviceN]
WITH options
```

The options available to the BACKUP LOG statement include all of the options available to the full backup statement and adds the following three new options:

- **WITH NO_TRUNCATE**   This is a very important option. When you perform a log backup with NO_TRUNCATE, the full transaction log is backed up, but the inactive portion of the log is not truncated. When you use this option, the backup process doesn't call a checkpoint. You use this option when you need to back up the transaction for a database that has experienced a failure in one of its data files. If you tried to perform a normal log backup in this situation, it would fail because SQL Server cannot call a checkpoint unless all of the data files are accessible (since this process must write changes back to the disk).

- **WITH TRUNCATE_ONLY**   This option is a bit misleading. Although you include the BACKUP LOG statement, if you include the

TRUNCATE_ONLY option a backup does not take place. Instead, the inactive portion of the log is deleted without being saved. In SQL Server 7 this option writes an LSN to the log indicating that the backup is running at that point. In SQL 2000 it does not call a checkpoint or write anything to the log.

- **WITH NO_LOG** In SQL Server 2000 this option is identical to WITH TRUNCATE_ONLY. In SQL Server 7 there was a marked difference. In both versions, the WITH NO_LOG option truncates the log without actually performing a backup. However, it does not attempt to perform a checkpoint or write an LSN to the log. This option is used to empty transaction logs that have become 100 percent full. A normal transaction log backup will fail if it cannot perform the checkpoint and write the LSN to the log.

Backing Up Files and Filegroups

To perform a filegroup of file backup, you use syntax very similar to that of the full backup. However, you need to reference the logical name of the file or filegroup. You also need to make sure you keep regular transaction log backups. The syntax for a file backup is as follows:

```
BACKUP DATABASE databasename
FILE = filename TO backupdevice
WITH options
```

To back up a filegroup, you would use the same syntax with one change, as follows:

```
BACKUP DATABASE databasename
FILEGROUP = FileGroupName TO backupdevice
WITH options
```

Backing Up a Database
Using Enterprise Manager

All of these options can be set using Enterprise Manager.

To backup a database in Enterprise Manager, follow these steps:

1. Expand the Management folder.

2. Right-click the backup icon and select Backup a Database.

Alternately, you can right-click on any database and select All Task | Backup Database. Both of these options will open the backup window (see Figure 6-1).

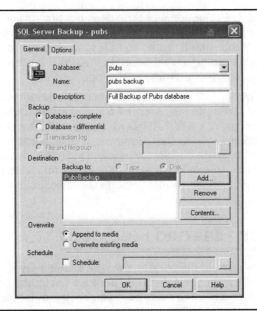

Figure 6-1. The backup window in Enterprise Manager

In this window, select the database that you want to back up from the pull down menu. You can give the backup a name and description (this sets the WITH NAME and WITH DESCRIPTION parameters). You can then choose the type of backup you want to perform. If any of the types are invalid (for example, you could not perform filegroup backup on a database with one data file and no filegroups) it will be grayed out in the window. You can then use the Add button to add one or more database devices or data file locations. These values represent the TO value of the backup. Next you can choose to Append to media or Overwrite existing media. These options are equivalent to the WITH INIT and WITH NOINIT. You can also schedule the backup to run at a later time.

If you click on the Options tab, you have further control over the backup (see Figure 6-2). On this tab, you can choose to verify the backup and to create a media set label (which sets the WITH MEDIANAME and WITH MEDIADESCRIPTION parameters). You can also set your tape options on this form. If you don't have a tape drive installed, these options will be grayed out (as in Figure 6-2).

Performing Dumps in SQL Server 6.5

The discussion of backup types and syntax applies to SQL Server 7 and 2000, but not to SQL Server 6.5. SQL Server 6.5 did not have anything equivalent to a differential backup and does not support filegroups. SQL Server 6.5 did allow you to create backup devices with the

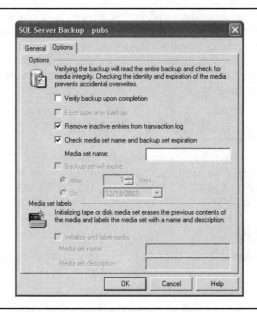

Figure 6-2. The backup Options tab

sp_addumpdevice stored procedure. To back up SQL Server 6.5, you
use the DUMP DATABASE statement with the following syntax:

```
DUMP DATABASE databasename TO device
WITH options
```

The WITH options available in SQL Server 6.5 were WITH INIT and NOINIT
as well as the tape options, as discussed earlier in this chapter. SQL Server 6.5
supported backing up to multiple backup devices and supported backups
without a device using a similar syntax, as follows:

```
DUMP DATABASE database_name TO {disk |tape |Floppy | Pipe}
= 'full path to backup location'
WITH options
```

Thankfully, later versions of SQL Server do not support backing up to
floppy disk.

To back up a transaction log, use the DUMP TRANSACTION statement.
It supports the same options as SQL Server 7. It supports NO_TRUNCATE
and TRUNCATE_ONLY (which writes an LSN) and NO_LOG (which does
not). SQL Server 6.5 also supports a DUMP table statement with the
following syntax:

```
DUMP TABLE database.owner.tablename
TO device WITH options
```

This option is no longer supported in SQL Server. It has been largely replaced by the differential backup. The rationale behind this statement was that you could back up only tables that have changed to reduce the time it takes to perform a full backup. The differential backup handles this in SQL 7 and 2000 (without the risk of out-of-sync tables that was a problem in SQL 6.5).

Automating SQL Server Backups

Backups happen regularly and on a predictable schedule. This makes them excellent candidates for automation. You can easily create a SQL Server Job that executes a BACKUP DATABASE or BACKUP LOG statement. SQL Server 7 and 2000 also include a Database Maintenance Wizard that allows you to automate a number of common database maintenance jobs, including backups.

To start the Wizard in Enterprise Manager, follow these steps:

1. Expand the Management folder.

2. Right-click the Database Maintenance Plan icon and select New Maintenance Plan.

3. Select which databases to maintain.

4. Choose your re-indexing options.

5. Choose your database integrity options.

6. Set the schedule and options for your database backups (the wizard only configures full backups).

7. Specify the directory where the data backups will be stored.

8. Set the schedule and options for your transaction log backups.

9. Specify the directory where the log backups will be stored.

10. Specify where the reports generated by the maintenance plan will be located.

11. Specify how much historical information should be stored.

12. Click Finish to create the plan.

Once you complete the wizard, it will add a number of jobs to run the automation. These jobs should be edited and maintained through the wizard.

NOTE   *Automation is discussed in detail in Chapter 9.*

Chapter 7

Restoring and Recovering Databases

As you saw in Chapter 6, planning and implementing an effective backup is important to protect your data. However, in the event of a failure (particularly a catastrophic failure), you must have a procedure for getting your backups back onto the server so that the data is accessible. This is the restoration process. A good backup strategy needs to consider the restoration process. As a DBA, you will be responsible for considering not only your backup strategy but also your recovery plan. Different backup types can make restoration faster or slower. How you restore your backups can also impact the amount of data loss. This chapter will provide a solid overview of the restoration process and will show you the steps you need to take to restore both user databases and system databases (like **master** or **msdb**). It will also introduce you to the automatic recovery process, and discuss why having a good understanding of how recovery works is important for performing effective restorations.

7

Overview of SQL Server Recovery

Microsoft SQL Server is a transaction database management system. When a transaction occurs, it must complete entirely or not at all. Chapter 4 mentions the ACID test for a transaction. Transactions must be Atomic (all or nothing), Consistent (always follow the same rules), Isolated (multiple users are unable to modify the same record at the same time), and Durable (able to withstand a failure). For our current purposes, let's examine durability. Consider the following situation. You have a process that transfers money between two bank accounts. This operation consists of two Transact-SQL UPDATE statements. The first statement removes money from one account and the second UPDATE statement adds the same amount of money to another account. If SQL Server was not durable, and if it crashed between the two statements, the debit would occur but the credit would not (and you would lose money).

Luckily, this is not the case. SQL Server uses its transaction log to record the activity of transactions (even if the database is in Simple recovery mode). Before each transaction begins, a marker is placed into the log and assigned a transaction identifier. All activity in the transaction is then logged. If all steps in the transaction complete successfully, then a second marker is added to the log indicating that the transaction is complete. A transaction is not committed until this second marker is written to the log. Eventually these transactions are written back to the data file. When the checkpoint process occurs, committed transactions are flagged to be written back to the data files. When a transaction is written back to the data file, it is considered inactive. The rest of the operations are kept in the active portion of the log. The active portion is everything from the checkpoint prior to the oldest uncommitted transaction.

TIP *For a more complete discussion of transactions, see the "Transactions Explained" section in Chapter 4.*

Each time the SQL Server service starts, it *recovers* all databases as a means of ensuring durability on the server. Whenever SQL Server starts, it is not aware of the reason why it was last stopped. It could have been stopped by a DBA or the server could have crashed. In either event, there may be transaction issues (remember that data modifications take place in cache and are later written back to the data file). When the SQL Server service stops (for whatever reason), the caches are cleared. Because of this there could be committed transactions that have not yet been written to disk. There could also be actions that were started and not completed at the time when the service stopped. The recovery process covers both circumstances.

The purpose of recovery is to ensure that all transactions are brought to a consistent state. To recover a database, the SQL Server service reads the active portion of the transaction log (remember that the inactive portion contains committed transactions that have already been written back to disk and can be safely ignored). It reapplies all committed transactions by rewriting them to the cache. It also rolls back all transactions that were uncommitted. Because the instructions for the incomplete transactions were also stored in memory and lost when the service stopped, there is no way to recover the steps needed to complete these transactions. Therefore, rolling back the incomplete transactions is the only way to make them transactionally consistent. Because transactions are all or nothing, SQL Server will, in these cases, choose nothing. Consider the previous bank transfer example. If the SQL Server were to fail between the two steps, when the system recovered, it would roll back the first operation and place the debited amount back into the account. This means the transfer will, in effect, never have taken place. It also means, however, that you won't lose any money either. This maintains both the atomicity and the durability of a transaction.

NOTE *The frequency of checkpoints is determined by the recovery interval configuration parameter. Essentially, the recovery interval is the longest period of time SQL Server will allow for recovery. A recovery interval of one does not mean that the database will perform a checkpoint every minute. Instead, it will call the checkpoint process each time the number of transactions in the transaction log would take more than one minute to recover.*

The recovery process is automatic. It happens every time the SQL Server service starts. Until recovery is complete, SQL Server will not allow users access to a database. This prevents users from accessing data from incomplete transactions. If a database has not been recovered, it will appear to be offline. Until the database is brought online it cannot be accessed. It is also possible to manually control the recovery process during a database restore. When you restore, you can choose to restore and recover a database automatically, or you can choose to restore but not recover the database. As you will see later in the chapter, you will need to leave the database unrecovered to restore certain backup types. By default, the restore process will always recover the database after it has been restored to bring the restored database to a transactionally consistent state.

One final aspect of recovery to be aware of is the mechanism SQL Server includes to speed up recovery of servers that have been intentionally stopped. To speed up the recovery process, when you manually stop and restart the SQL Server service, it automatically performs a checkpoint on shutdown. During this checkpoint, any committed transactions that have not yet been written to disk will be flushed to the data files prior to the server stopping. This is only true, however, if it is the SQL Server service that initiates the shutdown. The SQL Server service will initiate its own shutdown when you stop the service using either SQL Enterprise Manager or the SQL Server Service Manager. If you stop the server using the net stop command or the Windows Services Utility, SQL Service will not perform a checkpoint before stopping the service. For this reason, you should always use the SQL Server tools to stop the SQL Server service.

Restoring and Recovering Databases

Restoring a database is different than *recovering* a database. Restoration is the process of taking a database backup and using it to replace or re-create a damaged or missing database. The SQL Server restoration process starts with a number of safety checks. These safety checks are as follows:

- Does the database name in the backup differ from the database being restored?
- Does the backup set have a different file structure than the database being restored?
- Is the backup set complete?

These checks are designed to avoid accidentally overwriting existing databases.

First the restore process tests to see if the name of the database you have included in your RESTORE statement matches the name of the database recorded in the backup set. If they differ, the restore process checks to see if a database with the new name exists. If there is no such database, SQL Server will simply create a new database with the new name. Backing up a database and restoring it with a different name is a good way to create a duplicate copy of a database (on either the same server or a different server). If a database with that name does exist, however, SQL Server will not perform the recovery. This check prevents you from accidentally restoring one database with a backup taken from another database.

Next, the restore process checks the file information in the backup set and compares it to the current database that you are restoring. If the number of files is different or if the file path is different, SQL server will not allow you to restore the database. SQL Server remembers where a backup was taken from and will attempt to restore to the same file path. Again, this check is to prevent accidentally overwriting files.

The final check is most relevant if a backup has been performed across a media set. Remember that each member of the set will have only part of the backup because the data is striped evenly across all members of the set. If one member of the set is missing, then the restore process will not have all of the data from the backup. This test will be performed even if there is only one backup device. In this case, the restore process will simply test if the backup file is readable.

Each of these safety checks can be controlled through the use of options. The options will be discussed later in the "Controlling Recovery During the Restore Process" section of this chapter. When the backup set passes all of these tests, the restore process begins. In SQL Server 7 and 2000, the restore process will drop the existing database (including all physical data and log files) and re-create the database entirely from the backup. This means that after the database has been restored, it will appear exactly as it did at the point in time when the backup ended. This also means that if a drive failed and was replaced, the restore process will recreate the missing database files on the new disk automatically. This only requires that a folder with the same path name as the original data and log folders exists so that the restore process can place the newly re-created files in the correct file path. In order to restore a database, you must be a member of the **sysadmin** or **dbcreator** fixed server role.

Both Transact-SQL and the Enterprise Manager have tools for restoring databases. As with the backup utility, the restore tools are installed automatically when you install Microsoft SQL Server. Now let's look at the steps to restore a database from different backup types. First, there are some very important pre-restore tasks that must be performed.

NOTE *The information in this chapter does not apply to SQL 6.5. SQL 6.5 uses a LOAD DATABASE and LOAD LOG statement to perform its restore. However the process is very different. Consult the SQL Server 6.5 help for information on using the LOAD statement.*

Pre-Restoration Tasks

Before you restore a database, there are three steps that you must perform to ensure that the restore proceeds properly and that a minimum amount of data is lost. These steps are as follows:

1. Close and limit user access to the database.

2. Back up the transaction log.

3. Verify the backup set.

The first step is essential if the database you are planning to restore is currently online. The SQL Server restore process cannot drop and re-create the database if users are connected to it. For this reason, you must first close the connections of any connected users. It is best to have the users save their work and disconnect themselves. If you simply kill user processes, any unsaved changes will be lost.

Once all of your users have disconnected from the database, you can prevent new users from connecting by changing the access level to the database. In SQL Server 7 this is achieved by setting the database to **DBO user only** mode. In SQL Server 2000, the process is the same but the option has been renamed **Members of db_owner, dbcreator, sysadmin.** To set this option using Transact-SQL, use the following statements:

For SQL Server 2000:

```
ALTER DATABASE <database name>
SET RESTRICTED_USER
```

For SQL Server 7 (will also work in SQL Server 2000):

```
EXEC sp_dboption [@dbname = ]' <database name>',
[@optname = ] 'dbo use only', @optvalue= {TRUE | FALSE}
```

Use the following steps to change access options using Enterprise Manager:

1. Expand the Database folder.

2. Right-click the database you plan to restore and select Properties from the Context menu.

3. Click the Options tab.

4. If the database is running on SQL Server 7, click the dbo Use Only check box. If the database is running on SQL Server 2000, click the Restrict Access check box and select the Members of db_owner, dbcreator or sysadmin radio button.

5. Click OK.

SQL Server will not allow you to restrict access if any nonadministrative users are still connected to the database. Make sure they are all disconnected before you change the database access level.

Once database access has been restricted, you should back up the transaction log for the database. This step is only necessary if your database is using the Full or Bulk logged recovery models. If your database is using the Simple recovery model, you will not be able to perform any transaction log restores, so SQL Server will not allow you to back up the transaction log. You should back up the log because the restore process drops and re-creates both the data files and the log files for a database. If you have transactions in your log that have not been backed up, they will be permanently lost once you perform the restore. When you back up the transaction log, you should also use the WITH NO_TRUNCATE option. Because the log will be dropped and re-created, there is no need to truncate the log as part of the backup. Also, if data files are missing or corrupt (which may be the case depending on the reason for restoring the database), you will be unable to back up the transaction log unless you use this option.

NOTE *Recovery modes are described in detail in Chapter 6.*

Finally, you should verify the backup set that you plan to use for the restore. Check that you have the correct backup set for the database you need to restore. Verify that the set contains the most recent backup. If the backup device contains more than one backup, you will need to record which backup file(s) within the device you will need. Make sure that the backup is readable by SQL Server and complete. If you used a volume set to back up the database, check that you have all members of the volume set. To verify the backup in Enterprise Manager, use the following steps:

1. Expand the Management folder.
2. Click the Backup icon.
3. In the right pane, double-click the backup device containing the backup you plan to restore.
4. Click View Contents.
5. Use the scroll bar to review the contents of the device, as shown here.

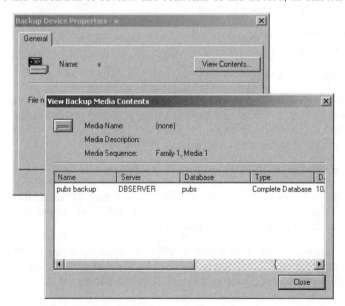

SQL Server includes four Transact-SQL statements that can be used to get more detailed information about each backup device than is included in Enterprise Manager. There are four verification statements that are used with the RESTORE statement. They are listed in Table 7-1.

Any user can execute these options. It is important to note that none of them verify the condition of the actual data. They simply return information about the backup device. If the data was corrupted before the backup, none of these options will detect this error. The syntax for each is as follows:

```
RESTORE <verify option>
FROM '<backup device>' [, <device 2>, …<device n>]
[WITH] options
```

Option	Description
VERIFYONLY	This option tests to see if a backup device is readable. If you are testing a media set, it will also test to see if the set is complete.
HEADERONLY	This option reads the header for each backup held within a device and returns the following: —The name and description of each backup set —The type of backup performed as an integer (1 = full backup, 2 = transaction log backup, 4 = file or filegroup backup, 5 = differential database backup, 6 = differential File backup) —When the backup ran —On which server the backup ran —When the backup expires —The Log Sequence Number (LSN) positions for the backup (useful when determining the restore order for multiple transaction log backups)
FILELISTONLY	This option returns information about the physical files contained within the backup set, including the following: —The logical file names —The physical path to the files —The size of the backup file —The maximum size of the data file (backups do not store unused space in the data file, but this space will be re-created when the file is re-created) —Filegroup membership
LABELONLY	This option is used to display the labels for backup devices. It is used primarily with backup sets on tape. This option returns the following: —Media name —Media description —Media family information (if the device is a member of a media set)

Table 7-1.   The Verification Options for the Restore Statement

For most of these verify options, information about all backup files in the backup device will be displayed. The exception to this is WITH FILELISTONLY. This option will, by default, only display file information for the first backup in the device. If you want to find file information about other backups, you need to use the WITH FILE = x option. This option will be discussed in detail in the "Restore Options" section of this chapter.

Restoring a User Database

Now that you have completed all of the pre-restore tasks and verified your backup, you are ready to start the restore process. How you restore the database will depend on what type of backup you are restoring from. The following section looks at all of the backup types individually.

Restoring a Full Backup

With the exception of file and filegroup backups, all restores must start with the restoration of a full backup. The full database restore is a baseline. Using this restore, the corrupt or damaged database is deleted and a new copy is created from the backup set. Not only are the physical data files re-created, but the transaction log files are also re-created. At the end of a full database restore, the database will appear as it did at the moment that the full backup completed (including any uncommitted transactions that were in the transaction log at the time). Full database restores can be used to replace damaged databases or replace data files that have been lost because of hardware failure. If the database was lost because of data corruption (either accidental or intentional), you will still need to use a full database restore to bring the data back to a non-corrupt state. For this reason, the full database restore is one of the most important activities you may be called upon to perform as a DBA.

A full backup restore can be performed using either Enterprise Manager or the RESTORE statement. To restore a database using the Transact-SQL RESTORE statement, use the following syntax:

```
RESTORE DATABASE  databaseName
[FROM < backup device> [,<device 2>, … <device n>] ]
[WITH <options>]
```

The backup device parameter will be either the name of a backup device or, if you performed a full backup without using a permanent device, the path to the backup (including the media type). For example, if you wanted to restore a database called **salesrecords** from a backup device called **FullBackupNovember**, you would use the following statement:

```
RESTORE DATABASE salesrecords
FROM FullbackupNovmember
```

When this statement is executed, the restore process will locate the file information from the devices from the **master..sysdevices** table and get the backup set. If the backup was made to a media set, you must include each device that was used in the media set. For example if you had backed up **salesrecords** to four devices labeled BackDev1 through 4, you would use the following syntax:

```
RESTORE DATABASE salesrecords
FROM backdev1, backdev2, backdev2, backdev4
```

If any members of the media set are missing, the restore will fail.

If you had backed up **salesrecords** directly to a disk file, you would use the following syntax:

```
RESTORE DATABASE salesrecords
FROM DISK = 'd:\tempBackups\salesback.bak'
```

This ad hoc restore uses the same device types as the BACKUP statement (DISK, TAPE or PIPE). Because the RESTORE statement has no reference for this backup, you must include the full file path to the backup file, including the drive letter (or the drive label in the case of a tape backup).

To restore a database using Enterprise Manager, you would use the following steps:

1. Right-click either the Databases folder or the specific database which you want to restore.

2. From the Context menu, select All Tasks | Restore Database.

3. In the Restore Database window, make sure the database you want to restore is in the Restore as Database list box.

4. In the Show Backups of Database list box, select the database that you want to restore (this will produce a list of backups available to restore).

5. Use the check boxes in the lower pane to select the backups that you plan to restore from, as shown here.

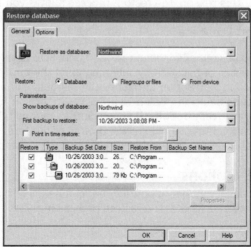

6. If the backup you want to restore from is not present, click the From Device radio button and select the device, as shown here.

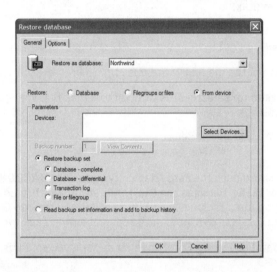

Controlling Recovery During the Restore Process

As was mentioned in the "Restoring a Full Backup" section of this chapter, when a full backup is restored, the transaction log is also restored. The transaction log contains all transactions that occurred while the backup took place. This means there may be incomplete transactions in the log. To maintain transactional consistency, the restore process, by default, also recovers the database after it is restored. There may be times, however, when you don't want to recover the database. If, for example, you have transaction log backups to restore, the database must remain unrecovered. This will prevent data loss because transactions that began during the full backup may be committed on a subsequent log backup. If you were able to recover the full restore before the log restore, you would lose all of those transactions. For this reason, the restore process allows you to control when recovery takes place. The RESTORE statement has three options to control recovery. They are listed in Table 7-2.

Recovery can also be controlled when restoring from SQL Enterprise Manager. If you restore a series of backups by selecting all of the applicable backups in the Recovery tool, SQL Server automatically restores all but the final backup in sequence using the WITH NORECOVERY option. You can also manually set the recovery options. If you click the Options tab, there is a Recovery Completion State section at the bottom of the form. Table 7-3 lists the three options available and the recovery options to which they correspond.

The RESTORE Options

SQL Server also has a number of options that can be used to selectively override the safety checks that the restore process imposes to protect

Option	Description
WITH RECOVERY	This is the default option. If you specify this option, the restore process will recover the database. You should specify this option if you are only restoring the full backup or if this is the final backup restore in a sequence.
WITH NORECOVERY	This option allows the restore to complete but does not recover the database. SQL Server neither rolls back nor commits any transactions that are in the transaction log for the current backup. While in this state, the database will remain offline. However, you will be able to restore subsequent backups.
WITH STANDBY	This option does not recover the database. Instead, it allows it to be accessed in a read-only fashion while still allowing subsequent restores against the database. This is a key component of a procedure called Log Shipping. Log Shipping is discussed in Chapter 14.

Table 7-2. The Recovery Options for the RESTORE Statement

Enterprise Manager Option	Recovery Option Equivalent
Leave Database Operational. No Additional Transaction Logs Can Be Restored	WITH RECOVERY
Leave Database Non-operational, But Able to Restore Additional Transaction Logs	WITH NORECOVERY
Leave Database Read-Only and Able to Restore Additional Transaction Logs	WITH STANDBY

Table 7-3 The Recovery Options in the Enterprise Manager Restore Utility

databases from accidental restores. Each of these options are included in the WITH clause of the RESTORE statement. The options are as follows:

- **WITH REPLACE** This option overrides all safety checks that relate to the database. Using the WITH REPLACE you could, for example, overwrite a database with a backup taken from another database. WITH REPLACE will also allow you to restore a database with a backup set that has a different number of database files. You should use caution when using this option. One place where you might use WITH REPLACE is when rolling a test database back to an earlier version using an old backup. The command does not require any parameters.

- **WITH FILE**   Allows you to specify which backup within a single device to use to restore a database. Remember that one of the advantages of creating permanent backup devices is that you can append multiple backups to a single device. If you don't specify the WITH FILE option, it will always default to 1 and restore the first backup placed in the backup device. The best way to find the correct value for the WITH FILE option is to consult the position value returned by the RESTORE HEADERONLY command. The syntax for this option is FILE = x (where x is the numeric value of the file within the backup device).

- **WITH RESTART**   Use if a recovery is interrupted (such as with a tape load error). This command will locate the point where the restore was interrupted and continue from that point forward. This command does not take any parameters.

- **WITH MOVE... TO**   Use to override the safety check that attempts to re-create the physical database and log files in the same location where they were backed up. Using this option, you can specify an alternate path and file name for each file. If you are moving a database to a new location (such as creating a copy of a production database on a test server), you must use this option unless the test server has the exact same folder structure. The syntax for this option is MOVE 'logical_file_name' TO 'physical_file_path'.

---

*TIP   This option provides one of the best ways to change the physical location of database files. All you need to do is back up the database and restore it using the Move...to option. This option updates both the **master** database and the file header for the database files. You can use the method to move both data and log files.*

The options can be combined in a single statement as long as a comma separates each statement. For example, suppose you had backed up a database called **FinProd**, and you wanted to restore it on a different server and rename it to **FinQC**. The target server already has a **FinQC** database but you want to overwrite it. You also want to change the file path for the **FinData** and **FinLog** files. The backup you want to restore is the third backup stored in a backup device. You also plan to restore a transaction log once the backup restore is complete. You would use the following statement:

```
RESTORE DATABASE FinQC FROM backupdevice
WITH FILE = 3, REPLACE,
MOVE 'FinData' TO 'd:\datafile\findata.mdf',
 MOVE 'FinLog' TO ' d:\logifles\finlog.ldf', NORECOVERY
```

Restoring a Differential Backup

The process of restoring a differential backup is almost identical to restoring a full backup. You use the same syntax in the RESTORE DATABASE statement, and you can use all the same WITH options that you saw in the last section. However, in order to restore a differential backup, you must first perform a full restore of the database and make sure to include the NORECOVERY option. When the SQL Server restore process detects that the device referenced by the RESTORE DATABASE statement contains a differential backup, it checks to see if the database is currently in an unrecovered state. If it is not, you will receive a message instructing you to perform a full database restore with the NORECOVERY option and the restore will fail. If the restore process finds the database in a non-recovered state, it will apply the backup. Differential backups only contain changes made since the last full backup so they are much smaller than the full backup, yet much faster to restore than a series of transaction log backups.

After the differential restore is complete, not only are all changes recorded back to the database but the transaction log is also updated to the state it was in when the differential backup was run. This means that you can restore subsequent transaction logs to the differential backup. To do this, you must use the NORECOVERY option when restoring the differential backup so that you can apply the transaction log backups. If you don't specify NORECOVERY, SQL Server will automatically recover the database after the differential restore is complete.

Restoring the Transaction Logs

In order to restore a transaction log backup, the database must be in a non-recovered state. Therefore, all transaction log backups must start with a full backup including the NORECOVERY option. You can also restore transaction logs after a differential backup, again, as long as it does not recover the database. If you have multiple transaction log backups to restore, they must be restored in order. Each backup records the first and last Log Sequence Number (LSN) of the portion of the transaction log that it stores. These LSNs must match so that the final LSN of one backup is next to the starting LSN of the next backup. You can use the RESTORE HEADERONLY statement to view the first and last LSN values of each backup.

The restore process will take all transaction log backups, knit them together into one long transaction log, and then recover the entire log to bring the database to a transactionally consistent state. For this reason, if a backup file is damaged, missing or unreadable, you will not be able to restore any subsequent transaction log backups and will lose data after the end of the last intact backup. If the final log backup is the one that you make just prior to starting the restore process, you should be able to minimize your data loss to only those transactions that were incomplete at the point in time when the system failed or became corrupt. This is why the Full recovery model provides the best coverage for preventing data loss.

In Transact-SQL, the syntax for restore transaction logs is slightly different from the other restores you've seen so far. The syntax is as follows:

```
RESTORE LOG database_name
[FROM < backup device> [,<device 2>, … <device n>] ]
[WITH <options>]
```

The options in the WITH clause are the same as those in the full backup. When you restore multiple transaction log backups, make sure that you specify NORECOVERY for all but the final log backup. To restore transaction logs in the Enterprise Manager, you follow the steps that were included in the full backup. Because this tool graphically represents all backups, simply select the full backup that you want to start from, and all of the transaction logs that you want to include as part of the restore.

The transaction log also has one WITH option that is not available to the other backup types; this is the WITH STOPAT option. The STOPAT option allows you to perform a point in time recovery. For example, suppose that one of your advanced users accidentally issues an UPDATE statement on the pricelist table without including a WHERE clause. This statement will set all products in the product table to the same price. Because this is a valid statement and the user has UPDATE permission on the table, the rows update. SQL Server logs and commits each row update separately. There is no error, so the system proceeds normally. You know that the update took place at 2:35 P.M., because the operator, noticing his mistake, notes the time on the system clock. Because the transaction log records all changes, you can (assuming you are using the Full recovery model) back up the current transaction log, and restore the database, including the final backup, to the point where the data corruption occurred. The syntax for this final restore would be as follows:

```
RESTORE LOG productDB FROM bkdevice
WITH STOPAT = 'October 27, 2003 2:34', RECOVERY
```

Bear in mind that this process will not only roll back the **products** table. The entire database will be rolled back to the state it was in at 2:34 and any data that was entered into the database after that time will be lost. You can duplicate this functionality in Enterprise Manager by selecting the Point In Time restore check box in the Parameters section of the General tab and setting the Stop At Time in the text box. If your database is in Simple recovery mode, this option will be grayed out.

You have one other option, available only in SQL 2000, that can be very useful. If you are going to perform an action and you are not sure if it will work or cause further problems, you can include a marker in the transaction log. You do this by using the BEGIN TRANSACTION WITH MARK 'pointer name' statement. The mark saves you from needing to know the exact time that a transaction executed. If you have a mark in the log, you can reference it directly using the STOPATMARK or STOPBEFOREMARK options. The difference between the two statements is that the STOPATMARK will stop the recovery immediately *after* (that is including) the marked transaction, whereas the STOPBEFOREMARK will stop the restore immediately *before* the marked transaction (and exclude it from the recovery). For example, if you execute a transaction on the **productDB** database including a marker called 'test1' and you decide to undo the change, you would use the following statement as your final transaction log restore:

```
RESTORE LOG productDB FROM bkdevice
WITH STOPBEFOREMARK = 'Test1', RECOVERY
```

You cannot perform this operation from Enterprise Manager.

Restoring Files and Filegroups

File and filegroup backups are different from the rest of the backup types because they do not require an unrecovered full backup in order to proceed. Using file and filegroup backups is a way to avoid restoring entire full backups for very large databases if only part of the database is damaged or corrupted. You can, therefore, restore a single database file or a single filegroup while leaving the rest of the database intact. This may seem to open up the possibility of synchronization problems within the database. Suppose you had a database with one filegroup that is two days older than the rest of the filegroups in the database. This would cause serious data consistency errors. Luckily, SQL Server will not allow this condition to exist.

Prior to starting a file or filegroup restore, you *must* back up the current transaction log. If SQL Server detects a portion of the log that is not backed up, it will not allow you to perform a file or filegroup restore. You will restore the file or filegroup without recovery and will then reapply the transaction logs. SQL Server is smart enough to apply the logs only to the file or filegroup that is sitting in the unrecovered state.

The syntax for performing a file or filegroup restore is as follows:

```
RESTORE DATABASE  databaseName
{File = 'file_name' | Filegroup = 'filegroup_name'}
[FROM < backup device> [,<device 2>, … <device n>] ]
[WITH <options>]
```

For example, if you wanted to restore a filegroup called **HRTables** from a database called **VLDB**, you would use the following statement:

```
RESTORE DATABASE  VLDB
Filegroup = 'HRTable'
FROM backupdevice
WITH NORECOVERY
```

Again, make sure that you include the NORECOVERY option when you restore the filegroup so that you can apply your transaction log backups.

Restoring and Recovering System Databases

The discussion so far has focused on user databases. However, as a DBA you must also maintain your system databases. The backup procedure for system databases like **master** and **msdb** is the same as for any other database, but the recovery process can be very different. This is particularly true with the **master** database. **Master** is how SQL Server knows about itself. It contains key metadata about databases and also includes things like the **sysdevices** table which contains information about backup devices. Very often, if **master** has become corrupted to the point that it needs to be restored, the SQL Server service will not start. This poses a special challenge because the SQL recovery process is performed by the SQL Server service.

Luckily SQL Server includes a stand-alone executable called rebuildm.exe. This utility is used to re-create the **master** database from your SQL Server installation CD. Essentially, running rebuildm.exe returns your **master** database to the state it was in when you first installed SQL Server. However, it allows you to start the SQL Server service and run the restore process to restore **master**.

The restorem.exe file is located in the \Program Files\Microsoft SQL Server\ 80\tools\binn\ folder in SQL Server 2000 and \MSSQL7\Binn folder in SQL Server 7. Before you begin the rebuild, make sure you have a full backup of the **master** database. To rebuild a corrupt **master** database using rebuildm.exe, follow these steps:

1. Insert your CD and copy the \x86\data folder to your local hard drive.

2. On the local drive, change the properties for each file so that it is *not* read only.

3. Click Start | Run and type rebuildm.exe. This will start the rebuildm utility.

4. In the Source Directory Containing Data Files text box, enter the path to the local copy of the data folder.

5. If you have multiple instances on the computer, make sure you set the context to the database that you plan to restore.

6. Click Rebuild to re-create the system database. You will receive a warning informing you that all system databases will be overwritten. Click OK to complete the rebuild.

Now that the **master** database has been re-created, you can use your backup to return it to the state it was in prior to the failure. There is, however, one extra step that you need to perform. Remember that because the restore process drops and re-creates the data file, you need to remove all user connections from the database prior to starting the restore. Unfortunately, with **master**, the SQL Server service is a connected user which locks the database. This means that you cannot start a restore while the service is running. The solution to this is to start the database in single-user mode. To start your SQL server in single-user mode:

1. Stop the SQL Server service.

2. Open the command editor and browse to the \Program Files\Microsoft SQL Server\80\tools\binn\ (for SQL Server 2000) or \MSSQL7\Binn (for SQL Server 7).

3. Run the following command: **sqlservr.exe –c –m.**

The -c switch starts the server in single-user mode and the -m switch runs SQL Server as an application without placing it in the control of the Service Manager. Note that when this command runs, it will not give you a command prompt backup until the service stops. Therefore, once the text stops scrolling, you can open Query Analyzer or Enterprise Manager to perform the restore of the **master** database. If you backed up **master** to a database device, the reference to that device will now be gone. Before performing the restore, re-create the device and point it to the existing physical tape or file. This will not overwrite the device; it will simply re-create the missing entry in **sysdevices**. After **master** has been restored, stop and restart the service and everything should be back to normal.

NOTE *The rebuildm.exe command rebuilds all system databases so you must restore both the **msdb** and the **distribution** databases after SQL Server restarts.*

7

Chapter 8

Loading and Extracting Data

Having a properly functioning SQL Server is important—getting the data into a database on the server is equally important. Depending on the purpose or function of the database, users may add data over time (such as order data for an online retailer), or you can import it from another system (uploading a new product and price list table to the same online retailer, for example). As a DBA you may be called upon to set up and oversee these data imports or exports. You might even be required to schedule them to run automatically.

More than just moving data, however, you may need to clean or modify the format of the data as you transfer it from one system to the next. Microsoft SQL Server ships with a number of useful data migration tools. This chapter looks at the need to transform data and examines all of the tools available for performing imports and exports.

SQL Server Tools for Extraction, Transformation, and Load

As a DBA you may need to draw data from many sources. You might simply import data from one SQL Server database into another. However, your data might come from other data sources such as Microsoft Access, a series of Excel spreadsheets, or text files exported from a mainframe system. It might reside on a heterogeneous data source like Oracle or DB2. You might also need to modify that data as it moves from one data source to another. This process of moving and modifying data is known as extraction, transformation, and load (ETL).

As the name suggests, there are three parts to the ETL process. The first part addresses connecting to a data source. There is no difficulty moving data between databases on the same server, as both share the same SQL Server service. Also, provided the SQL Server service on two servers has a common security context, there is no problem moving data between SQL Servers (even between versions of SQL Server). This becomes more difficult when you deal with heterogeneous data sources, however, since you need to determine how to connect to the remote data source (using ODBC or OLE-DB, for example) and under what security context.

You will also need to know how the data is presented, or what form the data is in. This can be a simple or complex problem. If you are dealing with a comma-delimited text file, for example, the connection can be quite easy.

167

There will be no security to deal with (other than file-level NTFS security), and the data will all be in text format with typically a well-known structure.

If your data source is another RDBMS, the connection will be more complex. First, you will have to resolve security and connection issues to allow SQL Server to connect to the remote data source. The second problem is that many RDBMS use non-standard (according to the ANSI SQL standard) data types (SQL Server is also guilty of this). As a result, you may have difficulty mapping data to SQL Server data. This leads to the second part of ETL—data transformations.

Sometimes, it becomes necessary to alter data before you load it so that it matches what the target server expects. This is particularly important if you are loading data from multiple sources into a central destination. The following are reasons for choosing to transform data:

- **Re-mapping data**   This type of transformation occurs frequently when you bring data from a heterogeneous data source, or when you combine data from multiple data sources. For example, a remote data source might store telephone numbers as integers, whereas the destination stores them as character data. Re-mapping can also involve more detailed data type issues. For example, you might need to handle incompatible date formats or mapping data types that don't have a direct correlation on the target database (such as the Oracle **raw** data type or Access's YesNo data type). Re-mapping ensures that you will be able to successfully move data from the source to the destination.

- **Changing data format**   Changing format means altering the way information is stored. For example, you may have a Boolean field in a data source like a Yes/No or True/False column. Because SQL Server doesn't have a Boolean data type, different database designers may come up with different ways of representing these values. Suppose you are merging customer data from several data sources. In the customer profile there is a value, ReceiveCat, indicating that the customer wishes to receive your catalogue. This field would be Boolean. There are only two options, yes they want it or no they don't. Suppose, however, one source uses 1 and 0 to indicate customer preference, another uses the string "True" and "False," and a third uses "Y" and "N." Clearly you cannot import all three directly into your destination table. If you did, you would need to search for all three values—1, "True," and "Y"— to find each customer when you want to put a customer mailing list together. Instead, you could select one format ("True," for example) and change the incoming data so that all columns present the information the same way. In this example, all 1s and "Y"s would be converted to "True."

- **Aggregating data**   Depending on the reason you are moving your data, you might want to aggregate your data and only store the results in the destination table. Aggregating data simply means summarizing or calculating values based on the data in the source location. For example, suppose you are moving data from a point-of-sales (POS) system to a reporting database. The POS stores the price of each item, the quantity purchased, and any discount. It does not physically store a total purchase amount. In the reporting database, you might want a total sale column to save you from calculating this value every time you run a report.

• **Validating data**   Validating data is an important transformation. What may be acceptable data at the data source may not be acceptable at the destination. For example, if the source destination allows NULLs for a column, but the destination doesn't allow columns with a NULL, your inserts will fail. Similarly, if you move data from a text field on the source to a numeric field on the destination, you may have illegal characters (such as a "-" or "$"). The transformation process should detect these rows and, if possible, correct them (such as stripping the "$" from numeric values or supplying a default for the NULL values). Validation is particularly important when you have foreign keys on the destination table. If a value is entered in a FOREIGN KEY column that is not in the referenced PRIMARY KEY or UNIQUE constraint, the insert will also fail. Validation in this instance can mean both checking to see if a corresponding value exists, and possibly generating a key (such as taking a first name and last name from the source and looking up a customer id in the destination database).

• **Ensuring data consistency**   Data consistence can be an issue when you are pulling data from multiple sources. Consider a city column in a customer database that is being fed by three separate data sources. The first refers to New York as "NYC," the second uses "New York City," and the third uses simply "New York." To SQL Server, all three values are different (that is, SQL interprets these as three different cities). This problem may be compounded by spelling errors (like NewYork and Nw York). If you do not maintain consistency in your data, it will be very difficult to locate all of your New York customers (in this example) from the destination database.

The third part of ETL is the Load into the destination database. As with source location, you must consider how you will connect to the destination database. You must also consider the security on the destination. Remember that whatever process you use for your ETL, you will need read permission on the data source, but will need read and write permission on the destination. Also, if the tables to hold the transformed data do not exist on the destination, the ETL process will also need object creation privileges on the destination.

Microsoft SQL Server includes a number of tools and processes to help with ETL: the BCP utility (bcp.exe), which has existed since the earliest days of SQL Server; the BULK INSERT process; and, for SQL Server 7 and 2000, there is a much more powerful tool—Data Transformation Services (DTS). As you will see in the next section, only DTS is a true ETL tool because it is capable of both data import/export and data transformation.

The Data Transformation Service

DTS is sometimes referred to as a data pump. Like a water pump, DTS connects to both a data source and a data destination. It draws data into itself from the data source and then pushes it to the destination. DTS can also perform transformations on the data as it moves it between the source and destination. DTS uses OLE-DB to connect to the data source and the destination. Therefore, any data source that is accessible by OLE-DB can serve as a source or destination for DTS. Neither the source nor the destination needs to be SQL Server. You can use DTS to move data from a DB2 database to an Oracle database, for example (not something intended by Microsoft, but a useful feature nonetheless. Data sources (and destinations) can also be accessed through third-party OLE-DB providers. SQL Server ships with a number of OLE-DB providers allowing you to connect to both relational and non-relational data sources, such as the following:

- Oracle
- Microsoft Access
- Microsoft Excel
- Active Directory
- Delimited text files
- Any ODBC-accessible data source

The OLE-DB connection object manages security for each connection. You can configure the DTS package to authenticate to both the source and the destination data sources without requiring manual intervention. If you are using the ODBC provider for OLE-DB, you can set authentication information in the DSN you create for the ODBC data source. You can also schedule DTS to establish regular data transfers.

DTS is also able to move the table structure (the schema) with the data. Unless you are moving between SQL 7 and 2000 data sources, however, you can only move tables using DTS. You are not able to move other objects like views, triggers, or indexes between data sources, unless both data source and destination are SQL 7 or 2000. SQL Server 2000 also allows you to move more than just schema. It also allows you to move users, jobs, alerts, user-defined errors, and even entire databases.

DTS jobs are constructed as packages. Each DTS package is a self-contained unit that can include multiple data sources. A package will contain connections to all data sources and can also contain a number of transformation tasks. Each task is a unit of execution within the package that provides the transformation functionality. These tasks include such activities as executing ActiveX scripts, SQL Server statements, or command-line programs and batch files.

You can also control the order in which the individual tasks execute when the package is run. Tasks can run in serial or in parallel. Tasks running serially can have the control of flow from one task to the next task specified. That is, DTS allows you to determine if job steps run serially (one after another) or in parallel (at the same time). Furthermore, if you are running serially, a job step can be configured to run as follows:

- On successful execution of the previous step
- On failure of the previous step
- On completion of the previous set (regardless of success or failure)

A DTS package can also be configured to run transactionally across steps in the package. If there is no order specified, operations can run concurrently. It is also possible to have two paths run in parallel, and then combined into a single operation. For example, you could have a data import from a large number of files loading into different database tables at the same time. Then have all of the load paths converge on a single task that performs a transformation on the data and loads it into central reporting tables (as shown in Figure 8-1). At the end of this package, you could create two e-mail tasks: one stating the job succeeded and one stating that it failed. You could then run one on success and the other on failure. At the end of the job, only one e-mail would be sent—which one would depend on whether or not the job ran successfully.

When you create your DTS package, you can save it in a number of different formats. These are described in Table 8-1.

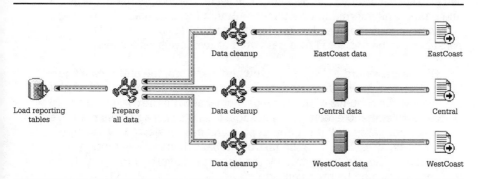

Figure 8-1. A DTS package executing in parallel

Package Type	Description
A local SQL Server package	These packages are stored in the **msdb** database of the local SQL Server. They can be manually executed from the server, or be scheduled to run automatically by the SQL Server Agent service.
A Visual Basic file	The package can be saved as a BAS file and loaded as a code module into a Visual Basic application. The BAS files will use the DTS object model.
A COM file	This option allows the DTS package to be saved as a structured storage file with a .dts extension. This type of DTS package is not stored within SQL Server. It can be called by an outside process and can be shared between SQL Servers.
Inside the SQL Server Meta Data Services	This option stores the package inside the SQL Server meta data repository. Adding the package to the repository allows you to store meta data about the package and to track the history of all loaded and transformed data. This is commonly referred to as tracking the data lineage. This is a useful feature if you need to track data sources and transformations. The meta data repository is stored in the **msdb** database of a SQL Server where the package resides.

Table 8-1.   Options for Saving DTS Packages

If you store the package as a local SQL Server package or a COM file, you can also set security on the package. The security encrypts the package and protects all information contained within it (such as user id and password information used to connect to remote data sources). DTS packages can be protected by a password at two levels, as follows:

- **Owner password**   If you set an owner password, the entire package will be encrypted. Only someone with the owner password will be able to view the contents of the package. Someone with the owner password can also edit and execute the package. If a DTS package does not have an owner password, it is unencrypted and can be viewed by anyone who has access rights to the **msdb** database. Because encryption is based on the password and not the user, it is important to use a strong password to protect the package.

- **User password**   You cannot set a user password without first setting an owner password. Anyone with the user password can execute the package, but will be unable to view or edit its contents. With a valid user password, you can execute the packages manually using SQL Enterprise Manager or run them through the DTSRUN command (which is discussed in the "Automating Data Loads" section of this chapter).

DTS is accessed through a suite of tools that include the following:

- The DTS Import/Export Wizard
- The DTS Designer
- The Copy Database Wizard

Each tool has specific functions, but all three utilize the same underlying service. The easiest of these to implement is the DTS Import/Export Wizard.

The DTS Import/Export Wizard

The DTS Import/Export Wizard is used to perform simple transformation tasks. These tasks are simple in the sense that they only deal with a transformation between a single source data and destination. The wizard will allow you to copy multiple tables or views, and to create a new destination table based on the results of a query. SQL Server 2000 also allows you to define a transformation based on the output of a stored procedure. The wizard has the ability to create the destination schema and to run a single ActiveX script to provide some transformation functionality. If both the source and destination databases are SQL Server 7.0 or higher , the DTS Import/Export Wizard can also transfer objects between databases.

To use this wizard, follow these steps:

1. Open SQL Enterprise Manager and expand the server from which you want to run DTS.

2. Right-click the Data Transformation Services folder and select All Tasks | Import Data from the Context menu. (If you select Export Data from the menu, you will open the same wizard.)

3. Select the OLE DB provider from the data source list box. The type of connection you choose will determine the data required for the connection.

4. Fill in the connection information in the lower part of the window to describe the data source (including any necessary security settings). Click Next.

5. Select the connection type for the destination.

6. In the lower pane, input all connection information for the destination (again including any necessary security settings). Click Next.

NOTE *The DTS Import/Export Wizard tests connection information and if it cannot connect to either data source, it will prevent you from continuing until the connection can be established.*

7. Select the table(s) or query to use as the data source. If both objects are SQL Server 7.0 or higher databases, you will also have the option to transfer objects on this screen.

8. On the next screen, select the objects you want transferred, or enter the query that will be the basis of the transfer (depending on which option you chose in step 7). If you chose to use a query as your data source, you can use the Query Builder to help you build the SQL Query that will drive the results. Or, you can simply type the query into the form. Alternatively, if you compose the query in Query Analyzer and save it as a SQL file, you can then load that file into the package.

9. Once you have chosen your source, you must choose the destination. In the Destination Table box, you can choose an existing table on the destination data source or choose to create a new object (assuming you have the correct permissions). If you want to edit the newly created table or perform a transformation, you must click on the ellipsis button under Transform, as shown here.

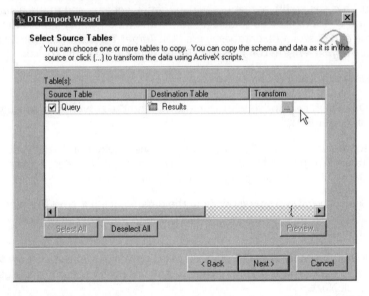

10. On the Column Mappings and Transformation form, click on the Column Mappings tab to edit the script to create a new table or to control how columns on the source will map to a preexisting destination. If you click on the Transformations tab, you can choose an ActiveX scripting language and enter the transformation script in the window. You can also create a VBScript file using another editor and load it into this window using the Browse button.

11. Click OK to confirm all mappings and translations.

12. Click Next.

13. On the next screen you can decide to have the package execute immediately, create a DTS package for replication, or schedule the package to run later. You can also save the package. SQL Server 7 can save the package as a SQL Server package into the repository or as a Visual Basic code file. SQL Server 2000 also gives you the option to save the package as a structured storage (COM) file. Click Next to continue.

14. If you opt to save the file, you will be asked where to save it and be prompted to add an owner password and a user password. If you don't add the passwords, the package will remain unencrypted. Click Finish to save and run the package.

The DTS Designer

The DTS Designer allows you to create much more complex DTS packages. To open the DTS Designer, right-click the Data Transformation Services folder in SQL Enterprise Manager and select New Package from the Context menu. This will open the designer window. On the left side of the window, you will see a list of all available OLE DB providers and all available tasks (as shown in Figure 8-2). Start by dragging the relevant data objects to the work area. As you drag a data object onto the work area, a property sheet will open that allows you to configure and name the connection. It is a good idea to change the connection name from the default, particularly if you will have multiple instances of the same type of data object.

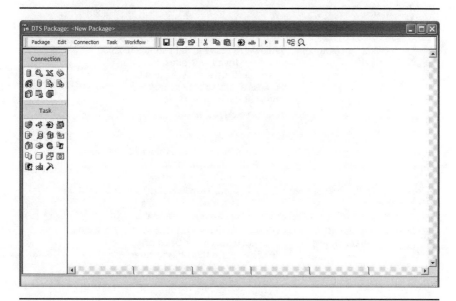

Figure 8-2. Using the DTS Designer

To build a package, you will drag all required tasks to the work area. Again, a property sheet will open for each object that will allow you to configure the task and possibly associate it with a particular data object. Finally, if you click on one object, hold down SHIFT, and click on a second task or data source, you can choose the workflow relationship between the two objects by selecting the type from the Workflow menu. The package will execute from the first icon you selected to the second. An arrow will indicate in which direction the steps will move.

When you have added and configured all data sources and tasks, select Package | Save to save the package. At this point you can also determine which type of package to save (for example, a SQL Server object or VB Script) and set the owner and user passwords.

DTS Data Objects   There are a number of possible data objects that you can choose from in the DTS Designer. These are listed in Table 8-2.

Icon	Data Source	Description	Availability
	OLE-DB Provider for Microsoft SQL Server	This data source can be used to connect databases from any SQL 7 or 2000 Server. If you are connecting to multiple databases on a server, you will need one connection object for each database.	7.0, 2000
	Microsoft Access	Allows you to connect to a single Microsoft Access MDB file.	7.0, 2000
	Microsoft Excel	Allows you to connect to a single Microsoft Excel XLS file.	7.0, 2000
	dBase 5	Allows you to connect to dBase 5 databases.	7.0, 2000
	HTML file (source)	Allows you to read data supplied by data-driven web sites. In essence, it uses an ASP page to access a remote data source and present the data as HTML.	2000
	Paradox 5.*x*	Give access to Paradox 5.*x* data files.	7.0, 2000
	Text file (source)	Creates a link to an existing TXT or CSV file that will serve as a data-transformation source.	7.0, 2000
	Text file (destination)	Creates a link to an existing TXT or CSV file that will serve as a data=transformation destination.	7.0, 2000
	Microsoft OBDC Driver for Oracle	Allows you to use ODBC to connect to an Oracle Database. In order to use this object, the Oracle networking client must be running locally on the computer executing the DTS package.	7.0, 2000

Table 8-2   Data Objects

Icon	Data Source	Description	Availability
	Microsoft Data Link	This connection type uses the old DB-Library DLLs. It can be used to link to SQL Server 6.x databases.	7.0, 2000
	Other connection	Allows you to connect to any ODBC-accessible data source. You must create the DSN connection to the data source prior to configuring this object.	7.0, 2000

Table 8-2. Data Objects *(continued)*

DTS Task Objects There are also a large number of transformation tasks available to the DTS Designer. SQL Server 2000 included some additional objects that are not found in SQL Server 7. All available tasks are described in Table 8-3.

Icon	Task	Description	Availability
	ActiveX Script	Allows you to run an ActiveX script within a DTS Package. This allows you to use VB Script, Jscript, or any other supported active scripting language to perform complex transformations on your data.	7.0, 2000
	Transformation	This is the actual transformation task. It establishes the connection between the source and destination. You can embed an ActiveX script transformation within this task for more complete transformations.	7.0, 2000
	Execute SQL	Allows you to execute a SQL statement within the package. This task can perform operations such as creating or dropping SQL Server objects or executing stored procedures.	7.0, 2000
	Bulk Insert	A very fast but inflexible way of moving data into a SQL Server table. In order to use this task, the destination must be a SQL Server 7 or 2000 database. This task uses the Transact-SQL BULK INSERT command (see the "Using BULK INSERT" section later in this chapter).	7.0, 2000
	Execute Process	Allows you to execute CMD, BAT, or EXE files as part of the DTS package.	7.0, 2000

Table 8-3. Available DTS Tasks

8

Icon	Task	Description	Availability
	Copy SQL Server Objects	Allows you to copy tables, views, stored procedures, defaults, rules, user-defined data types, and user-defined functions (in SQL Server 2000 only).	7.0, 2000
	Data-Driven Query	Allows you to perform a record-by-record test on all data being moved (for example, applying a 5 percent, 10 percent, or 15 percent discount, depending on the price of a product).	7.0, 2000
	Send Mail	Allows you to automatically send an e-mail to a specified recipient. This is a good way of reporting the outcome of a DTS package.	7.0, 2000
	Execute Package	Allows you to call another DTS package from the current DTS package.	2000
	Transfer Error Messages	Allows you to transfer user-defined error messages (the ones created with **sp_addmessage**).	2000
	Transfer Master Stored Procedure	Allows you to transfer any stored procedure from the **master** database to any SQL Server 2000 database.	2000
	Transfer Job	Allows you to transfer jobs from one instance of SQL Server 7 or 2000 to a SQL Server 2000 server.	2000
	Transfer Database	Allows you to transfer a SQL Server 7 or 2000 database to a SQL Server 2000 destination server.	2000
	Transfer Logins	Transfers logins from a SQL Server 7 or 2000 server to a SQL Server 2000 destination.	2000
	Dynamic Properties	Dynamically sets values from an INI file or a global variable. This object allows you to pass in values and make them available when the package runs.	2000
	FTP	Allows you to receive a file from an FTP site. This file can then become a data source in the package.	2000
	Message Queue	Allows your package to communicate with other processes using the Microsoft Message Queue service.	2000

Table 8-3.   Available DTS Tasks *(continued)*

The Copy Database Wizard

A new tool added in SQL Server 2000 is the Copy Database Wizard. Although not immediately evident, this wizard actually uses DTS (and in particular, the new object transfer tasks in DTS) to migrate an entire database from one server to another (or between named instances on the same server). This tool cannot be used to create a duplicate database on the same instance of SQL Server.

To access the Copy Database Wizard, follow these steps:

1. Right-click the Database folder and select All Tasks | Copy Database Wizard from the Context menu.

2. Select the source server or instance and provide all necessary login information.

3. Select the destination server or instance and provide all necessary login information.

4. Select the database you want to transfer and select Move or Copy. If you select Move, the database will be dropped from the source server when the transfer is complete. Click Next.

5. Reconfigure the data files for the new location. If you don't make any changes on this screen, you must have a file path on the destination server that is identical to the path used by the SQL Server for the data and log files on the source server.

6. Choose which other objects to transfer (such as logins, jobs, or user-defined error messages).

7. Finally, you can save the package to run at a later time.

8. If you choose to run the package immediately, the database transformation will occur as soon as you click Finish.

Using DTS for ETL

DTS is an excellent ETL tool. With a single package, you can connect to multiple data sources and destinations. With the ability to use ActiveX scripts, execute SQL statements, and perform row-by-row operations through the data-driven query tasks, you have a powerful set of tools with which to perform transformations. In essence, you are only limited by your experience with these tools. Also, through the control of flow mechanisms, you can include error handling within your packages. If a step fails, you can configure tasks designed to remedy common sources of failure, or at least provide useful logging on the source of the failure and fail gracefully.

DTS is also very useful because you can configure all connect and login settings within the data source objects. This means DTS is able to authenticate to remote data sources without user intervention. Also, because DTS uses OLE-DB, there are very few data sources that are not accessible. You can also use many third-party providers, and the inclusion of an ODBC provider makes older data sources available.

The BCP Utility

The SQL Server Bulk Copy program (BCP or bcp.exe) is available in all versions of SQL Server. It is a very fast, yet limited, means of moving data into and out of SQL Server databases. BCP has two functions: moving data from SQL Server tables, views, or queries into delimited text files, and importing delimited text files into SQL Server tables. BCP is a command-line tool that can be executed manually or included in a Windows batch script. The syntax for this command is as follows:

```
bcp.exe {{table_name | view_name} | "query"}
{in | out | queryout | format} data_file [switches]
```

The ability to generate output files from views or SQL queries is available only in SQL Server 7 and later versions. If you draw data from a query, you must include the QUERYOUT option. Specify IN if you are loading a table from a text file or OUT if you are exporting to a text file. You can load data into a view, but only if the view does not contain any derived values (such as an arithmetic operation or a group by clause) and references only one table. The FORMAT option allows you to create a format file based on the formatting switches that you include (see Table 8-4). If you do include the FORMAT option, you must also include the -f switch.

There are a number of switches that allow you to control how data is loaded and exported. They are listed in Table 8-4.

Switch	Description	Available in 6.x
-m *number*	Maximum number of errors permitted before SQL Server cancels the BCP process. Each row that cannot be inserted is counted as an error.	Yes
-f *file_path*	Allows you to specify a format file that replaces the -n, -c, -w, -6 and -N switches. This file is generated when BCP is run with the FORMAT option. You must include the full path to the file.	Yes
-e *file_path*	Allows you to specify an error file to track problems. This file contains all rows that cannot be loaded from the file.	Yes
-F	Allows you to specify which row in the specified data file is the first row to bulk copy. If you don't include this switch, BCP will default to 1.	Yes
-L	Specifies the row number for the last row to bulk copy from the data file. If this switch is not included, BCP will load all rows from the starting point to the end of the file.	Yes
-b *number*	Indicates the number of rows to include in each batch. Each batch runs as a separate transaction. If you don't include this switch, the entire data file will be processed as a single transaction.	Yes

Table 8-4. The Options for bcp.exe

Switch	Description	Available in 6.x
-n	Indicates that SQL Server should import data in its native data types. This can cause incompatibility between versions of SQL Server—particularly with dates—in the format of the data. If the data does not match SQL Server's internal data types, an error will occur. This switch is intended to transfer data between SQL Servers on the same hardware platform.	Yes
-c	Indicates that all data in the data files should be treated as character data.	Yes
-w	Indicates that all data in the data file should be treated as Unicode text (**nchar**). Data exported with the **-w** switch cannot be imported into SQL Server 6.x (which doesn't support Unicode).	No
-N	Indicates that SQL Server should use the native data types for non-character types, and Unicode for character data (**nchar**). This option provides better performance than **-w** but still allows you to send Unicode character data. As with **-w**, data exported with the **-N** switch cannot be imported into SQL Server 6.x.	No
-V{60 | 65 | 70} (SQL Server 2000)	Instructs SQL Server to perform the bulk copy using data types from earlier versions of SQL Server. This switch can be used in conjunction with **-n** and **-c**. The **-V** option will not, however, convert **datetime** and **smalldatetime** data types to earlier formats. These will always be exported and imported using the ODBC canonical format. The **-V** is only available in SQL Server 2000.	No
-6	Performs the same as **-V** but is supported by SQL Server 7. In SQL Server 2000, it is only present for backwards compatibility and **-V** should be used instead.	No
-q	Turns on QUOTED_IDENTIFIERS between the database and BCP. This will allow you to use double quotes (") as character delimiters instead of the normal square brackets ([ ]).	Yes
-C *code_page*	Allows you to specify how to respond to code page differences for character data. The values for *code_page* are —**ACP** ANSI (ISO 1252). The SQL Server detail code page. —**OEM** Uses the code page of the client (this is the default). —**RAW** No code page conversion. This is fast but introduces the possibility of data error if the wrong code page is used. —Specified code page number.	No
-t *terminator*	Allows you to specify which character will be used as your column (field) delimiter. The default is **\t**, which is the tab character. You could replace it with any character (like a comma or semicolon).	Yes

8

Table 8-4.   The Options for bcp.exe *(continued)*

Switch	Description	Available in 6.x
-r *terminator*	Allows you to specify which character will be used as your row delimiter. The default is the \n (new line) character.	Yes
-i *file_path*	Allows you to specify a file which will provide answers to the command prompt if you are running BCP in interactive mode. This file will have responses for -n, -c, -w, -6, and -N switches.	Yes
-o *file_path*	Allows you to specify the output file that will receive the data if you are using the OUT option.	Yes
-a *packet size*	Allows you to control how many bytes of information the SQL Server will send to the client running BCP in each call. Packet can be any size from 4096 to 65535 bytes. This option will override any server settings.	Yes
-S *servername\ instancename*	Used to specify which SQL Server will be contacted by BCP. This switch is necessary if you are running BCP against a remote server. If you don't specify this option, BCP will look for a default instance of SQL Server on the local computer.	Yes
-U *username*	Used to determine which user ID will be used to connect to SQL Server. As an outside process, BCP must authenticate to SQL Server before it can execute.	Yes
-P *password*	Allows you to submit a password for the login account you specified with -U. Keep in mind that this password is sent in clear text. Whenever possible, you should authenticate with the -T option to make communication more secure.	Yes
-T	When you use this switch, BCP passes the security credentials of whichever Windows user executes the command. This means that if you execute BCP from the command line with this switch, your logon credentials are passed to the SQL Server. Therefore, you will need to ensure your Windows userid or global group has a valid login in the SQL Server to perform whatever actions BCP is attempting to perform.	Yes
-v	Returns the version of BCP running on the local machine. Knowing the version is important because not all switches will work with all versions. For example, the BCP version shipped with SQL Server 6.5 handles dates differently than the version shipped with SQL Server 7.0 and later.	Yes
-R	Enables regional settings for BCP. Regional settings can affect the way that SQL Server and BCP handle currency date and time data. By default, BCP ignores the regional settings. -R will use the regional settings of the local computer running BCP, not the regional settings on the remote SQL Server.	No

Table 8-4.   The Options for bcp.exe *(continued)*

Switch	Description	Available in 6.*x*
-k	Overrides defaults set on columns when NULLs are passed in from the data file. Whenever a NULL is encountered, the column will remain null.	No
-E	Specifies that the data file contains data that should be inserted into a column that has an IDENTITY property. Without this switch, SQL Server ignores any values passed to the IDENTITY property column and instead automatically generates a value for the column.	Yes
-h *hint[, hint2]*	Provides directives as to how BCP should execute. There are a number of available hints and you can include more than one of them with this switch. They are as follows: —**Order(col1 [ASC | DESC] [, col2])** Indicates the sort order of the data file. If the table receiving the data contains a clustered index and the data file is stored in the correct sorted order, this option will greatly increase the load speed. If either condition is not met, this option is ignored. —**ROWS_PER_BATCH = n** This option specifies the number of rows in each batch (and therefore, each transaction), which allows for better optimization of the data load. —**KILOBYES_PER_BATCH = n** Lists the appropriate number of kilobytes per batch. This option will also improve optimization. —**TABLOCK** Sets a table-level locking hint. This option greatly improves the speed of the data load because the bulk load process does not need to worry about running into locks held by other processes (locking contention). However, while the table lock is in place, no other processes will be able to access the table until the lock is released when the entire bulk copy is complete. —**CHECK_CONSTRAINTS** In normal operations, CHECK constraints are ignored during the bulk copy process. This hint forces CHECK constraints to be verified for reach row. —**FIRE_TRIGGERS** If you perform a load through BCP with this switch, in conjunction with the IN option, all insert triggers on the table will fire. By default, insert triggers are ignored during a Bulk Copy operation.	No

Table 8-4. The Options for bcp.exe *(continued)*

NOTE *As with most command-line SQL Server tools, BCP's command-line switches are case sensitive.*

Using BULK INSERT

The BULK INSERT statement is similar in functionality to BCP. BULK INSERT is used to load data from a delimited file into a SQL Server table or view. However, unlike BCP, this statement is controlled by the SQL Server service and is executed entirely within Transact-SQL. The BULK INSERT statement is not available in SQL Server 6.*x*.

The syntax for BULK INSERT is as follows:

```
BULK INSERT {'table_name' | 'view name'} FROM 'data_file'
[WITH
(
[ BATCHSIZE = number],
[CHECK_CONSTRAINTS],
[CODEPAGE = {'ACP' | 'OEM' | 'RAW' | 'code_page'}],
[DATAFILETYPE = { 'char' | 'native'| 'widechar' | 'widenative' }],
[FIELDTERMINATOR = 'terminator_character'],
[FIRSTROW= first_row],
[FIRE_TRIGGERS],
[FORMATFILE = 'format_file_path'],
[KEEPIDENTITY],
[KEEPNULLS],
[KILOBYTES_PER_BATCH = kilobytes_per_batch],
[LASTROW = last_row ],
[MAXERRORS = max_errors],
[ORDER ( { col1 [ ASC | DESC ] } [ ,...coln ] ) ],
[ROWS_PER_BATCH = rows_per_batch],
[ROWTERMINATOR = 'terminator_character'],
[TABLOCK ]
)]
```

The *date file* option must include the full path to the location of the file. If the destination is a view, the view cannot contain any derived columns or reference more than one table. There are number of options that control how the data is loaded. Many of these options perform the same function as BCP switches. The options are described in Table 8-5.

Option	Description
BATCHSIZE	This option specifies the number of rows in a batch. The batch size is important because each batch runs as a transaction. As each batch completes, SQL Server commits the transaction. If there is an error, the entire batch is rolled back.
CHECK_CONSTRAINTS	By default, CHECK constraints are not tested when a BULK INSERT takes place. This option overrides that default behavior and applies CHECK constraints for each row.

Table 8-5.   The Options for the BULK INSERT Command

Option	Description
CODEPAGE	This option allows you to specify how to respond to code page difference for character data. The values for code_page are as follows: —**ACP** ANSI (ISO 1252). The SQL Server detail code page. —**OEM** Uses the code page of the client (this is the default). —**RAW** No code page conversion. This is fast but introduces the possibility of data errors if the wrong code page is used. —Specified code page number.
DATAFILETYPE	This option can have four possible values, as follows: —**char** Any column with a data type of **char**, **varchar**, or **text** is converted into the code page used by the SQL Server performing the bulk insert. —**native** Uses BCP to load data using **native** data types. —**widechar** Loads data from a data file containing Unicode. —**widenative** Performs a **native** bulk load on all data types except for character-based types (**char**, **varchar**, **text**). Character data types are loaded as Unicode.
FIELDTERMINATOR	This option indicates the column delimiter character used in the data files.
FIRSTROW	Indicates which row will be the start of the bulk load. The default is 1.
FIRE_TRIGGERS	Allows insert triggers to fire during the bulk load operation.
FORMATFILE	If the data file was created by BCP with the **-f** option, you can use the format file to assist in loading the data by using this option. You must include the full file path in the format file.
KEEPIDENTITY	Allows values from the data file to be loaded into a column with an IDENTITY property. If this option is not set, SQL Server will ignore the values in the data file and populate the column from the IDENTITY property.
KEEPNULLS	Inserts NULL for empty columns even if there is a DEFAULT on the column.
KILOBYPTES_PER_BATCH	Allows you to set the approximate number of kilobytes for each batch.
LASTROW	Indicates the last row to be processed by a batch. By default, the BULK INSERT will load all rows from the starting point to the end of the data file.

Table 8-5.   The Options for the BULK INSERT Command *(continued)*

8

Option	Description
MAXERROR	Indicates the maximum number of errors that can occur before the BULK INSERT fails. If this value is not set, the default is ten errors. Each row that cannot be loaded from the data file into the target table is considered an error.
ORDER	Allows you to indicate how the data in a data file is ordered. If the order matches the order of a clustered index on the table, this option will increase the speed of the insert.
ROWS_PER_BATCH	Allows you to specify the number of rows in a single batch. If no value is specified, the entire data file is loaded as a single transaction. Breaking a large file into smaller transactions allows for better optimization of the BULK INSERT, particularly when the table is indexed.
ROWTERMINATOR	Allows you to indicate the end of row delimiter. The default is \n (new line).
TABLOCK	This option places a table lock on the table during the BULK INSERT. This will reduce contention and speed up the data load. However, no other process will be allowed to access the table until the BULK INSERT is complete.

Table 8-5. The Options for the BULK INSERT Command *(continued)*

Attaching and Detaching Databases

All of the sections in this chapter so far have discussed migrating data from one data source to another. It is also possible to physically move databases from one SQL Server to another, provided both servers are running compatible versions of SQL Server. There are a number of reasons why you would want to do this. You might, for example, want to create a pre-populated development database based on a production system. You might also want to create a report server that can be more thoroughly indexed. There are a few tools to help with this operation. One way of making this change is to make a full backup of the database that you want moved and restore this backup on the target server. You can also use the Copy Database Wizard discussed earlier in "The Copy Database Wizard" section of this chapter.

Another way is to physically move the database files from one server to another. The data files cannot be simply moved or copied while the SQL Server service is running. The only way to copy or move the database files without stopping the service is to use a system stored procedure to disconnect the files. There are system stored procedures capable of detaching a database while the SQL Server service is running—**sp_detach_db** and **sp_create_removable**.

Using sp_detach_db and sp_attach_db

You actually need a pair of stored procedures to move physical database files from one SQL Server to another. The two stored procedures needed are **sp_detach_db** and **sp_attach_db,** of which a variation called **sp_attach_singlefile_db** can be used for SQL Server databases with only one data file. As the names suggest, you will use one procedure to disconnect the data files from the source server and the other to reattach the files on the destination server. The syntax for **sp_detach_db** is as follows:

```
sp_detach_db [ @dbname = ] 'database_name'
[, [ @skipchecks = {TRUE | FALSE}]
```

The @skipchecks option indicates whether or not **sp_detach_db** should run the UPDATE STATISTICS command before detaching the database files. If the value of @skipchecks is true, then the check is skipped; otherwise, the UPDATE STATISTICS is run. The default value for this option is NULL. If the reattached database is going to be read-only, it is a good idea to perform the update prior to detaching the database. Once you execute this statement, the record of the database is removed from the **sysdatabases** table in the **master** database. The physical database files and log files are not deleted (as they would be if you dropped the database) and can be moved or copied.

One thing to remember when detaching the database is that the logins for the source SQL Server exist in the **master** database. These are not copied when a database is detached. However, any database users in the detached database will have values in the local **sysusers** table that reference security identifiers (SID) in the **master** database. For this reason, you should make sure that **dbo** owns all database objects, including the database itself. This will allow a **sysadmin** on the remote server to access the reattached database (as **dbo** always points to the same SID on all installations of SQL Server). You should also drop all database users so there are no conflicts. If you don't, these database accounts will not be orphaned and will be unusable. You should also disable replication on the database (publications or subscriptions).

The **sp_attach_db** stored procedure is used to reattach data files. The syntax for this procedure is as follows:

```
sp_attach_db [ @dbname = ] 'dbname' ,
  [ @filename1 = ] 'datafile' [ , @filename2 = 'logfile.]
[, filename3..16 = n ]
```

This stored procedure will allow you to reattach up to 16 data and log files. If your database has more than 16 data and log files, the database cannot be reattached using this procedure.

NOTE *If you are running SQL Server 2000, you can reattach databases of more than 16 data and log files by using the CREATE DATABASE statement using the WITH ATTACH option.*

You must reattach at least one database and one log file. When you run **sp_attach_db**, you must include the full path to the data and log files. This stored procedure re-creates an entry in the **sysdatabases** table in the **master** database. Once the database is attached, the files are locked by the SQL Server service on the new server and cannot be moved or copied. If you forgot to remove replication before detaching the database, you can remove it after the database is reattached using the **sp_removedbreplication** stored procedure. The syntax for this stored procedure is as follows:

```
sp_removedbreplication [ @dbname = ] 'dbname'
```

These stored procedures are available in SQL Server 7 and 2000 only. You must be a member of the **sysadmin** fixed server role to execute any of these procedures.

Using sp_certify_removable and sp_create_removable

SQL Server 2000 also gives you the ability to create a read-only version of a database that can be copied to removable media (such as a CD-R or DVD-R). This is useful if you want to distribute a large amount of complex data that does not change frequently (such as a large price list or a database of technical specifications). The database file can span multiple media if necessary. However, all files must be available when the database is accessed. For example, if you distributed a database on two DVDs, the files on both disks would need to be available at the same time to reattach the database. Therefore, you should probably copy the files to the hard drive first.

Before creating the removable database, you must prepare the database using the **sp_certify_removable** system stored procedure. The syntax for this procedure is as follows:

```
sp_certify_removable [ @dbname = ] 'database_name'
[ @autofix = ] 'auto' ]
```

This procedure verifies that the database can be distributed successfully on removable media. When it certifies the database, it reports back if a user other than **dbo** owns any object in the database. If this is the case, the database cannot be certified for removal. If you use the **@autofix='auto'** option, the procedure will automatically reassign all objects to **dbo** and drop any existing database users. It also updates the statistics on all tables and then takes the database offline and sets the access attributes on the data files to read-only. This allows the **sp_create_removable** stored procedure to execute.

The **sp_create_removable** system stored procedure separates the database into at least three files, as follows:

- A system tables file

- One or more data files

- A transaction log file

Although the data in a removable database is read-only, the system tables and log file are not. This is meant to allow you to change settings on the database (such as adding database users) without allowing the data to change. The data files can remain on the removable media, but the system tables file and log file will be copied to the hard drive.

The syntax for **sp_create_removable** is as follows:

```
sp_create_removable [ @dbname = ] 'database_name',
[ @syslogical = ] 'logical_file_name',
[ @sysphysical = ] 'physical_file_path',
[ @syssize = ] files_size ,
[ @loglogical = ] 'logical_file_name',
[ @logphysical = ] 'physical_file_path',
[ @logsize = ] files_size,
[@datalogical1 = ] 'logical_file_name',
[ @dataphysical1 = ] 'physical_file_path',
[ @datasize1 = ] files_size,
...
[ @datalogical16 = ] 'logical_file_name',
[ @dataphysical16 = ] 'physical_file_path',
[ @datasize16 = ] files_size]
```

All three file types have three attributes: xlogical, xphysical, and xsize. The sys-prefixed values (syslogical, sysphysical, sysfiles) refer to the file containing the system tables. The log-prefixed values refer to the transaction log file, and the data1-prefixed through data16-prefixed values represent the data file(s). The **sp_create_removable** system stored procedure allows a maximum of 16 data files.

Once a file has been detached, you can reattach it using **sp_attach_db**. The newly attached database will be read-only, and you can attach files from the removable media without having to copy the files to the hard drive. Again, all files created by **sp_create_removable** must be present and accessible before you can reattach the database.

Automating Data Loads

Data loads and extractions are often repetitive tasks. If you are using DTS to populate a data warehouse or archive data, these tasks tend to occur regularly. All methods discussed in this chapter can be automated. The BULK INSERT process can be scheduled by creating a SQL Server job with a single Transact-SQL task. This job can be scheduled and executed by the

SQL Server Agent. The BCP command can be included in a batch file and scheduled using the Windows Scheduled Tasks utility. To automate BCP, use the following steps:

1. Create a batch file that calls bcp.exe with all required options.

2. Click open the Windows Scheduled Tasks tool in Accessories | System Tools.

3. Double-click on the Add Scheduled Tasks icon.

4. Select the batch file.

5. Set the schedule for the task.

6. Enter the username and password that the batch file will use to execute. If you have included the **-T** option, make sure the user account you enter here has permissions on the remote server.

7. Click Finish to save the scheduled job.

With DTS you have multiple options for scheduling. If you have saved your package as SQL Server or structured storage package, you can simply right-click the package in the Local Packages folder of SQL Enterprise Manager and select Schedule Package. This option will create a SQL Server job that can be scheduled just like any other job. The job steps to execute the package use the DTSRun command. DTSRun allows you to execute a DTS package outside of SQL Enterprise Manager. The syntax for this command is as follows:

```
dtsrun.exe  [/S server_name[\instance_name]
  { {/U user_name [/[~]P password]} | /E }]
{/[~]N DTS_package_name }
| {/[~]G guid of repository package}
| {/[~]V version guid of repository package}
[/[~]M user or owner password]
[/[~]F COM file name]
[/[~]R repository_database_name]
[/A global_variable_name:typeid=value]
[/L log_file_name]
[/W NT_event_log_completion_status]
[/Z] [/!X] [/!D] [/!Y] [/!C]
```

If you call an argument with the tilde (~) rather than a forward slash (/), it indicates that the data will be presented as encrypted hexadecimal text. The switches for this command are listed in Table 8-6.

DTSRun is a command-line utility and can be run outside of SQL Server. It can also be scheduled using the Windows Scheduled Tasks. As a DBA this would allow you to have your Windows administrators schedule transformation jobs without giving them access to your SQL Server.

Switch	Description
/S	The name of the server containing the DTS package.
/U	A user account that is able to access the SQL Server.
/P	A password used to access the SQL Server (in conjunction with the user account listed with the /U switch).
/E	Indicates that trusted authentication should be used to connect to the SQL Server.
/N	The name of the package to be executed.
/G	The globally unique identifier (GUID) of the DTS package (which can be retrieved from the repository or the **msdb** database).
/V	The version GUID of the package. Each time a DTS package is modified, it gets a new version GUID.
/M	The owner or user password associated with the package.
/F	If the DTS package is in a structured COM file, this switch must give the full path to the DTS file.
/R	If the package is stored in the repository, this switch must provide the name of the repository database on the SQL Server.
/A	If the package was created to use global variables, this option must be used to pass in values for these variables.
/L	Designates a log file for package execution.
/W	Specifies whether or not DTSRun should write the results of package execution into the application log in Event Viewer. Value can be True or False.
/Z	Indicates that the command line for the DTSRun command has been encrypted using the encryption found in SQL Server 2000.
/!X	This switch prevents the package from executing. This allows you to create an encrypted command line without having to run the package at the time of encryption.
/!D	Allows you to delete a package from an instance of SQL Server.
/!Y	Allows you to see the encrypted command used by DTSRun without executing the package.
/!C	Copies the execution command line for the DTSRun job to the Windows clipboard.

Table 8-6. The DTSRun Switches

Chapter 9

Automating SQL Server Administration

Microsoft SQL Server often plays a key role in mission-critical applications. As a result, these servers must be up and running 24 hours a day, 7 days a week. Maintenance activities (such as backups or data transfers) must be performed daily, and any problems that could impact performance or functionality should be dealt with as soon as possible. There are problems with this, however. Most maintenance jobs are performed during periods of low activity and these periods tend to be outside of normal working hours (generally late at night). Also, problems may go undetected for long periods unless you are constantly viewing error logs. Luckily, SQL Server has a number of built-in automation features that allow you to run these jobs and checks without human intervention.

SQL Automation—An Overview

Automation in Microsoft SQL Server consists of three distinct parts: jobs, alerts, and operators. Jobs are scheduled tasks that can be performed without any user interaction. They can have multiple steps and can be simple or complex. Jobs are used to handle routine tasks, saving you from spending your day manually performing everyday tasks like backups or batch jobs. Alerts are not scheduled. They are actions that respond to conditions on the SQL Server. Alerts are important because the server is generally aware of problems before you are. Alerts save you from having to constantly scan error and activity logs on your servers. Finally, operators are individuals that are known to SQL Server and are notified of defined events. As you'll see in the "Managing Operators" section later in this chapter, there are different methods that SQL Server can use to notify operators. The process of defining an operator is simply to provide contact information for the individual. Essentially, you are creating an address book for your SQL Server.

Jobs, alerts, and operators can work together to create an overall automation plan that will allow you to better manage, monitor, and maintain your servers. They can easily integrate because the SQL Server Agent service controls them all. Jobs can create conditions that will trigger alerts (such as a job step failing with a particular error message). Alerts can also start jobs. This interaction could, potentially, have a job raise an error on failure and have an alert fix the problem and restart the job (through another intermediary job). At any point, the SQL Server Agent service could also notify an operator.

9

It is the ability to combine alerts and jobs, and the ability to notify operators at any point that make SQL Server automation so useful. It also allows the DBA to make automations simple or complex. The first step is to understand the importance of the SQL Server Agent service.

SQL Server Agent and Automating Administration

Automation cannot occur without the SQL Server Agent service (which we'll simply refer to as the Agent). The Agent is installed automatically when SQL Server is installed. This Agent is what starts all automated jobs at their scheduled times, monitors the system, fires alerts, and sends notification to operators. If the Agent is not running, no automated task can occur.

For this reason, you should always ensure that the Agent is started. If you are relying on automation, you should also configure the Agent so that it starts automatically when the server is rebooted. By default, in SQL Server 7.0 and SQL Server 2000, the Agent is not started and is not set to start automatically. There are different ways to change this. You can change the Startup property of the Agent in the Services console located in the Administrative Tools folder (or in the Control Panel if you are working on an NT 4.0 server). You can also start the service and configure it to automatically start using the Service Manager tool that ships with SQL Server, as shown in Figure 9-1.

If you are running named instances on a SQL Server 2000 server, each instance will have its own Agent service. The service on the default instance is called the SQLServerAgent service. On a named instance, it is called SQLAgent$*instancename* (where *instancename* is the name of the instance). For example, if you had a named instance called Instance2 on a server named CorpSQLSrv, the Agent service would be SQLAgent$Instance2.

Figure 9-1. Configuring the Agent with the SQL Server Service Manager

The security context for the Agent service is also important. Remember that nothing in Windows occurs without a valid login, and this includes services communicating with each other and performing tasks. When you installed SQL Server, you were given two choices for the security context of the services: the local system account or a Windows user account. There are pros and cons to each option. Consider the following factors when choosing an option:

- The account specified needs local administrator rights to function properly
- The account may need to communicate with other servers (such as a mail server)
- The account requires System Administrator privileges on the SQL Server

Using the local system account will give the Agent local administrator rights and, if you have maintained the default BUILTIN\administrators group login, will also have System Administrator rights on the local SQL Server. However, this account has no security context outside of the local server. This means that the Agent will be unable to perform any task that requires access to another server (such as retrieving files from a remote file server, contacting an Exchange server, or connecting to another SQL Server). However, this local service account does not require any special maintenance.

If the Agent will need to interact in any way with other servers, you should consider choosing a Windows account for the service.

To create a service account, complete the following steps:

1. Create a dedicated user account (do not, for example, use your own account or the built-in administrators account).

2. Give the account a strong password (that is, a combination of mixed case letters, numbers, and special characters that cannot be easily guessed).

3. Add the account to the local administrators group for the Windows Server on which SQL Server is running.

4. Grant the account the Log On as a Service right.

5. Make sure that the account password is not set to Change Password at Next Logon.

6. Make sure that the account password is set to Never Expires.

If you remove the built-in\Administrator logon account from the SQL Server, you must create a SQL Server login for the account and add that login to the System Administrator server role.

TIP   *For more information on the built-in accounts and roles, see Chapter 3.*

When associating a specified Windows account with the Agent, it is essential that the password cannot expire. The service cannot start if the user account used by the service cannot log on to Windows. The service has no way of changing its own password and, if the password expires, the service will simply not restart. Once this occurs, all automated processes will cease to function.

Configuring the SQL Agent Mail Service

A useful feature of SQL Server automation is the ability to automatically send e-mail messages. Before you can use this feature, however, you must configure the SQL Server Agent mail service, called SQLAgentMail. To configure this service you need to create a mail profile for the service account. The easiest way to create the profile is to log on to the computer using the Agent service's login account (if you are not using the local system account) and start a mail program like Microsoft Outlook. In Outlook, create a mail profile that contains all information about the mail server used in your environment (including password information, if required). The mail server can be any MAPI compliant mail server product (such as Microsoft Exchange or UNIX SendMail). It must be accessible from the SQL Server, and you may need to create a mailbox for the SQL Agent account. Once the profile has been created, it will be used by the Agent to send and receive mail.

Finally, once the Agent profile has been created, you must tell SQL Server to use this profile.

To add the profile use the following steps:

1. Open Enterprise Manager.

2. Expand the Management folder.

3. Right-click on the SQL Server Agent icon and select Properties from the pop-up menu.

4. On the General tab, select the Agent's mail profile in the list box located in the Mail Session section, as shown in Figure 9-2.

Note that if the Agent doesn't detect a profile, it will show an empty list box. If you have created a profile for the Agent and it doesn't appear in the list box, stopping and restarting the service will generally cause the Agent to recognize the new profile. Once you have configured SQLAgentMail, it is immediately available to the automation processes.

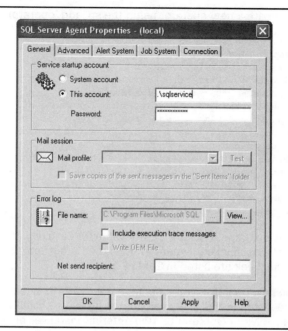

Figure 9-2.   Adding the mail profile

Managing Operators

Whenever a job runs or an alert is fired, you may want to send a notification. This notification can be as simple as informing an operator that a scheduled backup ran, or can be more serious, such as informing an operator that the transaction log is full. In order to have SQL Server contact a user, you must first define an operator. A SQL Server operator is simply an address book setting for the SQL Agent. All operators' contact details are saved in the **msdb** database and are available to the Agent service.

To add a new operator, use the following steps:

1. Open Enterprise Manager.

2. Expand the Management folder.

3. Expand the SQL Server Agent folder.

4. Right-click the Operators icon and select New Operator from the pop-up menu.

This will open the New Operator Properties form.

You can also create a new operator using the **sp_add_operator** system stored procedure. The syntax for this procedure is

```
sp_add_operator @name = ' Operator name',
[ @enabled = {1 | 0} --1 = enabled
[ @email_address = 'Operator e-mail_address'],
[ @pager_address = 'pager e-mail_address' ],
[ @weekday_pager_start_time = start_time for pager during weekday],
[ @weekday_pager_end_time = end_time for pager during weekday ],
[ @saturday_pager_start_time = start_time for Saturday ],
[ @saturday_pager_end_time = end_time for Saturday],
[ @sunday_pager_start_time = start_time for Sunday],
[ @sunday_pager_end_time = end_time for Sunday],
[ @pager_days = numeric days that operator can be paged],
[ @netsend_address = 'NetBIOS_address' ], ,
[ @category_name = ] 'Operator category' ]
```

The pager days parameter uses a binary value for each day of the week. You can add the decimal equivalent in the stored procedure. The codes for each day of the week are listed in Table 9-1.

To create the new operator, you must give it a name. This name must be unique to the instance of SQL Server. For example, you could have two operators called Night Operator on two different instances of SQL server on the same Windows Server, but not two in the same instance. The name is simply a way for the Agent to identify a specific operator. You also need to indicate how the operator is to be contacted. The choices available to you are

- E-mail address
- Pager e-mail address
- A computer name for the NET SEND command

In order to contact an operator via e-mail address or pager e-mail address, you must first have configured the SQLAgentMail service.

To enter the e-mail address or pager, browse the address book for the SQL Agent mail profile by clicking on the ellipsis. If you are using Microsoft Exchange, you can have this point to the global address book for your

Pager Day	Calendar Day
1	Sunday
2	Monday
4	Tuesday
8	Wednesday
16	Thursday
32	Friday
64	Saturday

Table 9-1. Pager Day Codes

domain. This simply reduces the possibility of mistyping an e-mail address. You should enter the full e-mail address for each operator (for example, Admin@haunting.com). SQL Server will try to resolve e-mail aliases from its address book, but it is unable to resolve e-mail aliases or display names if there are multiple names that begin with the same characters. For example, the Agent would not be able to distinguish between admin@haunting.com and administrator@haunting.com.

SQL Server will only allow you to enter one e-mail address per operator. However, there may be instances when you want the Agent to inform multiple users if an event occurs. For example, you may want only one operator notified if a backup runs successfully, but you might want to inform the entire operations group if the transaction log for a mission critical database becomes full. The way to create an operator that notifies multiple users is to create a distribution group alias on your mail server and use that alias for the operator's e-mail address. For example, you might create an alias called amOperators@haunting.com and add all of your daytime operators to the group. You could then create an operator called AM Operators and use this e-mail address, as shown in Figure 9-3. To the Agent service, there is no difference between an individual e-mail account and a distribution group. The New Operator Properties form also allows you to test the e-mail function. Clicking the Test button will send a test message to the specified user (via e-mail, pager message, or NET SEND pop up).

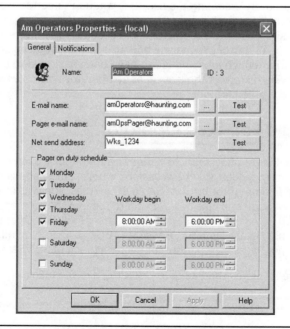

Figure 9-3. Adding an operator with a group alias

To use the NET SEND option, you enter the NetBIOS name for the operator's computer. When a message is sent, a pop-up window will appear on the desktop of the user. This is the least reliable means of communicating with operators, because it will be sent to the computer and not to the user. If the intended recipient is not working on the computer when the NET SEND occurs and another user hits the OK button on the pop-up window, the operator will never see the message. NET SEND should only be used for testing, or when there is no e-mail system available. To use the NET SEND option, the Windows Messenger service must be running on the Server.

If you enter a pager e-mail address, you can also specify when the operator is available. The New Operator Properties window allows you to choose the days and hours that the operator is available to be contacted via pager. If you specify weekdays, you can only select one set of available hours for the day. For example, an operator may work part-time and only be available on Tuesdays and Thursdays. The form allows you to select these two days. However, if he works during the day on Tuesdays and at night on Thursdays, there is no way to set different times on each day. The New Operator Properties window also includes a Notifications tab. This tab serves three functions. The first function is to allow you to assign the newly created operator to existing jobs and alerts. The second function is that it allows you to enable and disable operators. The ability to disable operators is useful if an operator will be unavailable for a prolonged period of time, and is a good alternative to deleting and re-creating operators. Suppose an operator was taking a six-month leave of absence, but would be returning after that period. By disabling the account, you don't need to worry about messages being sent to this operator accidentally. However, when the user returns, you also don't need to re-create the account. One interesting feature is the Send E-mail button. When you add an operator, you can send her an e-mail indicating which jobs and alerts have been assigned to her. Finally, this tab shows a history of the last time the operator was notified via each of the three possible methods.

Defining a Fail-Safe Operator

Because SQL Server allows you to define the availability of an operator's pager, there may conceivably be occasions where a message is triggered, but the specified operator is unavailable. If the message was critical, it is important that someone else be available to receive the message. SQL 7 and SQL 2000 give you the ability to designate a Fail-Safe Operator. This operator is only notified when the assigned operator is not available. There can be only one Fail-Safe Operator for each instance of SQL Server.

To designate a user as the Fail-Safe Operator, use the following steps:

1. Create an operator for the user who will become the Fail-Safe Operator.

2. Expand the Management folder in Enterprise Manager.

3. Right-click on the SQL Server Agent icon and select Properties.

4. Open the Alert System tab.

5. Select the Fail-Safe Operator from the Operator drop-down list (see Figure 9-4).

6. Click OK to finalize the selection.

Once selected, the Fail-Safe Operator will only be contacted if the designated operator is unavailable.

Creating SQL Server Jobs

SQL Server jobs allow you to have the Agent perform repetitive tasks at scheduled intervals. For example, if you perform a full backup of a database every morning at 2 A.M., you can create a job that will perform the backup automatically. This removes the need for a human operator to manually perform this task. Jobs can be simple (like the previous backup example) or complex. A complex job is one that contains multiple steps and can contain execution logic. For example, if step one fails, go to step two; if it succeeds, skip step two and go to step three.

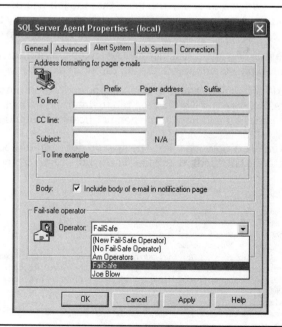

Figure 9-4. Selecting a Fail-Safe Operator

You can define a job in Enterprise Manager using the following steps:

1. Open Enterprise Manager.

2. Expand the Management folder.

3. Expand the SQL Server Agent icon.

4. Right-click the Jobs icon and select New Job.

This will open the New Job Properties window. This property form has four tabs, as follows:

- **General**   Allows you to name the job and to configure where and how it will run. The name you assign is used to identify the job and must be unique to the instance of SQL Server. On this tab, you can also set the job owner. The owner is important in determining the security context in which a job will execute. You can also determine where the job will run. By default, all jobs run locally. However, if you configure multi-server jobs, you can specify other target servers (multi-server jobs will be discussed in the "Defining Multi-Server Administration" section later in this chapter). The General tab also allows you to assign the job to a category. Categories simply allow you to group similar jobs together. Finally, the General tab gives you the ability to enable and disable jobs. Disabling a job maintains the job's settings but prevents it from running.

- **Steps**   Allows you to define the tasks that the job will perform. If the job performs multiple steps, it will also allow you to specify the order in which the steps are executed and what to do when a step completes.

- **Schedules**   Allows you to schedule the job and configure alerts. You can set multiple schedules for the job through this tab.

- **Notifications**   SQL Server jobs are able to report their outcome to operators. You use the Notification tab to determine which operators should be notified and how and when notifications should be sent.

You can also create a new job using the **sp_add_job** stored procedure, which is located in the **msdb** database. The syntax for this procedure is as follows:

```
USE msdb
EXEC msdb..sp_add_job @job_name = 'Job Name',
    @enabled = 1,
    @description = 'Job Description',
    @owner_login_name = 'owner name',
    @notify_level_eventlog = <flag indicating when to write to the event log>,
    @notify_level_email = <flag indicating when to e-mail an operator>,
    @notify_level_netsend = <flag indicating when to write to net send an operator>,
    @notify_level_page = <flag indicating when to write to page an operator>,
    @notify_email_operator_name = 'Operator to e-mail',
    @notify_netsend_operator_name = 'Operator to net send',
    @notify_page_operator_name = 'Operator to page',
    @delete_level = <flag indicating when to delete the job>
```

Flag	Description
0	Never
1	On Success only
2	On Failure only
3	On either Success or Failure

Table 9-2.   Return Flags for Notifying Operators

The parameters that require a flag use the same set of values. These are listed in Table 9-2.

The Importance of the Job Owner

The job owner is specified on the General tab. If you are a member of the System Administrator security role, you will see a list of all server logins and can select the owner of the job. If you are not a member of this role, the job will be created with your login as the owner, by default. We've already established that the SQL Server Agent service will execute a job on behalf of its creator. Under most circumstances, the Agent will have both Windows Administrator rights and SQL Server System Administrator rights. Essentially, there is very little that the Agent does not have the rights to perform. This could create a serious security concern if someone who was not both a Windows Administrator and SQL Server System Administrator was given the right to create jobs. In this situation, a user could have the Agent perform tasks that they were unable to perform themselves. Luckily, SQL Server does not allow this to occur. When the Agent executes a job, it operates under the security context of the job owner. If the owner is a System Administrator, it simply executes the job. However, if the job owner is not a member of this role, the Agent will impersonate the owner before executing the job. If the owner has permission to perform the job steps, the job succeeds. If the owner doesn't have permission to perform the steps, the job fails.

As you will see in the next section, the security risk could have been even greater because SQL Server jobs can include the execution of operating system jobs (such as .exe and .bat files) and the execution of ActiveX script files. By default, the SQL Server Agent will not execute operating system jobs or scripts unless the job owner is an administrator. As an administrator you can change this by creating a proxy account. The proxy account is a Windows user account that the Agent will impersonate when executing one of these commands.

To set a proxy account, use the following steps:

1. Create the Windows account that will be used as the proxy account.

2. Open Enterprise Manager.

3. Expand the Management folder.

4. Right-click on the SQL Server Agent icon and select Properties.

5. Click on the Job System tab.

6. Clear the check box in the Non-Sysadmin Job Step Proxy Account section at the bottom of the tab.

7. When prompted, enter the user name, password, and domain for the account you created in step 1, then click OK.

8. Click OK on the Main Property sheet to confirm the change.

You can also configure the proxy account using an extended system–stored procedure: **xp_sqlagent_proxy_account**. The syntax for this procedure is as follows:

```
xp_sqlagent_proxy_account N'SET',  N'Domain Name', N'proxy user name'
N'password '
```

Using the SET option, you will change the proxy account. You can also use the GET parameter to display the existing proxy account or the DEL parameter to delete the current proxy account.

CAUTION   *There is a danger with setting a proxy account. Not only will this account allow non system-administrators to execute operating system tasks, but it also gives the user the ability to execute the **xp_cmdshell** extended stored procedures. For this reason, you should create a dedicated user account for the proxy and keep the authentication information for this user secure.*

Defining Job Steps

All jobs have at least one step and can contain multiple steps. Each of these steps can be as follows:

- **A Transact-SQL script**   This can be any Transact-SQL operation. The operation could be as simple as executing a stored procedure, or executing a multiple-step script (including elements like cursors and looping structures).

- **An operating system command**   This can be any executable command-line object such as an .exe, .cmd, or .bat file. Again, to execute these types of job steps, you must be a member of the System Administrator role.

- **An ActiveX script**   This includes any VBScript or JScript scripts. When you add the script step, you will be prompted for the language the step will use, and then for the script itself. You can also use other scripting languages (such as Perl) if you have installed support for the language on the local server. VBScript and JScript are the only languages that are enabled by default.

- **A replication task**   SQL Server jobs can include calls to any of the replication agents to perform a replication task. The agents available include the Merge Agent for performing merge replication tasks, the Log Reader Agent for performing transactional replication jobs, the Snapshot Agent for snapshot replication tasks, and the Distribution Agent for publication and subscription tasks. If you are creating a job on SQL Server 2000, there is also a message queue reader available. For more information on the various replication agents, see Chapter 12.

A SQL Server job can contain one or more of these task types. For example, suppose you run a backup on your server to save to a local file. You want to archive the file to keep two days' backup, and you want to FTP the backup file to a remote location. You could create a three-step job that starts by running an operating system command to copy the current backup file to another location and delete the previous day's backup. In the second step, you could run a Transact-SQL script to perform the backup and, finally, in the third step, run an ActiveX script job to FTP the file to the remote location.

You can also perform branching logic in the execution of your job steps. You can set different next steps depending on whether a step succeeded or failed. In each case, you can have the job quit or go on to another step. For example, you could create a job that states if step one fails, the job should quit and report the failure. If it succeeds, step two should be run. Alternately, you could create a job that runs step one and, on failure, runs step two or, on success, runs step three.

Use the following steps to create a new job step:

1. Click on the Steps tab of the New Job Properties window.

2. Click the New button.

3. Give the step a name that is unique within the job.

4. In the New Job Step window, select the type of step and supply all the required information.

5. If you want to configure branching logic, click on the Advanced tab of the New Job steps popup window. This tab will allow you to configure different next steps based on the success or failure of the previous step. By default, if a step succeeds, it will move to the next step, and if a step fails, the job will exit.

6. Click OK to add the step.

At any time you can add or modify steps. The job will always execute from the top down—that is, from the first step in the list to the last. The Job

Steps tab allows you to move jobs up and down the list using the up and down arrows. The Steps tab is shown here.

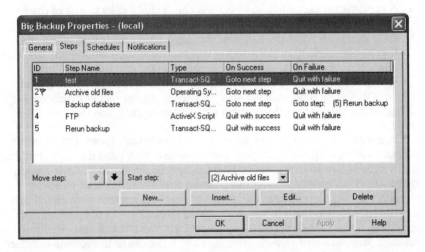

For both Transact-SQL tasks and ActiveX script tasks, you are required to supply the code for the step in the New Job Step window. It is possible to compose the code for both directly in the editor on the window. This is why both provide a Parse button that allows you to verify that the scripts are syntactically correct. It is a better idea, however, to create the scripts in another editor (such as Query Analyzer or Visual Studio) and import them using the Open button on the New Job Step window sheet. By creating the scripts in these other environments, you can manually execute them and ensure that they work as expected. The various IDEs also provide better tools for debugging.

Aside from using Enterprise Manager, you can also add job steps using the **sp_add_jobstep** stored procedure. The syntax for this procedure is as follows:

```
sp_add_jobstep [ @job_id = ] job_id | [ @job_name = ] 'job_name' ,
[ @step_id = ] step_id ],
[ @step_name = ] 'step_name' },
[ @subsystem = ] 'Step type' ],
[ @command = ] 'command string or file name' ],
[ @additional_parameters = ] 'parameters' ],
[ @cmdexec_success_code = ] code returned by cmd exc job ],
[ @on_success_action = ] <flag indicating success action>],
[ @on_success_step_id = ] <flag indicating next job step to execute>],
[ @on_fail_action = ] <flag indicating failure action],
[ @on_fail_step_id = ] <flag indicating next job step to execute>],
[ @server = ] 'server' ],
[ @database_name = ] 'database where TSQL steps will execute' ],
[ @database_user_name = ] 'user' ],
[ @retry_attempts = ] number of retry_attempts ],
[ @retry_interval = ] retry_interval ],
```

```
[ @os_run_priority = ] run_priority ],
[ @output_file_name = ] 'file_name' ],
[ @flags = ] <flag controlling output file> ]
```

The process flow flags used by this procedure are the same as the ones listed previously in Table 9-2. The subsystem parameter expects specific strings to indicate the type of job step. These values are listed in Table 9-3.

The flags parameter has three possible values—2 (append to output file), 4 (overwrite output file), and 0 (no option set).

NOTE *There are also a large number of variables available for the command parameter. For a full list, consult the **sp_add_jobstep** entry in Books Online.*

Scheduling Jobs

Once you have defined your job and configured all of its steps, you can schedule it to run. You can set the job schedule either through the Schedules tab of the New Job Properties sheet or by using the **sp_add_jobschedule** stored procedure. SQL Server allows you to schedule jobs as follows:

- Whenever the SQL Server Agent Service starts
- When the system is idle
- On a one-time only basis
- On a recurring basis

Also, the SQL Server job scheduler allows you to create multiple schedules for the same job. Why would you want to do this? Consider the following scenario: You are the administrator for a point-of-sales database that is very active during business hours, less busy at night, and even less busy on weekends. You want to back up the transaction log for the database every half hour from 6 A.M. to 6 P.M., and every two hours from 6:01 P.M. to 5:59 A.M.

Subsystem	Description
'ACTIVESCRIPTING'	Indicates that the job step is an ActiveX Script task
'CMDEXEC'	Indicates that the job step is an operating system command
'DISTRIBUTION'	Indicates that the job step is an Distribution Agent task
'SNAPSHOT'	Indicates that the job step is a Snapshot Agent task
'LOGREADER'	Indicates that the job step is a Log Reader Agent task
'MERGE'	Indicates that the job step is a Merge Agent task
'TSQL' (default)	Indicates that the job step is Transact-SQL task

Table 9-3.   The sp_add_jobstep Subsystem Parameters

You also want to back up the transaction log once every eight hours on the weekend. Rather than create three separate jobs that do the same thing, you can use a single job and assign it three separate schedules.

When you configure a recurring job you can schedule it to run Daily, Weekly, or Monthly. If you configure the job to run Weekly, you can choose which days of the week the job will run on. You can configure the job to run at a specific time or on an interval between a set start and end date (for example, every hour between 9 A.M. and 4 P.M.).

To create a new schedule, use the following steps:

1. Click on the Schedules tab of the New Job Properties sheet.

2. Click on the New Schedule button.

3. Give the schedule a unique name.

4. On the New Job Schedule form select the type of schedule you want to create.

5. If you are planning to create a recurring schedule, you must click on the Change button (unless you want to accept the default, which is Weekly on Sunday at 12 A.M.).

6. Use the Edit Recurring Job Schedule form to set the properties for the recurring schedule.

7. Click OK to add the schedule.

You can also set job schedules using the **sp_add_jobschedule** stored procedure. The syntax for this procedure is as follows:

```
sp_add_jobschedule [ @job_id = ] job_id assigned by sp_add_job,
    | [ @job_name = ] 'job_name',
[ @name = ] 'schedule name',
[ @enabled = ] enabled ],
[ @freq_type = ] flag for frequency of schedule ],
[ @freq_interval = ] flag for frequency of interval ],
[ @freq_subday_type = ] unit of interval ],
[ @freq_subday_interval = ] period of interval ],
[ @freq_relative_interval = ] interval within the month ],
[ @freq_recurrence_factor = ]number of weeks or month between reoccurrence ],
[ @active_start_date = ] active_start_date ],
[ @active_end_date = ] active_end_date ],
[ @active_start_time = ] active_start_time ],
[ @active_end_time = ] active_end_time ]
```

The Freq_type value is a numeric code indicating the type of schedule. The expected values for this parameter are listed in Table 9-4. Some of these types work in conjunction with the freq_relative_interval parameter. The expected values for this parameter are listed in Table 9-5.

Frequency Flag	Description
1	Occur once
4	Occur daily
8	Occur weekly
16	Occur monthly
32	Occur monthly based on the freq_interval value
64	Occur when the Agent service starts
128	Occur when the system is idle

Table 9-4. Expected Freq_type Values

When this flag is combined with the Freq_interval flag (which provides the day of the week), you can set values like Monthly on the first Sunday of each month. This would be @Freq_type = 32, @Freq_relative_interval = 1, and @Freq_interval = 1.

NOTE *The Freq_interval values have different meanings depending on the Freq_type value. See the Books Online entry for* **sp_add_jobschedule** *for all available settings.*

To schedule jobs to run when the system becomes idle, you first need to define the idle condition. Idle is determined by the system to be in a state where the system processor utilization falls below a certain percentage for a set period of time.

To configure the idle condition, use the following steps:

1. Expand the Management folder in Enterprise Manager and right-click the SQL Server Agent icon.

2. Select Properties from the pop-up menu.

3. Click on the Advanced tab and select the Computer is Idle When check box in the Idle CPU Condition section.

Freq_relative_interval Flag	Description
1	Occur on the first
2	Occur on the second
4	Occur on the third
8	Occur on the fourth
16	Occur on the last

Table 9-5. The Expected Freq_interval

4. Set a value for the average CPU usage and the time interval (in seconds).

5. Click OK.

The default setting is 10 percent utilization for 600 seconds (ten minutes). Set a value that reflects the normal utilization of your server. This schedule event is useful for running non-mission-critical maintenance jobs. By scheduling them when the system is idle, you never have to worry about these jobs interfering with more critical operations. In order to set a job to run on system idle, you must be a member of the Windows Administrators group as well as the SQL System Administrators role.

Setting Notification

Finally, once the job has been defined and scheduled, you can set notifications to be sent whenever it runs.

To set Notifications in Enterprise Manager, use the following steps:

1. Click on the Notifications tab for the job.

2. Select the check boxes for the means of notification that you require.

3. Select the Operator be Notified from the list box.

4. Select the condition under which the notification will be sent.

You can only assign one operator to each notification type. If you want more than one person contacted, you will need to create a group alias for the operator. Notifications can be sent under three conditions, as follows:

- Whenever a job succeeds
- Whenever a job fails
- Whenever a job completes

The options allow you to reduce the number of messages sent. For example, you may want to receive an e-mail indicating that a job ran successfully, but only be paged if a job fails.

TIP *In Transact-SQL, notifications are set as part of the **sp_add_job** stored procedure. See the section "Creating SQL Server Jobs" earlier in this chapter for the full syntax.*

Monitoring Job History

Aside from the notification system, SQL Server also keeps a history of all job activity. This log is stored in the **msdb** database in a table called **sysjobhistory**. Because it could get quite large if you have multiple, frequently occurring jobs, SQL Server limits the size of the history. The default setting is to store no more than 1,000 historical records and no more than 100 records relating to a particular job. This setting prevents the **sysjobhistory** table from filling the **msdb** database. As these maximum values are reached, older records are deleted.

You can change this default using the following steps:

1. Open the SQL Server Agent Properties sheet by right-clicking on the SQL Server Agent icon.

2. Click on the Job System tab.

3. In the Job History Log section, change the values for Maximum Job History Log Size and Maximum Job History Rows per Job.

4. You can clear the Limit Size of Job History Log check box. However, this will cause the log to grow unchecked and is not recommended.

To view the job history, you can either access the **sysjobhistory** table directly, or you can right-click any job in the Jobs folder and select View Job History. This will show all the records in the **sysjobhistory** table that relate to the selected job. It will also show if the job succeeded or failed and what the final error or message returned by the job was.

If the job is a multi-step job, you can get more information by selecting the Show Step Details check box in the top right-hand corner of the Job History form. This will show each step and whether that step succeeded or failed. It will also display the message or error returned by each step. This is an excellent tool for troubleshooting failed jobs.

Creating and Managing SQL Server Alerts

Aside from managing jobs, SQL Server has the ability to raise alerts. Unlike jobs that are executed at set intervals, alerts respond to events and conditions on SQL Server. These events could be either specific errors or conditions on the server (such as a transaction log exceeding 90 percent of allocated space). The advantage of alerts is that the Agent is instantly aware of events on the server and can bring issues to your attention. This saves you the trouble of constantly monitoring logs and watching performance counters.

Alerts can, obviously, be set to notify operators, and they can be configured to start jobs. This can be very useful to preemptively deal with potential problems. For example, while it is important to know that a transaction log has reached 90 percent of the allocated disk space, if you receive the page when you can't address the problem, the log may be 100 percent full before you are able to respond. It is better to have the alert start a job that backs up the log and truncates it immediately, and then sends you another page indicating that the backup ran successfully.

SQL Server allows you to set two types of alerts. Both are created using the same tools and can be programmed with the same responses. The difference between them is how they are triggered. The first type of alert responds to event ids written into the application event log. The second type of alert responds to performance thresholds. When you installed SQL Server, it loaded a number of SQL Server–related counters into the System Monitor. You can use the counters as the basis for condition alerts.

Creating Alerts on Events

The key to event-driven alerts is the application log in Event Viewer. The Agent constantly monitors new events as they are added to the log and checks the **sysalerts** table to see if any alerts have been defined for the new event code. In order for an alert based on an event to fire, therefore, the event must be written to the application log. If it does not appear in the log, the alert will never fire. This is important to understand, because it is possible for the application log to fill up. Windows and SQL Server will, however, continue to function normally without logging. If this happens, events may occur, but because they are not written into the application log, the alert will not fire. For this reason it is important to monitor the Event Viewer logs to make sure that they don't fill up. If event logging is critical for your system, you can configure the application log to overwrite log entries as needed. This ensures that events are always written to the log, but may mean events are overwritten without an administrator viewing them. In any event, it is important for someone to take ownership of the application log and make sure that it never fills up.

There are a number of ways for events to be written to the application log. SQL Server will write to the application log in the following cases:

- **Events have a severity of 19 to 25**   Severity is a number between 1 and 25. Events of severity 19 to 25 are considered errors (severity 25 events, for example, tend to be accompanied by a blue screen and a memory dump).

- **The event is configured to always write to the application log**   Some events are configured to always write to the application log. You can use the **sp_altermessage** stored procedure to configure any event id to automatically write to the application log

- **The event is raised using the RAISERROR WITH LOG command**   Events can be raised programmatically using the RAISERROR statement. If you include the WITH LOG option, these events will also be written to the application log.

- **The event is raised with xp_logevent**   This extended stored procedure allows you to write events directly into the application log.

You can create event alerts based on either severity or specific event ID. If you set an alert on severity, all events of that severity level will raise the alert. If you choose to raise an alert on a specific error number, you can also further limit the alert by specifying a text string that must appear in the event message. For example, you might set an alert on event 9002 (transaction log full) but specify the string **Northwind**. By adding this filter, the alert will only fire if the transaction log for the **Northwind** database becomes full. If the log for any other database fills, event 9002 will be raised (and read by the Agent) but will not meet the test set by the filter and will not trigger the alert.

You can create event alerts with Enterprise Manager and with the **sp_add_alert** stored procedure.

To create an event alert using Enterprise Manager, use the following steps:

1. Expand the SQL Server Agent icon in the Management folder.

2. Right-click on the Alerts icon and select New Alert.

3. In the New Alert Properties form, give the alert a name. This name should be unique to the instance of SQL Server.

4. In the Type list box, select SQL Server Event Alert.

5. Choose either the severity of the alert or the specific error number. You can optionally enter a filter string for the event message.

6. Click on the response tab.

7. If you want to have the alert automatically trigger a job, click Execute Job and select the name of the job from the drop-down list. (Note: This list contains all jobs that have been created on the local server and also provides a link that will open the New Job Properties windows.)

8. Select which operators will be notified when the alert is triggered and how they will be notified (notice that you can send notifications to more than one operator).

9. If you choose, you can add text to the alert message.

10. Set the interval between notifications. This is much more relevant when setting alerts based on performance conditions.

11. Click OK to create the alert.

The syntax for using **sp_add_alert** is

```
sp_add_alert [ @name = ] 'name',
[ @message_id = ] message_id ],
[ @severity = ] severity ],
[ @enabled = ] enabled ],
[ @delay_between_responses = ] delay_between_responses ],
[ @notification_message = ] 'notification_message' ],
[ @include_event_description_in = ] include_event_description_in ],
[ @database_name = ] 'database' ],
[ @event_description_keyword = ] 'event_description_keyword_pattern' ],
```

```
{ [ @job_id = ] job_id | [ @job_name = ] 'job_name' } ] ,
[ @raise_snmp_trap = ] raise_snmp_trap ],
[ @performance_condition = ] 'performance_condition' ],
[ @category_name = ] 'category' ]
```

These parameters are fairly self-explanatory. The @include_event_
description_in parameter indicates where the text of the event message
should be sent. This parameter expects one of four values which are listed
in Table 9-6.

Adding User-Defined Events

SQL Server also allows you to create your own user-defined events. This
allows you to programmatically raise events that can be trapped by the
alert system. You must assign this event a unique number that is 50001 or
higher. You will also give the event a description, set the severity level, and
choose whether or not it writes to the application log automatically. Custom
alerts are added to the **sysmessages** table of the **master** database. Once
added, they can be used by any database in the SQL Server instance. You
can create the event in Enterprise Manager or by using the **sp_addmessage**
stored procedure.

To add an event in Enterprise Manager, use the following steps:

1. Select Manage SQL Server Messages from the Tools menu.

2. Select the Messages tab and click the New button.

3. The error number box will automatically pre-populate with the next
available event number.

4. Enter a message text (you can use %s and %d to leave placeholders for
string or numeric values that can be supplied when the event is called).

5. Choose the severity.

6. Select whether or not the message should write to the application log.

7. Click OK to create the message.

Flag	Description
0	Do not include
1	Include in e-mail
2	Include in pager
4	Include in NET SEND

Table 9-6.   The @include_event_description_in option parameters

To create a new message with Transact-SQL, use the **sp_addmessage** stored procedure with the following syntax:

```
sp_addmessage [ @msgnum = ] msg_id ,
[ @severity = ] severity level ,
[ @msgtext = ] 'message text',
[ @lang = ] 'language' ],
[ @with_log = ] 'flag indicating whether or not to autolog' ],
[ @replace = ] 'replace' ]
```

The @with_log option should be set to 1 if you want the event to auto log or 0 (the default) if you don't. The @replace parameter allows you to replace an existing event with the new event. If you set this value to the message ID of an existing message, any call to the old event number would raise the new event.

The advantage to user-defined event codes is that it allows you to raise alerts on events that are not normally errors. For example, you might create an event "customer deleted." Deleting a record from a table is not an error or even an unusual occurrence. However, you could create a stored procedure for deleting customers which raises this event. You could then define an alert that would e-mail the Accounts Manager every time the procedure is fired.

To call a user-defined event, use the RAISERROR command with the following syntax:

```
RAISERROR ( { msg_id | text string } { , severity , state }
[parameter 1, parameter2 … parameter n )
[With Log]
```

If you included place holders in your error message (%s for strings and %d for numbers), you pass them as the parameters. You must supply the order in which they appear in the text message.

Creating Alerts on Performance Conditions

You can also create alerts based on performance conditions. The process of creating alerts on performance conditions is almost identical to creating event-driven alerts. The only difference is that, if you select SQL Server performance condition alert from the Type list box, the remainder of the section changes to allow you to choose a specific counter and object. You can only set SQL Server condition alerts on counters added by SQL Server. When you choose your counter and object, you must also select the condition. Conditions can be set when a counter value rises above, falls below, or is equal to, a particular value. For example, you can raise an alert if the number of deadlocks per second rises above 4 or if the amount of free space in a database falls below 1MB.

The responses are the same as the responses to event-driven alerts. When you set performance condition alerts, however, make sure you set a reasonable interval time between alerts. The interval determines how long after an alert is raised until it will be raised again if the condition still exists. For example, suppose you set an alert to fire when the free space in a transaction log exceeds 60 percent. If, after the interval time, the condition still exists, the alert will fire again. The default interval is one minute. This means that if you are 15 minutes from the console when you get the page generated by this alert, you will be paged 14 more times before you reach the console to fix the problem (or at least disable the alert). If the interval is too low, it can negatively impact performance because each alert must be processed by the Agent and sent to the operator.

Defining Multi-Server Administration

Up to this point, all of the jobs and alerts we have discussed have been local to a particular instance of SQL Server. If you monitor several SQL Servers, however, you can centralize management by configuring a multi-server environment. One thing you must understand is that all automation is local. The jobs must exist in the local **msdb** database and the local SQL Server Agent service must perform the automated tasks. What multi-server jobs allow you to do is create a job on a central server that has been designated as the Master Server and push those jobs out to target servers. The target servers will receive the jobs and execute them locally, but report the outcome back to the Master Server. The Master Server posts jobs in the **sysdownloadlist** table in the **msdb** database. The target servers consult this table periodically and download any new or altered jobs.

In order to create a multi-server environment, you must first promote one SQL Server to be the Master Server. This will also create a new operator called MSXOperator that will receive all notifications from the target servers.

To Create a Master Server in Enterprise Manager, follow these steps:

1. Right-click the SQL Server Agent icon in the Management folder.

2. Select Multi-Server Administration | Make This a Master.

3. In the Make MSX wizard, click Next.

4. Enter the contact information for the MSX Operator.

5. Specify which servers to enlist as targets (the servers must first be registered in Enterprise Manager). Click Next.

6. Enter a description for each server.

7. Specify how the SQL Server Agent service on the Master Server will authenticate to the target servers.

8. Click Finish to define the server as a master.

Once you have defined a server as the Master Server, a new icon will appear under the Jobs folder. You will now have the option to create local or remote jobs. You can create a job the same way that you created a local job, but you can now specify more than one target server for the job. Remember, however, that the jobs must run locally on the target server. If your job references a folder or a file that is not located locally on the target server, the job will fail on that server. For example, if you create an ActiveX step that calls a locally stored .bat file, the file must exist in the same file location on all of the target servers. Also, the job will appear in the job list of the target server but it cannot be edited from the target server. If you want to make a change to a remote job on a target server, you must make the change on the Master Server and then wait for the polling period to expire so that the target server can pull down the changes from the Master Server. Also, because all of the servers must interact, it is a good idea to use a common Windows account that has access to all of the servers to authenticate the SQL Server Agent on each computer.

Throughout this chapter, you have seen how to use SQL Server automation to perform routine tasks and to notify you of problems. All of the parts of automation can be combined to provide a more complex automated management. For example, if a performance condition (like a full transaction log) occurs, you can automatically run a job that truncates the log. You can also notify an operator both that the log filled and that the backup job ran successfully. In Chapter 10, you will take system monitoring a step further and examine the tools used to test system performance.

9

Chapter 10

Performance Tuning Part 1: Monitoring SQL Server Performance

One of the jobs that a database administrator is responsible for is ensuring the responsive operation of SQL Server. This means determining what is good performance, monitoring SQL Server to determine if those criteria are being met, and changing factors that are causing poor performance to improve the responsiveness of SQL Server.

The performance of a database is determined by a large number of factors, not the least of which is perception. One of my colleagues once mentioned that all our databases and computer systems would run perfectly fine were it not for one thing—the users. He's also the same guy that pointed out that there are only two industries that call their end customers "users": the computer industry and the drug trade. While this may be true, keep in mind that the users pay the bills. Without them, we would have no jobs (or fun tuning databases).

Factors Affecting SQL Server Performance

Generally, performance tuning of any computer system (not just SQL Server or databases) deals with monitoring the following four key areas:

- **Processor**   The processor or CPU executes each of the instructions passed to it by the operating system and applications. If the processor is too busy, applications will need to wait their turn to get access to it and this will slow down performance.

- **Memory or RAM**   The amount of RAM available to an application, and on the computer as a whole, directly impacts the performance of the application. A general rule of thumb is that more memory is better; lack of memory can increase CPU load. The operating system needs to page parts of an application's dormant memory back to disk to bring in additional memory needed by other applications. This process will also increase disk I/O. SQL Server can use available memory to cache Transact-SQL code and pages from the database, thereby improving performance.

- **Disk I/O**   Reading and writing from and to disk is one of the most expensive operations encountered by the operating system or database. Hard disks are generally slow in comparison to memory. An application will appear slow if a lot of hard disk I/O is taking place.

However, if data is not written to disk, and the computer fails, you will have lost data. One of the hardest things to do when monitoring performance is finding that balance between speed and safety.

- **Network**   In the old days, users connected directly to the computer running the database using dumb terminals, and all the code was on that machine. Today's applications are typically distributed among several servers, and users have their own PCs running the client application from which they access the database. A slow or poorly configured network will make the database seem slow.

The Pyramid of Performance

When deciding what factors will affect SQL Server performance, you need to look at the structure of SQL Server and its databases from the perspective of a pyramid, as shown in Figure 10-1. The base of your pyramid is the hardware and operating system on which SQL Server runs. As you go higher up the pyramid, the overall impact on performance of changes made in that area is less because you are getting more and more precise in your changes. This means that a well-tuned operating system (the base of the pyramid) will provide a better boost in performance than fixing a locking problem that was causing contention (the tip of the pyramid). The analogy here is simple: The base has more area than the tip, so it supports more of the weight (and performance load).

Operating System

Your first step in monitoring SQL Server's performance is monitoring how well your operating system is doing. This means monitoring the operating system for any performance problem in any of the four areas outlined previously—CPU, RAM, disk I/O, and network. Without starting SQL Server,

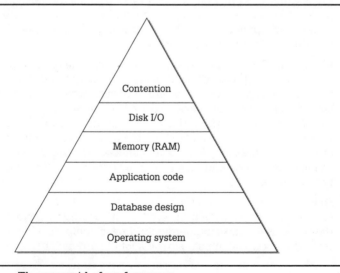

Figure 10-1.   The pyramid of performance

determine if the operating system is providing acceptable performance in these areas. If not, fix this problem before you go any further because, just like a pyramid, if the foundation is weak, the whole structure is weak and may crumble. Windows System Monitor and Windows Performance Logs are good tools to use here.

Database Design

Once you are certain that the operating system is working at its best, you need to then determine if the application design is optimal. This includes looking at the structure of tables and their relationships (primary and foreign keys), indexes, data types used, and so on. The approach used and what is an optimal design will be different for a database designed for online transaction processing (OLTP) versus one primarily used for reporting and decision support. Make sure that the design meets the database objectives and the business requirements it was intended to satisfy.

Ensuring a good database design exists is always a hard one for DBAs. Usually, the DBA responsible for maintaining the database was not involved in the design process. In many cases, the DBA becomes responsible for supporting a third-party, off-the-shelf application such as an ERP package or other line-of-business applications. The fact that the application runs slow becomes the database's problem.

SQL Server's ability to generate database diagrams can help you determine if an application is well designed, but often you will be unable to do much about it. If you are dealing with a good vendor you will get documentation outlining the architecture of the application and database, which may help. If your database was developed in-house, make sure that the design is sound. You will need to know something about designing databases or ensure that you have a good architect on board. Don't always trust the developer otherwise you may find yourself with an expense tracking system with one table called Expenses and columns named Expense1, Expense2, and so on.

Application Code

After you have determined that the operating system and database design are sound, the next area to investigate and monitor is the application code. You should investigate two levels of code: stored procedures, triggers, and user-defined functions in the database; and front-end application code written in other languages (Visual Basic, Visual C++, and so on) that is executing SQL statements against the database. This does not mean that you need to become a VB programmer overnight. You will not be worried about the VB code itself, but rather the SQL statements that it is sending across the network to the database. Be sure to do the following:

- Make sure that each statement does as much work as possible.
- Determine if the tasks being sent across could provide better performance if they were combined in a stored procedure.
- Make certain that a good balance between front-end (VB and so on) and back-end (SQL Server) execution exists.

SQL Server Profiler, as well as Windows System Monitor and Windows Performance Logs, are tools that could help you with the application code, as well as with the next three areas in the performance pyramid: memory, disk I/O, and contention. Chapter 11 details how you can determine if the application code is optimal.

Now that you have looked at the operating system, database design, and application code, you are left with three areas that typically have a lower impact on performance: the memory configuration of SQL Server, placement of SQL Server files in an effort to optimize I/O across the disks, and locking and other factors that cause contention. However, a database administrator has direct control over these. If you look at the area represented by these three items in the pyramid, you find that they make up only about a third of the total area of the pyramid. Manipulating these three areas alone (as is done by many DBAs) will not provide as much of a performance boost as dealing with the bottom three.

Memory (RAM)

Memory is the next area to address. Here we are talking about the memory directly under SQL Server's control—the memory used to cache database pages and Transact-SQL execution plans. You want to make sure that the buffer cache and procedure cache, respectively, are being used effectively. This means that cursors are being shared (for example, the same Transact-SQL statement is being used by many users) and most queries are satisfied from cache instead of going to disk to retrieve the data. Ensuring cursors are shared is as simple as minimizing the number of ad-hoc queries that users can issue by providing them with a front-end client application. This is more easily done in transaction processing environments, such as ERP systems, where users perform small transactions according to a process driven by a client application. In data warehousing or decision support environments, users will query large amounts of data and it is not as easy to pre-determine what those queries will be. In either case, you need to figure out what is acceptable performance. The goal is always to have as high a cache utilization as possible. This means allocating as much RAM to SQL Server as possible without causing paging at the operating system. Windows Performance Logs and System Monitor can help you monitor how well SQL Server is using memory.

Disk I/O

SQL Server will have to read data from disk at least once. While it is true that the best performing SQL Server database is one that can load all of its data and application code into memory, that data still must be read from disk at least once. In monitoring disk I/O you want to ensure that, if you have multiple disks, no one disk is overburdened with I/O. A nice even distribution across all disks is the key. This can be achieved using hardware and software, including the implementation of RAID arrays (Table 10-1 lists common RAID types), or within SQL Server through the use of filegroups. In general, if you can do it in hardware, do so because it requires less monitoring and tweaking.

RAID Type	Description
RAID 0	Disk striping without parity. Data is striped across multiple physical disks providing great read and write performance, but no protection against data loss. A single physical disk failure will cause the entire RAID 0 strip set to be lost.
RAID 1	Disk mirroring. Data is mirrored between two physical disks. If one disk fails, the other will continue to operate, resulting in no lost data (unless both disks fail). RAID 1 provides no performance improvements over writing to a single disk (it is only slightly slower).
RAID 5	Disk striping with parity. Data is striped across multiple physical disks providing great read performance. Writes are slower than on a single disk as they require that parity information be calculated and written to one of the disks each time a write occurs. All disks contain some parity information and the loss of one (and only one) disk will not cause the loss of all data. Losing a disk will require that the data be reconstructed on the fly from the available data and the parity information, which is sometimes referred to as "running in a reduced state." The capacity of one disk (out of a maximum of 32) is lost because of the need to store parity information.
RAID 10 also called RAID 1+0	Disk mirroring and striping. Consists of a series of mirrored disks (RAID 1) that are then configured into a stripe set (RAID 0). Best combination of fault tolerance (you can lose one disk from each mirrored pair) and performance, but also the highest costs—you need twice the number of disks. A variation of RAID 10 is RAID 0+1 where you mirror a set of striped sets. This is not as robust as RAID 10 because if you lose a single disk in one of the RAID 0 stripe sets, you lose half the mirror and are vulnerable if a disk in the other stripe set also dies. For this reason, using RAID 10 is preferred.

Table 10-1.   Common RAID Implementations

10

In using RAID, keep in mind that RAID 10 gives the best performance in all environments. In transaction processing scenarios, RAID 5 is not recommended because of the slowdown in performance when writes take place (unless the hardware-based RAID controller has a lot of cache RAM and a fast processor to perform the parity calculation). RAID 5 can be used in data warehousing and decision support scenarios since the write overhead only takes place when the data is loaded—a periodic occurrence typically.

RAID 1 is best for transaction logs so as to provide fault tolerance, and you should never use RAID 5 to store transaction logs because the write overhead transaction logs are the most write-intensive part of a database.

If you cannot afford the performance improvements RAID offers (and these days that is less and less the case as prices have dropped significantly), you can implement multiple disks and place data files for different filegroups on the disks. You will also need to determine which tables and indexes are heavily queried and cause the most I/O, and place them on separate filegroups whose data files are on separate disks. The goal is to even out the I/O across all disks by placing objects in different filegroups. If this seems harder than implementing RAID, it is. However, it may be sometimes necessary to use multiple filegroups and data files even if RAID is available because of database size or other factors, so be aware of this option.

Contention

Finally, at the top of the pyramid is contention. Generally, contention will not be an issue unless all other performance elements (operating system, database design, application code, memory, disk I/O) have been resolved. If everything else is working perfectly, you may get contention issues, but this rarely happens. In SQL Server, the number one area of contention is locking, which is usually caused by application code that performs manual locking. In general, don't do things manually that SQL Server does automatically, like deal with locking. Code short transactions (for example, to do all your error checking before you start the transaction,) so as to minimize the amount of time locks are applied. In other words, check your code first if you have contention issues.

Defining a Performance Baseline

The first step in monitoring SQL Server for performance is determining what an acceptable level of performance is. For this purpose, you need to set a performance baseline. A baseline gives you a starting point from which to measure what has changed in the database since the last monitoring session and also, if monitoring is done consistently and proactively, determine where future bottlenecks may exist and take corrective action in advance—at least that's the ideal we all strive for.

Before doing any monitoring to improve performance, set a baseline of what the existing performance is. Take out the tools you would use to determine bottlenecks and use these tools to record current levels of performance. Now, don't do this when usage is light (at night, for example) or when you are going through a period of intensive activity (month end for an order entry system). Instead, do this during "normal" operation so that you can record logs, which you can use later, that monitor a typical level of performance. You may want to leave the monitoring tools running over a 24-hour period to determine what are the low and peak activity periods, or even over a week to do the same for days. In any case, you need to know what you're starting with if you want to make improvements to it.

Once you have a baseline, you can then measure how effective changes that you have applied are. When you are satisfied that the changes you have applied have achieved the desired results, create a new baseline that can then be used to gauge future performance decreases or increases. You can monitor the database against the baseline to figure out where a bottleneck may occur and take corrective action before it happens. The only downside to this technique is that users won't know that you've done anything and will accept a well-performing database as the norm!

Tools for Monitoring SQL Server Performance

In monitoring SQL Server's performance, as well as the performance of the operating system, you will use a number of tools including the following:

- **Windows Event Viewer** Event Viewer is one of the main tools in troubleshooting issues with the operating system and its applications, such as SQL Server. SQL Server will log key events to the Windows Application event log and you can review the log to see what issues appear. You can also create alerts based on events in the event log that can notify an operator when a problem occurs, and even take corrective action.

- **SQL Server logs** Any warning and error that SQL Server encounters goes into the SQL Server logs, whereas only messages specifically marked in SQL Server to go to the Windows Application event log are sent there. Each time you restart SQL Server, a new log file is created. You can view the log files in Enterprise Manager or in the LOG folder for the instance (MSSQL\LOG under the root for the SQL Server 2000 installation for the default SQL Server instance). The most recent log is always called ERRORLOG and older logs have an incremental extension starting with 1, with the oldest log having the highest number extension.

- **Windows System Monitor and performance logs and alerts** Windows System Monitor allows you to view system and SQL Server performance counters in real time. You can also create performance logs of specific counters to view later and perform an analysis of database and operating system activity over time. Windows System Monitor events can also be configured to fire SQL Server alerts.

- **SQL Profiler** Allows you to record database activity, including all Transact-SQL statements sent to SQL Server for later review. Almost a "Big Brother" tool, SQL Profiler can be used in conjunction with server-side tracing or to record real-time activity.

- **System stored procedures, DBCC (Database Consistency Checker), and other Transact-SQL tools** Allow you to view current system status and activity, as well as enable or disable tracing and query current database status. These tools are useful when you have a specific problem to address.

10

- **SQL Enterprise Manager** The Current Activity Window in SQL Enterprise Manager allows you to see which users are connected and what Transact-SQL statements they are executing. You can also use it to determine if you have locking contention and kill any offending session to allow the transaction to complete.

- **SQL Query Analyzer** One of the best ways to determine if a Transact-SQL statement is efficient is to view its execution plan, which can be done in SQL Query Analyzer in either text or graphical mode. This topic will be dealt with in more detail in Chapter 11.

Windows Event Viewer

SQL Server and Windows will write events to Event Viewer when a critical problem is encountered, or when a warning is issued by the operating system or application. There are actually three logs in Event Viewer, by default. You may create additional logs by filtering events in one of the three base logs. The three base logs are as follows:

- **System log** Records events from Windows system components such as a driver or service failing to start.

- **Security log** Records security auditing events. You must enable auditing in Windows for events to be recorded to this log in versions prior to Windows Server 2003. Depending on the security policy of the computer in Windows 2000 and later, events may also appear in the security log.

- **Application log** A place for application programs, like SQL Server, to record important events such as errors or warnings, and information events such as server startup and shutdown. SQL Server will record these events. SQL Server Agent can use the recorded SQL Server events to fire alerts that can notify operators of problems, or launch jobs to correct issues.

Windows System Monitor and Performance Logs and Alerts

Perhaps the most useful tool in the DBAs arsenal for creating baselines, monitoring SQL Server and operating system performance and activity, and determining if corrective actions have had any effect, is Windows System Monitor. Windows System Monitor (previously called Performance Monitor) is part of the Performance MMC snap-in that also includes Performance Logs and Alerts. These tools together allow you to capture workload on the computer and determine if any bottlenecks might exist in Windows or SQL Server. This is possible because Windows and application programs like SQL Server will register performance objects and counters with Windows, which can then be logged, viewed, or have alerts configured through the Performance MMC snap-in. Using the Performance MMC snap-in, you can monitor each of the four key areas (CPU, RAM, disk I/O, and network) for the operating system or, if counters are registered, for each application.

Memory-Related Counters

When monitoring memory usage with System Monitor, you need to ensure that both Windows memory utilization and SQL Server memory utilization are optimal. Table 10-2 lists the key objects and counters to monitor in SQL Server 7 and 2000, and what to look for when gauging performance.

Object:Counter	Description	Guidelines
Memory:Available Bytes	Returns the amount of free memory at the operating system level available for programs.	Ensures that you always have at least 5MB of free memory—more is preferable. Getting too close to zero will result in high paging and poor performance.
Memory:Pages/sec	Returns the number of times per second that Windows had to move pages from physical RAM to hard disk (or vice versa).	This counter should remain low and never be steadily increasing or higher than zero. If the value for this counter grows or is greater than zero consistently, it indicates insufficient RAM in the computer.
Process:Page Faults/sec <SQL Server Instance>	Indicates the number of page faults caused by Windows trimming the working set (in-use memory) of the specific SQL Server instance.	Like the previous counter, a low value is desired, otherwise SQL Server or another process could be using too much memory, indicating a lack of RAM.
Process:Working Set <SQL Server Instance>	Displays the amount of memory used by the SQL Server process for the instance.	This value should always be greater than 5MB or what you configured as the minimum amount of memory SQL Server will use. It indicates the current amount of RAM used by SQL Server.
SQL Server Buffer Manager:Buffer cache hit ratio	Returns the percentage of requests for data satisfied from cache instead of going to disk to physically read the page.	This counter should be as close as possible to 100 percent. A value of less than 90 indicates insufficient RAM available to SQL Server.
SQL Server Buffer Manager:Total pages	Indicates the total number of 8K pages in the buffer cache.	This value should always be high and represent a significant portion (> 50%) of the total memory available to SQL Server (working set). If the value is low, add more memory to SQL Server.

Table 10-2.   Key System Monitor Counters for Monitoring Memory

10

CPU-Related Counters

In terms of processor monitoring, one of the important things to remember is that the CPU these days spends a lot of time waiting for requests. CPUs have grown so powerful in relation to hard disk speed and memory that CPU bottlenecks by themselves are rare. The usual culprit in CPU usage is lack of memory causing excessive paging, which makes the CPU work to perform the paging. Key processor and process-related counters are outlined in Table 10-3.

Counters for Monitoring Disk I/O

System Monitor also allows you to monitor physical (actual hard disk) and logical (volumes) disk activity. In order to get full disk monitoring on operating systems prior to Windows XP or Windows Server 2003, you will need to enable disk counters by issuing the diskperf –y command at the Windows command prompt and then rebooting your computer. Disk performance counters are disabled by default on computers using Windows 2000 or earlier operating systems because of their excessive overhead for the typical CPUs available at the time those operating systems were released. If you're not getting any values for a counter, ensure that you have enabled disk performance monitoring. In Windows XP and Windows Server 2003, disk performance counters are permanently enabled. Table 10-4 lists the key counters for disk monitoring.

Object:Counter	Description	Guidelines
Processor:% Processor Time	The granddaddy of CPU counters indicating how busy the CPU is overall.	This counter should fluctuate and never be consistently higher than 80 percent. If it is, you may need to get a faster or additional CPU.
System:Processor Queue Length	Indicates the number of threads waiting for access to the CPU.	If this counter is consistently greater than 2, you have a slow CPU and should get a faster one (or a second one). If this condition is combined with high CPU utilization and large amounts of disk activity, it probably means your system has insufficient RAM causing paging.
Processor:% Privileged Time	Returns the percentage of time the CPU is doing privileged operating system tasks instead of running user processes.	If this value is high, and you also have high physical disk counters, you may have a slow disk subsystem or insufficient RAM.
Processor:% User Time	The percentage of time the CPU spends executing user process tasks. SQL Server is a user process.	This value should be higher, on average, than the % Privileged Time, and indicates that the CPU is spending most of its time with user applications.

Table 10-3.   System Monitor Counters Dealing with CPU and Processes

Object:Counter	Description	Guidelines
System:Context Switches/sec	Indicates the number of times that a process has switched execution between threads.	If CPU utilization is high and this value is high (8000 or more) and you are running on a multi-CPU computer, you may want to enable SQL Server fiber mode switching by setting the SQL Server **lightweight pooling** parameter to 1. With fiber mode switching enabled, SQL Server manages some of the overhead of switching internally by using fibers instead of relying upon Windows to switch between threads, which is an expensive operating system operation requiring a user to kernel mode switch.

Table 10-3. System Monitor Counters Dealing with CPU and Processes *(continued)*

Object:Counter	Description	Guidelines
Physical Disk: % Disk Time	The percentage of time spent in reading or writing to the hard disks. This is the sum of Physical Disk: % Disk Read Time and Physical Disk: % Disk Write Time.	This counter should be less than 90 percent in all cases with a lower value being preferred. If you have a lot of disk I/O, determine if it is read or write I/O or if you have a lot of paging, indicating a memory problem. More RAM will reduce disk I/O in most cases.
Physical Disk: % Disk Read Time	The percentage of all disk activity used for reading data from the hard disk.	Most disk I/O should be reads on data warehousing or decision support systems. If this value is low in relation to Physical Disk: % Disk Time, then you have a write-intensive system.
Physical Disk: % Disk Write Time	The percentage of all disk activity spent writing data to the disk.	In OLTP systems, this may be close to Physical Disk: % Disk Read time, but should always be lower.
Physical Disk: Disk Writes/sec Physical Disk:Disk Reads/sec	Indicate the rate of I/O performing read and write operations on the disks.	These counters together and individually should be less than the theoretical maximum for your hard disk hardware. The appropriate values will vary by hardware type (SCSI, Serial ATA, IDE, etc.).

Table 10-4. System Monitor Counters for Monitoring Disk I/O

10

Object:Counter	Description	Guidelines
SQL Server Buffer Manager: Page reads /sec SQL Server Buffer Manager: Page writes /sec	These counters return the amount of I/O performed by SQL Server for read and write operations.	OLTP databases will have higher values for writing to the disk because of transaction log activity, whereas data warehouses should have higher values for reads. If the cache hit ratio is low, use these counters to determine if read or write operations are causing the problem. Increase memory or tune the application to reduce the amount of I/O.

Table 10-4.   System Monitor Counters for Monitoring Disk I/O *(continued)*

Counter for Monitoring Network Issues

The final (often forgotten) component that needs to be included in monitoring SQL Server is the network. You need to ensure that the network is not a bottleneck nor the network card a problem when it comes to SQL Server performance.

I recall a situation where a client spent a large sum of money on a new server to host SQL Server databases, only to find that users still felt the databases were slow. Investigating disk, CPU, and memory counters, they found that there was plenty of room to spare with memory and CPU, and the disks were hardly touched. When they finally looked at network counters, they found that the network card was saturated and could not keep up with the workload. There were two lessons learned here: don't forget the network and don't put a $30 network card in a $40,000 server.

Table 10-5 lists some network counters to monitor on your server. Many other counters exist, especially when it comes to SQL Server's activity and processing of Transact-SQL statements. These counters will be covered in more detail in Chapter 11.

A Very Important Counter

One SQL Server-based System Monitor counter that should be monitored, and does not nicely fit into any of the above four areas, is SQL Server Databases:Percent Log Used. This counter has an instance value for each database on the server and allows you to monitor how full a transaction log is for a specific database or for all databases. You can use this counter, and set an alert on it, to let you know when a transaction log is 80 percent full, for example, allowing you to run a job to expand the transaction log or back it up before it becomes full and causes the database to stop. Automating monitoring and setting alerts is covered in the "Automating SQL Performance Monitoring" section of this chapter.

Object:Counter	Description	Guidelines
Network Interface: Bytes Total/sec	Indicates the total amount of traffic sent and received through the network interface. Network Interface: Bytes Sent/ sec and Network Interface: Bytes Received /sec are subsets of this counter.	The total amount of data passing through the network interface should be well below the theoretical maximum. The maximum may also vary depending upon the network adapter in the computer so it is possible to reach the maximum on one card whereas the same value for a different card may be all right.
Network Interface: Current Bandwidth	For varying rate interfaces (e.g., wireless), returns the available bandwidth used; for permanent interfaces (Ethernet Card), returns the bandwidth used.	This value should be well below the theoretical maximum for the network card type. For 100Mb Ethernet, it should represent less than 75 Mb/ps.

Table 10-5.   System Monitor Counters Providing Network Performance Information

SQL Profiler

A very useful tool to generate workload for the database and also figure out what types of Transact-SQL statements are being sent to SQL Server is SQL Profiler. SQL Profiler allows you to log or trace server and database activity including Transact-SQL statements executed, login actions, and much more. You can also save the captured activity to the database or an operating system file for later analysis and even replay the Transact-SQL captured activity in the same or different database. The ability to replay captures is useful when you are making changes in a test environment and want to be sure that they have had some effect on the types of commands issued by users.

When using SQL Profiler, you should use the templates provided to focus your tracing. Enabling tracing of all events is not a good idea for two reasons. First, it introduces significant overhead on the server and slows everything down. Second, the data you get does not provide any useful information without significant review. You may find yourself looking for the proverbial needle in a haystack when more focused tracing would make the haystack smaller or the needle bigger. Besides, if the provided templates do not give you what you want, feel free to create your own to capture the trace activity you need. Figure 10-2 displays a sample of SQL Profiler output using the SQLProfilerTuning template.

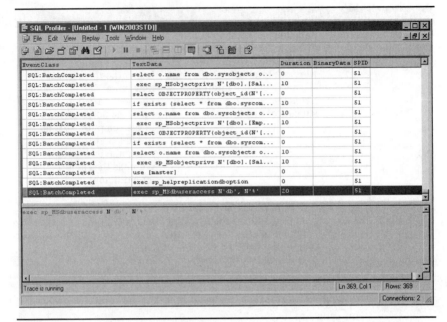

Figure 10-2.   SQL Profiler provides a record of Transact-SQL activity
against the server.

The types of events that you can capture and view with SQL Profiler
include timing information and code of executing queries, user activity in
the database, locking performance, CPU utilization for each Transact-SQL
statement, logical reads and writes, connection failures, and much more. It
can provide a lot of information, but the more you have it capture, the more
overhead it requires.

SQL Profiler also works in conjunction with SQL Server's tracing ability.
Using the **sp_trace_create** system stored procedure, you can enable tracing
of specific events on the server and then use SQL Profiler to review those
events or replay some or all of them on a different database. Furthermore,
in SQL Server 2000 you can use the TRACE_PRODUCE_BLACKBOX option
of the **sp_trace_create** stored procedure to create a 5MB trace of the last set
of events on the SQL Server.

Should SQL Server fail for any reason, the black box trace will provide
information on what was happening before it failed. Black box tracing uses
two files: blackbox.trc and blackbox_01.trc, which are stored in the default
data location for the instance. Use SQL Profiler to review the contents of
these files.

The syntax for the **sp_trace_create** system stored procedure is as follows:

```
sp_trace_create [ @traceid = ] traceid OUTPUT
    , [ @options = ] optionvalue
```

```
, [ @tracefile = ] 'tracefile'
[ , [ @maxfilesize = ] maxfilesize ]
[ , [ @stoptime = ] 'stoptime' ]
```

The @**options** parameter takes several possible values, with TRACE_
PRODUCE_BLACKBOX, whose option value is 8, being one that cannot
be used with any other value. Other possible values for @**options** include
(TRACE_PRODUCE_ROWSET), indicating that the trace will produce a
rowset compatible with data entry to a table; (TRACE_FILE_ROLLOVER),
indicating that once the @**maxfilesize** parameter's value has been reached
to close off the old filename and place further trace information into a new
file with an incremental number (*filename_1.trc, filename_2.trc*, etc.);
and (SHUTDOWN_ON_ERROR), instructing the trace to tell SQL Server to
shutdown should it not be possible to write to the trace file for any reason.

Monitoring Real-Time SQL Server Activity

Whereas SQL Profiler is great to get an idea of activity on the server over a
period of time, if you need to get a quick look at what is currently happening
on the server, or determine who has a particular row or table locked, the
Current Activity Window in SQL Enterprise Manager, system stored
procedures, and the DBCC command may be of help.

The Current Activity Window in SQL Enterprise Manager provides a
graphical view of activity on the server and the ability to see what the
last command issued by a process was, and which users have locks on
which resources. Figure 10-3 shows a list of processes and users on the
server (double-clicking on one will bring up the last Transact-SQL statement
issued by the user, giving you the ability to send a message to that user or
kill the process). Other information available includes locks held by each
process, as well as objects with locks and the processes that are holding
those locks. The one annoying thing about the Current Activity Window
is that it does not refresh automatically—you need to do it yourself by
right-clicking on Current Activity.

10

If you need to get current activity information out through Query Analyzer
or incorporate this ability in your application, you can make use of a number
of system stored procedures, including the following:

- **sp_who**   Provides information on currently connected sessions, logins,
  computers connecting from, databases connected to, and Transact-SQL
  statements executing. A complementary system stored procedure,
  sp_who2, provides this and timing information in a better format.

- **sp_lock**   Displays current active locks, blocking session, and deadlock
  information.

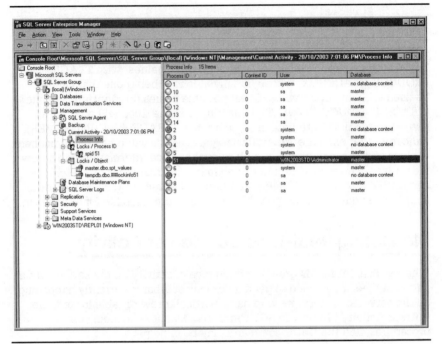

Figure 10-3.   The Current Activity Window of SQL Enterprise Manager
provides information on current processes and locking.

- **sp_spaceused**   Returns the space used by the current database's data
  files and transaction logs. If passed the name of a table or an index,
  provides information on the space used by the object.

- **sp_monitor**   Displays a text-based set of information on SQL Server CPU,
  logical I/O, and connection information since **sp_monitor** was last run.

- **sp_statistics**   Returns current statistical information on indexes of the
  table whose name was passed as the parameter to the procedure.

- **sp_helpdb**   Displays a list of current databases, compatibility level,
  and current running options for each database defined on the server
  when no parameters are passed. If passed a database name, it provides
  the same information as well as the name and location of data and log
  files and filegroups.

A system stored procedure that has been around a long time and includes
many options is **DBCC**, which stands for Database Consistency Checker. A
number of these options (or statements) are useful when monitoring SQL
Server activity as well as determining if structural problems exist, as shown
in Table 10-6.

DBCC Statement Option	Description and Syntax Example
CHECKDB	Performs a check on the allocation and structural integrity of all objects in the database specified on the command line. DBCC CHECKDB (Northwind)
CHECKFILEGROUP	Verifies the structural integrity of all tables and data files in the specified filegroup of the chosen database. Switch to the appropriate database before executing the command. If you do not specify any parameters, the PRIMARY filegroup is checked. USE Northwind GO DBCC CHECKFILEGROUP
CHECKTABLE	Verifies the integrity of all pages allocated to the table. Pages can be used to store data, index, and large object (text, ntext, image) information. DBCC CHECKTABLE ('pubs..authors')
SQLPERF	Displays statistics since the server was started. Available options include transaction log space usage for all databases (LOGSPACE), disk I/O (IOSTATS), buffer cache utilization (LRUSTATS), and network performance (NETSTATS). DBCC SQLPERF (LOGSPACE) DBCC SQLPERF (LRUSTATS)
SHOW_STATISTICS	When passed a table name and index name as parameters, will display information on the selectivity of the index, which can help determine if the index will be used when a query is executed against the table. DBCC SHOW_STATISTICS ('pubs..authors', UPKCL_auidind)
TRACEON	Enables a trace flag for the server. Available trace flags are 260 (version information for extended stored procedures); 1204 (types of locks involved in deadlocks and the offending commands); 2528 (disable parallel execution of DBCC CHECKDB, DBCC CHECKTABLE and DBCC CHECKFILEGROUP command); and 3205 (disable default support of hardware compression on tape drives during SQL Server backups). Once a flag is enabled, it is not disabled until TRACEOFF is run with the same trace flag number. This means that trace flags are persistent between restarts. DBCC TRACEON (2528)
TRACEOFF	Turns off a trace flag turned on by TRACEON. DBCC TRACE OFF (2528)
TRACESTATUS	Displays the status (0 for off and 1 for on) for the specified trace flag. To get a list of all trace flags enabled and their status, issue a DBCC TRACESTATUS (-1). The -1 option means all trace flags. DBCC TRACESTATUS (2528)

Table 10-6.   DBCC Commands Useful in Monitoring SQL Server

10

Automating SQL Performance Monitoring

Being able to monitor SQL Server is a nice feature, but who wants to sit there and manually start and stop monitoring, or always watch the server in case anything goes wrong. To make the job easier, SQL Server provides an automated event monitoring and alert facility that can be used to configure automatic notification of critical SQL Server or Windows Performance/System Monitor events, as well as the ability to automatically initiate a job to take corrective action.

The process of automating SQL Server monitoring requires the following three key configuration steps:

1. For SQL Server events, ensure that the SQL Server error message generated when the event takes place is logged to the Windows Application event log, or ensure that the RAISERROR command that manually raises the error uses the WITH LOG option to write the event to the Application event log.

2. Create one or more operators in SQL Server to be notified when an alert fires because of a monitored event.

3. Configure alerts on SQL Server events or Performance counters you want to monitor and specify the threshold that will fire the alert. Also, specify whether to notify an operator and/or fire a corrective job when configuring the alert.

Another optional step is to configure an Alerts Management Server that will be sent notification of events not handled by the local SQL Server instance. Having an Alerts Management Server allows you to create alerts on one server and have another SQL Server instance send any event that was raised but not handled locally to the Alerts Management Server for processing. The downside of this approach is that if the Alerts Management Server is a SQL Server on the network, and many SQL Server instances are configured to use it, a lot of network traffic will be generated sending event information from each SQL Server for each event to the Alerts Management Server. This approach is great in small environments (and great in theory everywhere) but impractical in organizations with many busy SQL Servers.

(Chapter 9 covered how to perform each of the steps outlined above.)

Chapter 11

Performance Tuning Part 2: Tuning SQL Server

Did you ever notice that users of your databases seem to believe that they are the only ones using them? On top of that, each and every user wants the database to respond to his query as fast as possible. The fact that there are 100 or 500 other users using the same database is not something he worries about. And you know what, he's right!

As a database administrator, one of the most challenging, and most rewarding, parts of your job is to make sure that databases are performing to the satisfaction of users. At the same time, you also need to make sure that users have realistic expectations of performance. Setting Service Level Agreements (SLAs) and having everyone sign off, is a great idea, if you can make it work. When push comes to shove, your users think, "I want my data NOW!"

So, how do you fix it? First, find out what the problem is and then take appropriate action. Instead of immediately throwing a pile of money away on new hardware (since new and faster toys can fix anything—or so some of my clients believe), try monitoring the performance of the operating system, checking the database design, monitoring memory, and monitoring I/O usage first. Other important factors to understand include what the Transact-SQL statements are doing, how the SQL Server Query Optimizer determines the best way to satisfy a query, and how to restrict certain operations, and others.

11

Goals of Database Tuning

When tuning SQL Server, or any other database or shared application, you are primarily concerned about the following:

- **Response Time** The time it takes for a single query (a Transact-SQL statement, for example) to return a result to the user

- **Throughput** The number of simultaneous Transact-SQL statements that can be processed by the server while still providing acceptable response time for **all** users

At the most basic level, the goal of tuning is to assure the fastest possible response time for the most users. Sounds simple enough. But it is easier said than done because so many factors enter into the equation, including the operating system, database design, application code, SQL Server memory configuration, disk I/O, and locking issues. These should all sound familiar by now since these are all the components of the Pyramid of Performance introduced in Chapter 10. In this chapter we will focus on the impact of database design and application code in performance tuning.

Tools for Tuning SQL Server

Chapter 10 outlined many of the tools that can be used to monitor SQL Server performance, including Windows System Monitor, SQL Profiler, system stored procedures, and others. You can use these tools when diagnosing the design and performance of application code of your databases. The following additional tools can also provide insight into whether or not your databases are performing well:

- **SQL Query Analyzer**   Although the main reason you would use SQL Query Analyzer is to execute Transact-SQL against the database, it also provides the ability to turn on a couple of important features—SHOWPLAN output and graphical execution plan display. These tools allow you to determine how SQL Server is executing a specific statement and also gather statistics on disk and memory usage.

- **Index Tuning Wizard**   Creating indexes is easy. Finding out if they are being used is often not as easy. The Index Tuning Wizard can take a workload generated by tracing or SQL Profiler and analyze its contents to determine how queries were executed, which indexes were used, and which new ones should be created.

All the wonderful tools that Microsoft provides to monitor and tune databases notwithstanding, one of the best tools that a DBA has in tuning databases is a thorough understanding of what the application is doing and what database objects are being used for. I call this the *KYD Factor*—Know Your Data. You can easily plan a strategy to keep your SQL Server performing well if you know the following:

- The design of the database
- How the application uses the database
- The impact of both the database and the application on memory, disk, locking, and the operating system,

Unless you designed and wrote the application yourself, acquisition of this knowledge will take time. However, the more tuning you do, the better you get at it.

Windows System Monitor

In addition to the Windows System Monitor counters related to SQL Server that were discussed in Chapter 10, there are also counters available that deal with how efficiently SQL Server executes queries and what kind of operations it performs. Table 11-1 lists counters that are useful when diagnosing application performance and design issues.

Object:Counter	Description	Guidelines
SQL Server Access Methods: Full Scans/sec	The number of full table or index scans performed.	Full scans take the most time and should be avoided. If full table scans are performed, see if an index will help. Investigate the Transact-SQL code executing to see if it can be made more efficient.
SQL Server Access Methods: Index Searches/sec	The number of index searches started.	Should be higher than Full Scans/sec as data access in OLTP databases should retrieve small numbers of rows.
SQL Server Access Methods: Range Scans/sec	The number of index range scans that take place on the database.	Should be high in relation to Full Scans/sec in OLTP databases. May be less than Full Scans/sec in databases with very large tables or queries that return a large portion of the data.
SQL Server Access Methods: Page Splits/sec	The number of index pages that had to be split because of insufficient space for new index entries.	If this value is constant or increasing, you should rebuild the index using the DROP_EXISTING clause and set an appropriate FILL FACTOR.
SQL Server SQL Statistics: SQL Compilations/sec	The number of compiles of execution plans per second. Also includes compiles as a result of recompilation.	This number will climb after the SQL Server instance starts, but should level off after a time of normal running. If the number continues to climb, determine if ad-hoc queries are being executed or if procedures are explicitly recompiled on execution.
SQL Server SQL Statistics: SQL Recompilations/sec	The number of recompiles taking place on the server. Recompilations increase CPU load and should be avoided.	Generally, should be a low value when using OLTP databases and stored procedures. If a lot of ad-hoc queries are used, as in data warehousing, may be higher. Verify that stored procedures, triggers, and user-defined functions are not being explicitly recompiled on each execution.

Table 11-1.   Performance Counters for SQL Performance or Database Design

11

Execution Plans and the Query Optimizer

One of the questions that DBAs will need to answer when users complain about slow performance of a query is "What is happening when I execute this query?" In order to be able to answer that question, you need to understand what the SQL Server Query Optimizer is and how it works. After getting some idea of that topic, you will need to find out what steps are taking place when executing a query. When you need to determine how well a specific Transact-SQL statement is executing, one of the tools that you can use is SQL Query Analyzer. It can be configured to display either graphical or text-based showplan (execution plan) information, but we're getting ahead of ourselves a bit.

SQL Server Query Optimizer

A very important, integral part of SQL Server is the Query Optimizer. Its job is quite simple—to determine the most efficient way to satisfy a query within the parameters specified. In processing a query and formulating an execution plan, the Query Optimizer will:

- Figure out if one or more indexes can be used
- Determine the best way to process joins
- Calculate statistics on columns, if they are not available, in order to get better information to generate the execution plan
- Evaluate many possible execution plans to satisfy the query
- Calculate the lowest cost execution plan of the ones available and use it

In understanding how the Query Optimizer works, one fundamental concept that needs to be grasped is that of *cost*. Cost, from the viewpoint of the Query Optimizer, means the lowest combination of I/O and CPU processing. Essentially, the Query Optimizer is always trying to do what I, and probably most of you, want—to get the most amount of stuff for the least amount of effort. The difference between it and me is that I have to win the lottery to achieve that goal, whereas the Query Optimizer does this every time it executes a query. It is limited by the statistics available and any constraints in terms of available hardware, memory, and so on. It usually performs its task well, although you can guide it by using optimizer hints placed in your SQL code, which tell it whether or not to use specific indexes.

The optimization of a query and creation of an execution plan follows these phases:

- **Parsing**   The syntax of the Transact-SQL statement is checked and the query is broken down into its component parts such as select list, table list, join and where conditions, and so on. The end result is a parsed query tree.

- **Standardization** This process removes any redundant syntax found in the query and produces a standardized query tree.

- **Query optimization** Several possible execution plans are evaluated based upon the standardized query tree. In producing the execution plan, a number of steps take place, with the greatest impact in performance derived from query analysis (identification of search and join criteria), index selection (determination of available indexes and the usefulness of each), and join selection (determination of the best join strategy to use).

- **Compilation** This process produces the compiled execution plan that will be run.

- **Execution** Also referred to as Database Access Routines, execution actually runs the execution plan and returns the results to the user. This process also places the execution plan in the procedure cache.

Once an execution plan has been run and placed in the procedure cache, the following processes will reuse the same execution plan without going through the above phases of execution again (also known as recompilation): subsequent executions of the same SQL statements; execution of a procedure, function, or trigger; or the selection of data from a view. This is the desired effect because the process of evaluation, optimizing, and compiling an execution plan is CPU-intensive and will cause overhead on the server.

SQL Server's Query Optimizer will need to recompile the statement if

- A structural change on a table or view referenced by the query takes place. This includes any ALTER TABLE or ALTER VIEW statements, or the addition, removal, or rebuilding of an existing index.

- New statistics have been generated on a referenced object either automatically by SQL Server or using the CREATE STATISTICS or UPDATE STATISTICS commands.

- The procedure, view, user-defined function, or trigger was created with explicit recompilation specified, or the **sp_recompile** system stored procedure was invoked on a referenced object, or the WITH RECOMPILE option was specified with executing a stored procedure.

- A large volume of data was inserted, deleted, or updated in a referenced table, which caused many keys to be modified, essentially making previous information about an index useless.

If databases get very large, one of the things that you don't want to happen is for a query to take hours or days to execute. While this may be necessary in some very large database (VLDB) environments, you may want to specify a maximum time in which a query will be allowed to execute. In SQL Server 2000 you can specify a cost limit, either for the entire SQL Server and all its databases or for a specific session. This is done using the **query governor cost limit** SQL Server configuration option or by executing SET QUERY_GOVERNOR_COST_LIMIT for a session. The default for both of these parameters is 0, which means that any query will be allowed to execute no matter what the estimated cost is.

To set the **query governor cost limit** for the SQL Server, you need to perform the following two steps as a user with either the **sysadmin** or **serveradmin** role:

1. Enable advanced configuration options by setting the value of **show advanced options** SQL Server configuration option to 1. This can be done without restarting SQL Server, as shown here.

```
use master
EXEC sp_configure 'show advanced option',1
RECONFIGURE
```

2. Specify the maximum amount of estimated elapsed time, in seconds, that a query will be allowed to execute by enabling the **query governor cost limit** at the server level. The following example sets the cost limit for the server to 15 minutes (900 seconds).

```
use master
EXEC sp_configure 'query governor cost limit',900
RECONFIGURE
```

Because this is an estimated query time, any query exceeding this estimate during the building of the execution plan will not be allowed to execute. Instead of chewing up resources for 15 minutes and then being killed, the query won't event start if the Query Analyzer determines that it will take more than 15 minutes to run.

If you want to see what the current value for this, and all other configuration parameters, is on the SQL Server, execute the **sp_configure** system stored procedure without any parameter.

To set the maximum estimated time that a specific session's query can take, issue the command SET QUERY_GOVERNOR_COST_LIMIT, within that session, and include the number of seconds in which you want queries to execute, as in this example:

```
SET QUERY_GOVERNOR_COST_LIMIT 600
```

Determining the Execution Plan in Use

One of the hardest issues to track down is why a specific query is taking a long time to execute. Fortunately, SQL Server provides a few ways to determine what is actually happening during query execution by allowing you to view the execution plan of a query, either graphically or in text mode, as well as displaying statistical information for a query, such as the number of I/Os and CPU costs. These can all be viewed by using SQL Query Analyzer in SQL Server 7 and 2000. SQL Server 6.x does not provide graphical output of the execution plan, although a text-based version of the execution plan is available.

Graphical Execution Plan Display

So that SQL Query Analyzer can provide the graphical execution plan of any statement sent to the server, you need to enable execution plan output by selecting Show Execution Plan from the Query menu, or by pressing CTRL-K. This will execute the query you send to SQL Server and, for each line executed, provide graphical information on what the Query Optimizer selected as the execution plan for the query. If you do not want to have the query execute, but still want to have the execution plan provided, you can select Display Estimated Execution Plan from the Query menu and Query Analyzer will display the information in the Estimated Execution Plan tab of the results window. This is useful when you suspect that a query may take a long time to complete and you want to see what SQL Server will do, or if you want to test differences in optimizer hints and syntax without actually executing the query. An example of the graphical output provided when the display of the execution plan is enabled is shown in Figure 11-1. Notice that information on the percentage of total time taken by each step in the execution is provided along with the step. If you place your mouse cursor over a step, additional statistical information is also displayed.

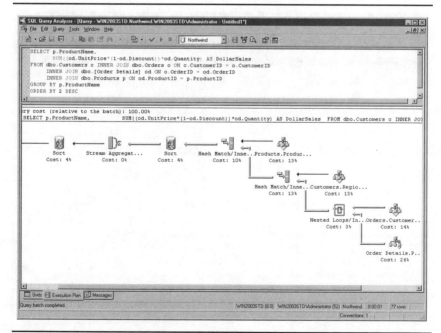

Figure 11-1. Graphical execution plan output in SQL Query Analyzer for a specific SELECT statement

Reading this output is done from the bottom up. In other words, the last step in the execution plan displayed (bottom right) is the first step that took place. If two steps appear at the same level, they are being executed at the same time, in order for that part of processing to complete. The top-left step shows the completion of the Transact-SQL statement and the return of the rowset to the user.

If the Transact-SQL statement you execute is a stored procedure, SQL Query Analyzer displays execution plan information for each line of executed code in the stored procedure. The same also holds true for DML statements that fire triggers, or user-defined functions. SELECTing from a view expands the statement to include all of its component parts. This is important to remember if you are wondering why a simple SELECT statement is causing several different tables to be read and other operations to be performed. Figure 11-2 shows an example where a simple SELECT statement caused many indexes and tables to be used.

Of course, understanding what each of the icons in the graphical execution plan output means is perhaps the most important part of deciphering what is taking place. Table 11-2 provides information on some of the most common operations displayed, though others exist.

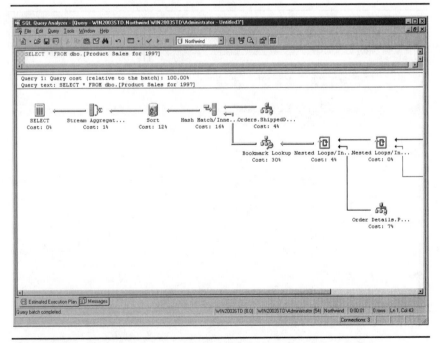

Figure 11-2.   Execution plans of views include information on how referenced objects are accessed to retrieve the data.

Graphical Showplan Icon	Operation Name	Description
	Bookmark Lookup	The operation used a row ID or cluster key to retrieve a record. This typically happens after an index scan or index seek to retrieve the appropriate rows.
	Filter	Evaluates each row returned by the previous operation to determine if they satisfy the selectivity criteria (that is, the WHERE clause).
	Hash Match	In a join, creates a hash table of the smaller rowset in the join computing hash values for each row. For each row of the other rowset in the join, a hash match computes the hash value of each row and scans the hash table for matches.
	Index Scan	Scans the entire non-clustered index for all rows satisfying the query. If a WHERE clause was specified in the query, non-matching rows will be eliminated during the scan.
	Index Seek	Performs a seek of the index for only those index entries matching the seek criteria. This operation differs from an Index Scan because the list of values needed is known, whereas for an Index Scan, every index entry must be queried.
	Merge Join	Used to perform inner and outer joins and UNION operations. Other operations (sort, index seek, index scan, and so on) may appear before the merge join to retrieve the appropriate set of data required for the merge join operation.
	Nested Loops	Used to perform inner join and left outer join operations by scanning data in one table, and then using an index or other method to retrieve all corresponding rows in the second table. This is less preferable to merge joins because of the performance costs associated with the repetitive I/O.
	Parallelism	Indicates that the operations to satisfy the query will be performed in parallel. Parallel query capabilities are available in the Enterprise Edition of SQL Server and can provide performance improvements with large volumes of data.
	Table Scan	The entire table will be scanned to determine the rows required to satisfy the query. If a WHERE clause was specified, only those rows matching the selectivity criteria will be returned. Generally, a table scan is the slowest method to retrieve data but is appropriate when the WHERE clause does not provide sufficient selectivity.

Table 11-2. Common Icons in Graphical Showplan Output

Graphical Showplan Icon	Operation Name	Description
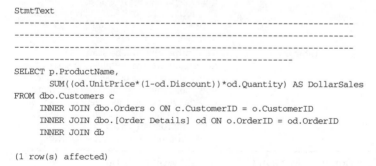	Sort	The data being returned is being sorted to satisfy the query. This can be as a result of an explicit ORDER BY or GROUP BY, or because of a DISTINCT, TOP, or UNION operation.
	Top	Indicates that only a subset of all rows that match the query predicates will be returned because a TOP operator was used.

Table 11-2. Common Icons in Graphical Showplan Output *(continued)*

SHOWPLAN_TEXT and SHOWPLAN_ALL

Sometimes the information provided by graphical execution plan output can be lengthy, or you may just need a more succinct piece of information that you can easily review or populate a table with for more thorough analysis later. In this case, or if you are using SQL Server 6.x, you can instruct SQL Server to provide text-based information from the execution plan for your Transact-SQL statements. The two following commands allow you to display execution plan information textually:

```
SET SHOWPLAN_TEXT [ON | OFF]
SET SHOWPLAN_ALL [ON | OFF]
```

SHOWPLAN_TEXT, when enabled, will display the information about the execution plan as a set of rows that can be inserted into a table, if needed, for later analysis. Execution plan output is returned in a hierarchical tree format representing steps taken by the Query Optimizer in executing the query, as well as estimated values of optimization for each step of the process. The information returned for each execution step includes indexes used on each table, join order of tables, temporary worktables used, and other relevant information. An example of SHOWPLAN_TEXT output for the query in Figure 11-1 is shown here, although actual display output may vary depending on word wrapping characteristics. Note that the SQL statement is actually truncated—that's the way it works.

```
StmtText
-------------------------------------------------------------------
-------------------------------------------------------------------
-------------------------------------------------------------------
----------------------------------------------------------
SELECT p.ProductName,
       SUM((od.UnitPrice*(1-od.Discount))*od.Quantity) AS DollarSales
FROM dbo.Customers c
     INNER JOIN dbo.Orders o ON c.CustomerID = o.CustomerID
     INNER JOIN dbo.[Order Details] od ON o.OrderID = od.OrderID
     INNER JOIN db

(1 row(s) affected)
```

```
StmtText
-------------------------------------------------------------------
-------------------------------------------------------------------
------------------------------------------
  |--Sort(ORDER BY:([Expr1004] DESC))
     |--Stream Aggregate(GROUP BY:([p].[ProductName])
        DEFINE:([Expr1004]=SUM(Convert([od].[UnitPrice])*
           (1-[od].[Discount])*Convert([od].[Quantity])))))
        |--Sort(ORDER BY:([p].[ProductName] ASC))
           |--Hash Match(Inner Join,
                 HASH:([p].[ProductID])=([od].[ProductID]))
              |--Index Scan(OBJECT:([Northwind].[dbo].
                 [Products].[ProductName] AS [p]))
              |--Hash Match(Inner Join, HASH:([c].
                 [CustomerID])=([o].[CustomerID]),
                    RESIDUAL:([c].[CustomerID]=[o].[CustomerID]))
                 |--Index Scan(OBJECT:([Northwind].[dbo].
                    [Customers].[Region] AS [c]))
                 |--Nested Loops(Inner Join,
                       OUTER REFERENCES:([o].[OrderID]))
                    |--Index Scan(OBJECT:([Northwind].[dbo].
                       [Orders].[CustomerID] AS [o]))
                    |--Clustered Index Seek(OBJECT:([Northwind].
                       [dbo].[Order Details].[PK_Order_Details]
                       AS [od]), SEEK:([od].
                          [OrderID]=[o].[OrderID])
                          ORDERED FORWARD)

(10 row(s) affected)
```

Like graphical execution plan output, SHOWPLAN_TEXT output is read from the bottom up. The last step displayed (bottom right) is the first step that took place, whereas the first row of output (top left) is the final result of execution. If two steps appear at the same level, they are being executed at the same time in order for that part of processing to complete.

The second option for displaying an execution plan textually is SHOWPLAN_ALL. This option provides the same output as SHOWPLAN_TEXT but with the addition of statistical information, including the estimated number of rows, I/O cost, CPU time, and average row size for a query. In this way, it is more similar to the information returned by the graphical execution plan output. The amount of data is quite extensive and returns rows of several hundred bytes in size, which are very hard to show in the pages of a book.

After turning SHOWPLAN_TEXT or SHOWPLAN_ALL on, it is important to remember to turn them off, since they will remain enabled for the session. Another way to enable and disable SHOWPLAN_TEXT, as well as the display of statistical information in text form (covered in the next section) in SQL Query Analyzer, is to modify the Connection Properties dialog box by selecting Connection Properties from the Query menu. This displays a dialog, as shown in Figure 11-3, where you can select a check box to enable or disable these options. If you select to display SHOWPLAN_TEXT (by checking the box titled Set showplan_text), you will notice that most other

11

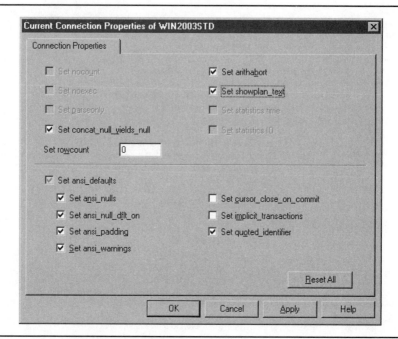

Figure 11-3. You can enable SHOWPLAN_TEXT from the Connection Properties dialog box of SQL Query Analyzer.

options become unavailable. Turning SHOWPLAN_TEXT on in this manner requires that you turn it off the same way. The same also holds true if you enable it, or any other option, from the command line. In other words, if you enable an option in code, you must disable it in code; if you enable an option through the Connection Properties dialog, you must disable it through the Connection Properties dialog.

Displaying Execution Plan Statistics

One important factor in determining how well a query is executing is to find out the disk I/O and CPU time it requires. With graphical execution plan output, you can get this information by placing your mouse cursor over any of the execution plan steps. When using SHOWPLAN_TEXT, this information is not provided, although SHOWPLAN_ALL will give you statistics for each step in the execution. However, it is useful to get statistical information only without the SHOWPLAN details just to get a quick glimpse of what a particular Transact-SQL statement is doing. SQL Server allows you to set the following three options to provide statistical information:

- **SET STATISTICS IO [ON | OFF]**—Provides information on logical and physical reads, read-ahead reads, and the number of times a table was accessed during the operation.

- **SET STATISTICS TIME [ON | OFF]]**—Shows the time, in milliseconds, used to parse, compile, and execute a Transact-SQL statement.

- **SET STATISTICS PROFILE [ON | OFF]]**—Provides information on the number of rows processed by the execution step. Also included are the SHOWPLAN_ALL statement for the step. You can use this in place of SHOWPLAN_ALL, with additional information.

You can enable each of these STATISTICS options using the appropriate SET command outlined above, or by using the Connection Properties dialog box of SQL Query Analyzer. You can set any or all of these options to ON and the output will be displayed until you set them to OFF again, or until your session ends.

Output of the query executed in Figure 11-1, when STATISTICS IO is the following on the author's server:

```
ProductName                                 DollarSales
-------------------------------------       ------------------------
---------------------------
Côte de Blaye                               141396.73522949219
Thüringer Rostbratwurst                     80368.671936035156
… <more data>
Genen Shouyu                                1784.8249969482422
Geitost                                     1648.125
Chocolade                                   1368.7125396728516

(77 row(s) affected)

Table 'Order Details'. Scan count 830, logical reads 1672,
    physical reads 0, read-ahead reads 0.
Table 'Orders'. Scan count 1, logical reads 4, physical reads 0,
    read-ahead reads 0.
Table 'Customers'. Scan count 1, logical reads 1, physical reads 0,
    read-ahead reads 0.
Table 'Products'. Scan count 1, logical reads 1, physical reads 0,
    read-ahead reads 0.
```

In this case, the fact that all reads were logical (from the buffer cache, for example) and none were physical (from disk) indicates that the query was operating efficiently because it was able to return all of the data to the user from memory. This is always preferable.

An example of the output for the same query when setting STATISTICS TIME to ON is as follows (be sure to turn off STATISTICS IO, as I did in this example, otherwise you will get its output, too):

```
ProductName                                 DollarSales
-------------------------------------       ------------------------
---------------------------
Côte de Blaye                               141396.73522949219
Thüringer Rostbratwurst                     80368.671936035156
```

11

```
... <more data>
Genen Shouyu                              1784.8249969482422
Geitost                                   1648.125
Chocolade                                 1368.7125396728516

(77 row(s) affected)

SQL Server Execution Times:
   CPU time = 50 ms,  elapsed time = 157 ms.

SQL Server Execution Times:
   CPU time = 50 ms,  elapsed time = 504 ms.

SQL Server Execution Times:
   CPU time = 50 ms,  elapsed time = 504 ms.

SQL Server parse and compile time:
   CPU time = 0 ms, elapsed time = 0 ms.

SQL Server Execution Times:
   CPU time = 0 ms,  elapsed time = 0 ms.
```

After the data is displayed, the final part of the output is the statistical information on CPU usage. Note, however, that multiple results are displayed. This is because each step during execution has a different CPU statistic, which can be seen with SHOWPLAN_ALL or STATISTICS PROFILE, the output of which is too long to display here.

Optimizing Queries

Once you have determined that a query is not performing as efficiently as possible, what should you do? The first step is to figure out which part of the query is executing slowly and see if you can speed that up. Before doing so, take a step back and determine what the query is accomplishing and see if you can get the same results by rewording the query. You also need to look at some SQL Server features that can help to speed up queries. While the literature on optimizing SQL queries is vast, with many books written on it, and the topic itself is complicated, some steps you should check and/or perform include the following:

- Create calculated columns and index those columns. Calculated columns are those whose data is based upon the result of an expression. If the expression is frequently used in a WHERE clause, indexing the calculated column could allow the Query Optimizer to use it and provide better performance.

- Use sparse indexes. If the columns you are frequently querying contain NULLs, you can index the column(s). Doing so will create an index with only the non-NULL data indexed. If you have a table with 100,000 rows and only 15,000 have non-NULL values in columns, your index will only contain 15,000 entries. This means that any query for a value (other than NULL) in the column will only scan 15 percent of the total data (15,000/100,000).

- Create non-clustered indexes that contain all columns frequently queried in a SELECT statement. This will allow SQL Server's Query Optimizer to use the index to completely cover the query and never touch the base table. This is explained in more detail later in the "Using Indexes to Cover a Query" section of this chapter.

- Create a clustered index on the columns that most frequently appear in the WHERE clause or JOIN condition when many columns in the table are being retrieved in each query.

- Create indexes on columns tables are joined by. In other words, remember to create an index on all FOREIGN KEY columns since PRIMARY KEY or UNIQUE constraints will create indexes automatically, but FOREIGN KEYs will not.

- Do not create indexes on small tables (less than eight pages) because they will provide no benefit. A full table scan is quicker on small tables because SQL Server performs full table scans by reading an extent (eight data pages) at a time.

- Formulate queries so that they do not return a majority of the table data (for example, only SELECT the columns you need and try to avoid SELECT *). If you issue a SELECT * or select many columns in a table, indexes created on the table may not be used because the Query Optimizer may decide that a full table scan or full cluster scan will produce less I/O and will be more efficient than scanning an index first, and then the data (may cause double the I/O).

- Verify that indexes are being used. The Index Tuning Wizard, discussed in the "Tuning Indexes" section of this chapter, can be helpful here when provided a working set of SQL Server trace information to analyze.

- Keep statistics up-to-date so that the Query Optimizer has the best information on the size and distribution of data in a table or index. Use the CREATE STATISTICS or UPDATE STATISTICS commands to manually create statistics when data volumes in a table change drastically to provide the Query Optimizer with the latest information. Better still, use the Database Maintenance Wizard in SQL Enterprise Manager to create a job that will automatically back up your database or transaction log and update statistics at the same time.

- Use optimizer hints when appropriate to override choices made by the Query Optimizer for specific queries that have been well tuned manually. Using optimizer hints, you can instruct the Query Optimizer on how to evaluate a query, which indexes to use, and so on. This will negate a lot of what the Query Optimizer is designed to do for you, so do this only after all other avenues have been exhausted.

- Test your changes to make sure they have had an effect.

In many respects, tuning SQL Server databases and queries is more of an art than a science. The basic tenets of tuning follow the scientific method we were all taught in high school science class (or earlier): formulate a hypothesis, design an experiment to test the hypothesis, test the hypothesis, record the results, compare the results with the hypothesis, document any differences, determine the factors that affected the outcome and did not produce the expected results, rework the hypothesis or design a new experiment, and repeat the process. It is kind of like the instructions you find on shampoo bottles for washing your hair—apply shampoo, lather, rinse, repeat—only it's a bit more complicated and takes a lot more time. We cannot go into fine detail on the topic in this book because this topic alone could fill two books.

Using Indexes to Cover a Query

One of the most useful features of SQL Server, and an important consideration when designing indexes, is its ability to satisfy a query without ever reading the base table's data pages. This can be accomplished if both of the following are true:

- All columns referenced in the query for the specified table appear in the index. For this reason, composite keys are often a good idea when creating indexes.

- The index being used is a non-clustered index. Using a clustered index does not provide any performance benefit because all of the table's data is stored at the leaf level of a clustered index, so scanning it is the same as performing a full table scan.

So how does this actually work? As an example, you have a table called Contacts with many columns including ContactID, CustomerID, LastName, FirstName, Telephone, and so on. You may also have other related tables such as Customers. You frequently issue the following, or similar, SELECT statement:

```
SELECT LastName, FirstName, CompanyName
FROM Contacts INNER JOIN Customers
ON Contacts.CustomerID = Customers.CustomerID
WHERE Contacts.LastName LIKE 'Sm%'
```

In designing indexes using this example, the general wisdom would state that you should create clustered indexes on the CustomerID column of the Customers table, an index on the LastName column, and perhaps a clustered index on the CustomerID column of the Contacts table. In doing so, you would ensure that SQL Server would scan the clustered index on both tables and probably not use the non-clustered index on the LastName column of the Contacts table. Now, what if you did the following:

- Created a non-clustered composite index on the Contacts table that included LastName, FirstName, and CustomerID.

- Created a non-clustered composite index on the CustomerID and CompanyName columns of the Customers table.
- Re-issued the query.

In this case, SQL Server would never have to touch the base table data of either table because all of the data elements needed to satisfy the query are available in the composite non-clustered indexes, as follows:

- The LastName and FirstName columns being returned to the user are in the composite non-clustered index on the Contacts table.
- The CompanyName column being returned to the user is in the composite non-clustered index on the Customers table.
- The CustomerID columns used to perform the join are in the composite non-clustered index in each of the tables.

If you had created the two composite non-clustered indexes (one per table), SQL Server's Query Optimizer would determine that all of the required data elements to perform the join and return the data to the user were available in the indexes, and would never touch the base tables. In the output of the execution plan (text or graphical) you would see the "Scanning a non-clustered index entirely or only a range" operation, but no operation to **touch** the base table.

So what is the main benefit of using non-clustered indexes that cover a query completely? SPEED! Because a non-clustered index only contains data for the columns making up the key value, as well as the Row ID of the row with the data, the amount of disk space taken up by the index is less than the table as a whole. It is not uncommon to be able to fit 20 or 30 or more key values in an index page when the base table can only accept three or four rows in a page. If you have to scan only ten percent of the pages to retrieve all of the data to satisfy a query, your query will run about ten times faster!

A second thing to remember is that if you are using grouping functions (COUNT, SUM, MIN, MAX, and so on) and all of the rows for which these operations are being applied exist in a non-clustered index, creating indexes that cover a query can also significantly speed up these operations, since the values to be aggregated also exist in the index. However, as soon as one column that does not appear in the index must be returned to the user, or appears in the WHERE clause, JOIN condition, or ORDER BY, then SQL Server must read the base table data, and the index cannot be used to fully cover a query. Therefore, designing your indexes with a view to using them to fully cover a query is beneficial in query-intensive environments with large amounts of data.

To determine which columns users are querying, and which columns are good candidates to cover a query, create a SQL Profiler trace. You can review it to see what columns are being queried in the SELECT statements being executed, or you can use the Index Tuning Wizard to help you design indexes.

Tuning Indexes

I have to admit that I am not a big fan of the wizards phenomenon that has swept the software industry in the last few years. I generally think that wizards hide too much of what is happening, making it harder to learn how to do things well yourself. Or, they just plain get things wrong. For these reasons, I was skeptical when Microsoft introduced a tool in SQL Server 7 to help you determine if your indexes are efficient—the Index Tuning Wizard. To a certain extent, the initial release of the Index Tuning Wizard in SQL Server 7 justified my fears. But, there was enough there to make it useful in designing better indexes, or removing indexes not being used, by analyzing queries being sent to the server. In SQL Server 2000, Microsoft has improved it so it is even more useful. So, despite my reservations about wizards, the Index Tuning Wizard is what I use to tune indexes in SQL Server 7 and 2000 databases.

The Index Tuning Wizard in SQL Server 2000 will perform the following functions:

- Analyze a provided workload by using the execution plan information and Query Optimizer costing information

- Determine which indexes were used and which indexes were not used in the workload provided

- Recommend ways to tune the database by suggesting indexes to be added, deleted, or modified (changing from clustered to non-clustered, adding or removing columns, and so on)

- Allow you to specify criteria in evaluating the workload such as whether to keep all existing indexes or not, the maximum number of columns for recommended composite indexes, the maximum amount of disk space to be occupied by indexes, and other choices

You can use the Index Tuning Wizard to make recommendations on user tables but you cannot use it to add or remove indexes in system tables. It also will not recommend that indexes used to enforce PRIMARY KEY or UNIQUE constraints be dropped, so be aware of these limitations.

To invoke the Index Tuning Wizard from the Management node of the dialog box that appears when you select the Tools | Wizards menu option in SQL Enterprise Manager, you must have been granted the **sysadmin** role. You should also have created a SQL Server workload either by using the server-based trace capabilities in SQL Server 2000 or via SQL Server Profiler. This workload will be fed to the Index Tuning Wizard for analysis and to make recommendations on index usage based upon the Transact-SQL statements in the trace.

The first screen that appears when you invoke the Index Tuning Wizard is an introductory screen that explains what the wizard does. Clicking Next presents a screen, shown in Figure 11-4, where you specify if you want to keep existing indexes, as well as the speed of analysis. For the most accurate

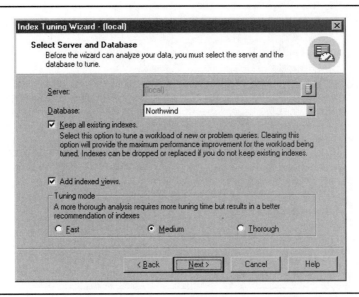

Figure 11-4. Running the Index Tuning Wizard, you can select whether or not to keep existing indexes and/or add new ones.

results, you should clear the Keep all existing indexes check box and specify the Thorough tuning process, though this will also take the longest. In SQL Server 2000 Enterprise or Developer Edition (but not in SQL Server 2000 Standard Edition).you also can specify whether or not the Index Tuning Wizard should recommend creating Indexed Views—generally a good idea.

Clicking Next brings up a screen where you must provide a SQL Server workload either as a SQL Server Profiler trace file or as a table within a SQL Server database with the same information, or a set of Transact-SQL statements in a SQL file on disk. If you invoked the Index Tuning Wizard from SQL Query Analyzer, you can use it to analyze index usage for one or more queries you have open. The Advanced Options button launches a dialog box, shown in Figure 11-5, where some of the more interesting selections can be made. You will be shown the current size of the index and table data in the database, and you have the option to limit the number of queries that the Index Tuning Wizard will examine (I generally uncheck this option—but be aware that it can take a long time for a big workload). You can also specify the maximum size for new recommended indexes (set according to existing data volume) and the number of columns for composite indexes (again, set according to your data structures).

The next step is to specify on which tables in the selected database to perform index tuning, and then click Next to set the Index Tuning Wizard to run. Depending on the workload and tables in your database, you may want to grab a coffee or lunch at this point. When you return, you will get a report of the tables and indexes analyzed, as shown in Figure 11-6.

11

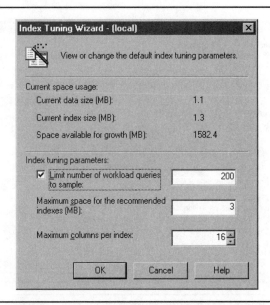

Figure 11-5. The Advanced Options dialog box allows you to further
control recommendations made by the Index Tuning Wizard.

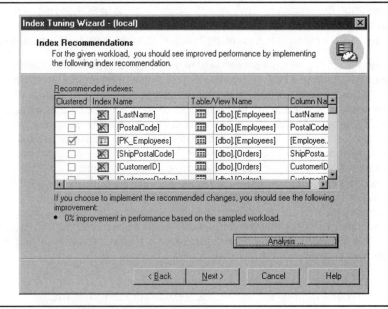

Figure 11-6. The Index Tuning Wizard will recommend adding or
dropping an index, based upon the workload.

The report will also indicate the performance improvements that existing indexes are providing, and recommend which indexes to drop and which to add. Clicking on the Analysis button will provide additional report types that can be viewed or saved to disk in text format (you really should save them so that the information can be reviewed carefully later).

The last step in the tuning process is to implement the recommendations, or save the script to disk so that you can implement them later. I don't believe in doing anything before testing it, so I always create a script that I can modify before actually applying it. By saving the script to disk, and because the Index Tuning Wizard can't spell table or column names wrong, it can save you a lot of time by sparing you from having to write the syntax yourself (and possibly creating typing mistakes).

All in all, the Index Tuning Wizard provides a good starting point for tuning your databases. You should test its recommendations, before implementing them in production, by seeing how the execution plan for problem queries is affected by adding or removing an index, as recommended by the Wizard.

11

Chapter 12

SQL Server Replication

If your organization is geographically dispersed—with offices across many building, cities, states, or countries—getting a complete picture of corporate information can be difficult. Each office or division may have a subset of the data, but no one office has all of the data. Or the reverse might be true. Perhaps data is centralized at one location, but the field offices do not have a complete picture of the organization's data, which makes it difficult for employees to do their jobs. For example, let's say a salesperson in Phoenix is not aware that technical support in New York has not dealt with an outstanding critical client issue. The Phoenix employee calls the client to make a new sale and gets an earful. This is only one example of why organizations are implementing solutions that distribute data among several SQL Server databases using replication.

Replication and Distributed Data

The most common questions asked by many smaller organizations are, "Why have data on more than one server? Doesn't that cost more money with additional servers and such?" These are valid questions, and it is quite likely that smaller organizations may not require that data be distributed between multiple SQL Servers. If, for example, you are part of a company that has a single office with 10, 20, or even 50 employees, having two physical servers to replicate data may cost more money than it is worth. You may be better off spending money on a faster server with plenty of fault-tolerance built in instead. However, with SQL Server 2000 you don't need to have two servers. You can have replication between instances on the same server, which can be useful, such as when you need to keep a second copy of the data for test purposes.

12

Before we get into replication in a big way, you need to understand what is meant by distributed data and why it is advantageous. SQL Server supports two ways to distribute data across multiple databases or data sources—replication and distributed transactions (see Chapter 13). You can accomplish some of the following goals, in a broad sense, with either method:

- **Bring data closer to the user** In larger organizations with many offices, if you have a large central database that is accessed by everyone, a number of problems can crop up, with speed of the database being at the top of the list. If everyone is hammering the same set of disks, memory, and CPU, things will be slower.

Furthermore, if the network between the remote office and the central location goes down, some of the users will not be able to access the database, thereby causing losses in productivity. Moving data closer to the user can alleviate some or all of these problems. This leads me to the next advantage of replication and distributed transaction—site independence.

- **Site independence** With both distributed transactions and replication, if one of the sites or servers goes down, you can still work. In distributed transaction scenarios, this means that you cannot execute a Transact-SQL statement that would modify data on other servers, but there is nothing stopping you from modifying data only on your own server. Similarly, cross-server queries won't work. With replication, since all servers have a copy of at least part of the data, sites are virtually autonomous.

- **Separates reporting from transaction processing** A common problem in many organizations is using the same database for high-volume transactions (OLTP) and reporting (DSS). When this happens, the amount of locking increases and concurrency decreases. You can increase performance by replicating the data from the OLTP database to a reporting database, which can be on a different server. Users that need to run reports can use the DSS/reporting database server without impacting the OLTP users.

Whether you choose to implement distributed databases or replication, and, in the case of replication, which type you choose to implement, depends on the following factors:

- **Latency** Does the data need to be in sync on all servers at the same time, or can you live with some latency between the time a transaction is committed and the time the data appears on the other database? If you cannot live with any latency, you need to configure distributed transactions. If you can live with it, depending on the degree of acceptable latency, then one of the replication types may be useful.

- **Site autonomy** Is it acceptable to have data on one SQL Server that may be out-of-sync with other servers (for example, does all data across all servers need to satisfy relational integrity defined using primary and foreign keys)? If the answer is no, then distributed transactions need to be used. Otherwise, a replication type will suffice.

- **Transactional consistency** Does all the data need to be consistent with other related data? This is not really an issue with either distributed transactions or replication because data will not be available to the other database until the transaction is committed.

Using distributed transactions ensures that all data is in sync on all servers at the same time. But distributed transactions do have a downside: What happens if one of the servers is not available? The transaction cannot complete and must be rolled back on all servers, which can be problematic if the servers are distributed across the country or if you have unreliable networks between them. However, the advantages of distributed transactions include the ability to partition a complex application so that users have quick access to their data (on the local server) while always getting results that are 100 percent accurate for all data across the collection of servers on which data is distributed. Furthermore, by using views in SQL Server 2000, you can "federate" your data so that each server has a different part of the database, but queries can span data sources and be transparent to users.

Replication, on the other hand, is far more flexible, but does not guarantee that data on all servers will be in sync 100 percent of the time, and requires that you accept some latency. However, it can provide for varying degrees of site autonomy. It also lets you do such cool things as allowing field sales to enter orders on a notebook computer, which get merged back to the central database nightly through replication. It is, by far, the more flexible of the two options.

SQL Server Replication Architecture

Microsoft SQL Server replication allows the distribution of data between two or more SQL Servers, or other data sources. When planning replication, a database administrator needs to consider what data will be published, who will receive the data, how often the data must be synchronized, the underlying network, and other physical characteristics.

Microsoft SQL Server supports replication between various data sources including SQL Server, Oracle, Access, and any OLE-DB or ODBC data source conforming to SQL Server subscriber requirements for replication. In other words, SQL Server replication can be used to replicate data between a SQL Server database and an Oracle database. However, when using any data source outside of SQL Server, limitations do exist. For example, any OLE-DB or ODBC data source can act only as a subscriber to SQL Server data and cannot publish information back to SQL Server when using SQL Server replication (third-party products do exist that will do this, but they are expensive). Further, not all SQL Server data types may be supported by a third-party data source, which may prevent certain information from being replicated. Bi-directional replication, the capability for two or more servers in a replication scenario to publish to one another, is supported only between SQL Servers.

If you're deciding upon a replication strategy, you must consider the following two elements: the replication model to be used and the type of replication to be performed. Replication models deal with the relationship of the server that will be sending out, or publishing, the information to other servers in the replication scenario. The model is the physical implementation of your replication strategy. The type of replication employed determines what will occur when replication takes place and provides the functionality that outlines how replicated data will be maintained.

12

SQL Server Replication Models

Replication models use a publisher/distributor/subscriber metaphor, as shown in Figure 12-1. The server whose data will be replicated is the *publisher*; the server physically sending out changes to other servers is the *distributor*; and the server receiving the data is the *subscriber*. You can compare this process to the process of ordering a magazine, such as *Time*. When you subscribe to *Time* magazine, the publisher (Time/Life Publications) creates the publication and places it in the mail. The post office, the distributor, receives the publication (the copy of the magazine) from the publisher and distributes it to you, the subscriber, via your mailbox.

There are three basic replication models that SQL Server supports, as follows:

- Central publisher/distributor model
- Single-subscriber/multiple-publisher model
- Multiple-publisher/multiple-subscriber model

All other replication models that can be configured are variations on these three basic models.

When choosing a replication model, you must take into account which SQL Server instance will make the data available to others (the publisher), which one will send this information to the subscribers (the distributor), and which servers will receive the information (the subscribers). It is possible for a single SQL Server instance to hold all three roles (for example, it could publish from one database to another database on the same SQL Server, using itself as the distributor).

The actual data to be published also follows the publisher/distributor/ subscriber metaphor. The smallest unit to publish is an article. A publication is a collection of articles. An article can be a single table in a database, a subset of that table containing only certain columns (vertical filtering), a subset of a table containing just certain rows (horizontal filtering), or just certain columns and certain rows in a table (vertical and horizontal filtering).

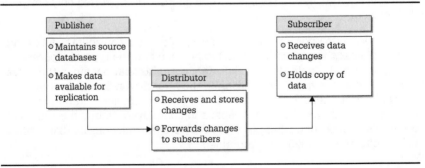

Figure 12-1.   The publisher/distributor/subscriber metaphor

In SQL Server, publications cannot span databases. If several different databases from one SQL Server (the publisher)) need to be replicated, multiple publications must be created on the SQL Server. However, it is possible for the database being published to have several publications for the same or different data. For example, you might want to publish just the inventory stock level tables from the order-entry database in one publication, and publish a separate publication that contains order information from the same database. Because you can configure security (such as which servers are allowed to receive the published data) for each publication, these two publications might be available to the same, or different, sets of subscribers.

Central Publisher/Distributor Model

The central publisher/distributor model is the most common and, very often, the easiest to implement. This model is used when a single SQL Server instance contains information that should be replicated to other SQL Server instances in the enterprise. In this model, one server is configured as the publisher/distributor. It is responsible for both publishing and sending articles to all those SQL Servers that have requested subscriptions to the available publications, as shown in Figure 12-2.

This is useful, for example, in an organization with a central SQL Server that stores all the information on customer orders. In this case, the server is used by the order-entry clerks to enter customer orders, but the data may also be useful to sales managers for generating sales reports, to accounting managers for sales and expense tracking, and so on. A performance problem may arise if a sales manager decides to run a report during a very busy time of the day because SQL Server's processing of the report will impact the entry of new orders. To alleviate this, replication could be configured between the order-entry SQL Server (the publisher) and another machine running SQL Server that will subscribe to the sales data and can be used to process the reports. The benefit of this configuration is that a sales manager will not slow down the order-entry process if he decides to run a lengthy sales report.

12

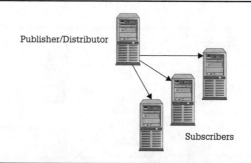

Figure 12-2.   The central publisher/distributor replication model

The central publisher/distributor model can be used in any situation where data from a central source needs to be available to users at other locations. The main reason for using this model is to lessen the impact of additional processing on the central SQL Server by allowing a subset or the same data to be available on another machine.

Single-Subscriber/Multiple-Publisher Model

The single-subscriber/multiple-publisher model, shown in Figure 12-3, can commonly be found in organizations with multiple offices, each of which manages data on its own. In this example, corporate headquarters needs to get information on activity in each location and needs to do company-wide roll-ups and reporting to gauge overall progress toward company goals. In this scenario, each office replicates the data it generates to the central subscriber (the head office) where it can be combined with data from other offices, thus allowing management to have an overall status.

When planning for the single-subscriber/multiple-publisher model, make sure the structure of the database takes into account that a single table at the central subscriber SQL Server instance may have data from several publishers. You need to add a column to every table participating in replication that identifies from where the data in the table originated. For example, assume you have an order-entry system in which each region enters its own orders, but replicates this information to the master orders table in the head office database. Because each region is responsible for generating its own order numbers, a mechanism has to be implemented to distinguish order number 1000 in region 1 from order number 1000 in region 4. To accomplish this, you would just assign a region code to each table. When orders are entered in region 1, the region code column would contain 1, whereas an order in region 4 would show 4 in the region code column. When this data is replicated to the head office, the region code distinguishes the same order number and allows a proper roll-up to be performed. Without a region code, depending on the time each region replicates with the head office, it is possible for region 1 to overwrite information already replicated from region 4. Generally, in these situations, the primary key for the table would be a composite key that includes the order number and region code.

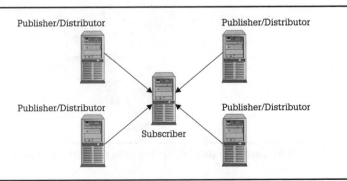

Figure 12-3.   The single-subscriber/multiple-publisher replication model

The Multiple-Publisher/Multiple-Subscriber Model

The multiple-publisher/multiple-subscriber model of replication consists of several SQL Servers publishing data to one another and subscribing to data from one another, as shown in Figure 12-4. This model is the most difficult to implement because you must carefully plan for, and configure, what is to be published, and to whom. You need to make sure that each publisher is not publishing to itself, thereby creating a potentially endless loop.

The multiple-publisher/multiple-subscriber model allows for all servers to see all data, assuming that is the desired result, or a subset of data not originating locally, depending on the filtering applied. This model might be useful in organizations that operate on a very distributed fashion, with each office needing to get information from others for a complete enterprise picture. This is the closest to a fully-distributed system that replication allows.

An international sporting event, such as the World Cup or the Olympics, is one scenario in which the multiple-publisher/multiple-subscriber replication model might be implemented. Because activities take place at several different venues, each venue would store its data on a different SQL Server. However, information about the results of all activities taking place in the World Cup or Olympics need to be available at all locations so that all participants, spectators, and officials can track the progress of the entire event. Each of the servers at each location would publish its changes to all other servers at all other locations so that all servers had a combined picture. Users accessing the data at one location would receive a complete picture of all activities for the event.

A similar scenario can also be used for a farm of SQL Servers servicing web sites that publish the results of each event. Due to the volume of transactions, the data may need to be available on several different servers at the same time, with the results from one server being replicated to all others. When data is accessed through the web site, the web server could connect to any of the SQL Servers to present the data to the user and no one server would then be a bottleneck.

12

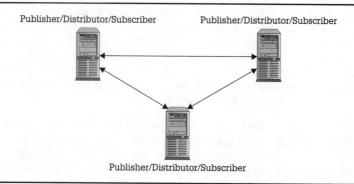

Publisher/Distributor/Subscriber   Publisher/Distributor/Subscriber

Publisher/Distributor/Subscriber

Figure 12-4.   The multiple-publisher/multiple-subscriber replication model

In this replication model, the data to be published must be horizontally filtered. In other words, only rows that have been entered at that server should be sent to all the other servers. Because each server acts as both a publisher and a subscriber, an improperly configured server could replicate information back to a server that originally sent it. If this occurs, the entire process breaks down, and replication will probably have to be reconfigured. For example, a region code can be used to designate the origin of data for replication. Each server publishes to all other servers only data that contains its own region code; it does not publish information that it did not originate. This ensures that region 1 does not end up publishing region 2's information back to region 2, and so on.

Remote Distribution Server

In all the models so far, we have assumed that the same SQL Server computer performs the publisher and distributor roles. In actuality, while any one SQL Server can be a publisher, distributor, and even subscriber, it can be beneficial to separate the task of distributing data from that of publishing it for performance, and other, reasons.

When using a remote distributor, the database administrator configures the publisher to send its changes to another SQL Server, the distribution server. The distribution server can accept published data from one or more publishers and can send this information to one or more subscribers. Just as the post office acts as a distribution vehicle for Time/Life Publications, *Newsweek*, and many other periodicals, a distribution server in SQL Server replication can accept data from, and send data to, many other servers participating in replication.

Figure 12-5 shows a situation in which a remote distributor would be beneficial. In this scenario, a server in New York contains information that users in London, Paris, Rome, and Dublin need to perform their jobs. One way that replication could be configured to provide these users with the necessary information is for New York to publish and distribute the data to all of the European offices directly. However, doing so would increase the communication costs and require New York to send the same, or similar, data to all four sites individually, which obviously would create four times the bandwidth across the Atlantic. To make this process more efficient, New York could publish to London and use London as a distributor for the rest of Europe. This would reduce the transatlantic bandwidth requirements (data would only need to be sent once to London). This configuration might even provide for better performance and more timely data as it is more than likely that communication lines between London and Paris are quicker than those between New York and Paris.

Even in situations where servers are physically closer than in the above example, using a remote distributor may improve performance. The publishing server only needs to send its changes to the distributor, which can worry about getting it out to the many subscribers. The publisher is then able to use its processing power for processing user requests instead

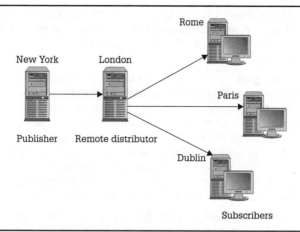

Figure 12-5. Using a remote distributor in replication

of using it to send the data to 10, 20, or 100 other SQL Servers. This is particularly useful when you want to separate OLTP databases from those used for reporting. Using a remote distributor ensures that a publisher spends its time doing what it should—processing user requests—and not managing distribution of data for replication.

Replication Mechanics

In processing replication, SQL Server uses a number of agents that are all part of the SQL Server Agent service, which must be started in order for replication to work. These agents perform the actual work of ensuring that data is replicated between the publishers and subscribers, and no changes get lost. Because many of the agents can reside on the publisher, distributor, or subscriber, support for both push and pull subscriptions (described later in the "Push and Pull Subscriptions" section of this chapter) is available in SQL Server.

Replication Agents

The agents that SQL Server uses when performing replication tasks include the following:

- **Snapshot Agent**   Typically running on the distributor, the Snapshot Agent is responsible for preparing the schema information and initial data files that will be transferred to the subscriber when a snapshot refresh takes place, or when transactional or snapshot replication is initiated. It records when snapshot refreshes took place and also creates the stored procedures on the subscriber for immediate or queued updating subscribers (covered in the "SQL Server Replication Types" section of this chapter).

12

- **Distribution Agent**   Used in snapshot and transactional replication, the Distribution Agent moves the data to the subscribers. The Distribution Agent runs on the distributor for push subscriptions and on the subscriber for pull subscriptions.

- **Log Reader Agent**   As changes are made to the published tables, the Log Reader Agent monitors the transaction log for those changes in transactional replication. It then copies those transactions to the **distribution** database on the distributor, where they are stored until sent to subscribers. Until a transaction has been sent to a subscriber, its data will be held in the **distribution** database, but the publishing server will be able to truncate the transaction log as soon as the Log Reader Agent copies the changes to the **distribution** database. Each published database has its own Log Reader Agent.

- **Merge Agent** (SQL Server 7 and 2000 only)   Used to apply the initial snapshot to the subscribers when merge replication is configured. After the initial snapshot is loaded, the Merge Agent is responsible for ensuring that updates on the subscriber are propagated to the publisher and vice versa. The Merge Agent runs on the distributor for push subscriptions, and on the subscriber for pull subscriptions. Each merge subscription has its own Merge Agent.

- **Queue Reader Agent** (SQL Server 7 and 2000 only)   Running on the distributor, the Queue Reader Agent is responsible for taking messages from a queue and applying them to the published database. It is used when queued updating subscribers have been configured on snapshot or transactional publications, or if queued updating has been specified as a failover for immediate updating subscribers.

- **Miscellaneous agents**   A number of additional agents, varying by SQL Server version and replication types used, also exist to perform housekeeping chores. These include Subscription Cleanup Agent, Distribution Cleanup Agent, and others.

Push and Pull Subscriptions

After choosing a replication model that meets the business requirements, you need to decide which will initiate the subscriptions: the publisher (push subscription) or the subscriber (pull subscription).

Push subscriptions are used in environments where the publisher wants to have greater control over who will receive the information. In this scenario, when defining publications and articles, the database administrator decides which servers will receive the publication and configures the subscribing server—including the database in which the replicated data will be stored—from the publishing console. In this way, the DBA of the subscribing server need not worry about configuring replication at the receiving end, as it will all be done from the publisher. This is useful if the data is of a sensitive nature, and the load on the distributor is of secondary importance. Push subscriptions do require the distribution server to use more processor time and perform more work to ensure that the data is "pushed" out as configured.

Pull subscriptions, on the other hand, are most useful in environments where security of the data being published is of secondary concern, or when the data has been vetted to contain only those elements that can safely be published to other servers. For example, any branch of the company may want to always have an up-to-date phone list. The Human Resources Department at corporate headquarters may provide this information in a publication that any branch can subscribe to and store on its own SQL Server. In this case, the DBA of the subscription server determines to what data to subscribe and in which database to store it. The DBA of the publishing server doesn't have to worry about who actually receives the data, thereby lessening her workload.

SQL Server Replication Types

Once a replication model has been selected, the type of replication to be performed must be planned. Replication types control how much data will be transferred and when. Microsoft SQL Server 7 and 2000 support three basic types of replication: snapshot, transactional, and merge. SQL Server 6.*x* supports snapshot and transactional replication. Which replication type you choose depends on the physical characteristics of the network, and how recent or "fresh" the data must be at the subscription sites.

In SQL Server 7 and 2000, snapshot and transactional replication types also support immediate or queued updating subscribers. The idea with updating subscribers is that most of the time users on the subscribing server will be reading data. Once in a while, they will need to make changes to the data (INSERT, UPDATE, or DELETE, for example). When those changes occur, they should take place on both the publisher and subscriber. With immediate updating subscribers, the change occurs on both at the same time, and the Microsoft Distributed Transaction Coordinator (MSDTC) ensures that the updates on both are successful. MSDTC will be described in more detail in Chapter 13. If a change cannot be made to both the publisher and the subscriber, it cannot take place, unless the immediate updating option has been configured with queued updating as a failover.

When queued updating subscribers is selected, the change takes place on the subscriber first and is then queued to take place on the publisher. This means that the subscriber will have more recent data than the publisher for a short time. The queue can either be a SQL Server table, when defined to be stored in the database, or a Microsoft Message Queue (MSMQ) v2 message queue, in SQL Server 2000. Triggers that are created on the replicated tables when the subscription is defined on the subscriber perform the placement of data changes to the queue location (table or message queue). If a publisher cannot accept changes when they occur, the changes will be held in the queue until the publisher is available again.

Any of the replication models outlined above will support any replication type. Furthermore, more than one replication type can be supported by the same database, though a publication can support one, and only one, replication type.

12

Snapshot Replication

Snapshot replication is useful in environments where subscribers generally require read-only access to the data, and will not be publishing data back to the server from which the snapshot was received. You can, however, use immediate or queued updating subscribers to propagate changes. Snapshot replication is most often employed in the single-publisher/multiple-subscriber and single-subscriber/multiple-publisher replication models. Figure 12-6 shows the process for snapshot replication.

With snapshot replication, a bulk transfer of all data within the publication is sent to each subscriber. This includes all the data at the time the snapshot is published. In other words, subscribers get a complete refresh of all the information in the publication. This replaces the data that already exists in the subscription databases with the current data at the publisher. The snapshot folder can be a folder on a Windows-based computer accessible using a UNC name, or, in SQL Server 2000, by using the FTP protocol. By default, the snapshot folder is located by using the administrative share (C$, D$, and so on) of the drive where SQL Server is installed, though this can be changed when creating a publication.

Snapshot replication is best used in situations where the publisher and subscriber are connected by a high-speed network link. The distribution server in this scenario does not store the snapshot data, but keeps track of the fact that a snapshot is required or has been completed. In a push subscription, the Distribution Agent, a part of the SQL Agent service, runs on the distributor and builds the tables, indexes, and data on the subscriber server. In a pull subscription, the Distribution Agent runs on the subscriber. In all cases, the Snapshot Agent runs on the distributor to track the status of the snapshot.

Snapshot replication can work well in cases where data latency (having data that is slightly older than from where it originates) is not much of an

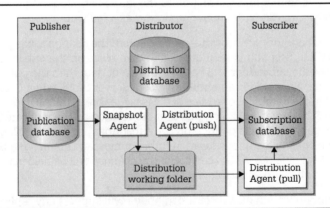

Figure 12-6.   Snapshot replication

issue. Furthermore, because subscribers have their own copy of the data, no locking issues or potential replication conflicts exist, since the data only originates on one server—the publisher. When using immediate updating subscribers, locking can be an issue if the publisher is busy and changes are being made to data. This is why queued updating subscribers are preferred and offer more flexibility—but greater latency. Snapshot replication can be scheduled to occur at off-peak hours to minimize potential network bottlenecks.

Transactional Replication

With transactional replication, as incremental changes to the data are made at the publisher, they are sent to the subscriber. Transactional replication with immediate updating subscribers provides all subscribers with the most up-to-date information (minimal latency). This replication type can be used with all models, including multiple-publisher/multiple-subscriber.

In transactional replication, changes to tables that are designated for replication are tracked in the transaction log. When data in those tables is modified, the Log Reader Agent (a part of the SQL Agent service) reads the changes and stores them temporarily in the **distribution** database. The Distribution Agent then sends the changes to the subscribers (in a push subscription), or the Distribution Agent reads the changes on the subscriber from the **distribution** database (in a pull subscription), as shown in Figure 12-7.

Transactional replication most often runs in real-time and works best when a constant network connection is available between all servers participating in this type of replication. In cases where a subscriber in transactional replication is down, changes for that server will remain in the **distribution** database until it becomes available.

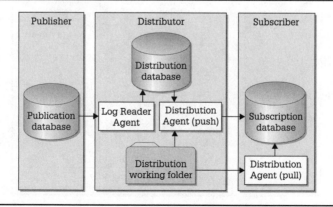

Figure 12-7.   Transactional replication

Note that in order for transactional replication to work, an initial snapshot of the published data must be sent to each subscriber. This is used to provide a starting point for both the publisher and subscriber to ensure that they are both in sync. When both servers have the same data, changes to the data can be applied as additional transactions. Furthermore, the snapshot can be scheduled to occur at regular intervals to ensure that a refresh of the data takes place to bring both sides in sync, if they are not. Immediate or queued updating subscribers can also be configured when using transactional replication in SQL Server 2000.

Merge Replication

Merge replication is somewhat of a compromise between snapshot replication and transactional replication. In a merge scenario, changes are not applied to the subscriber database as they are made on the publisher; instead, a Merge Agent applies changes to the database, either periodically or on demand. The end result, at the time of the merge, is that the data on all servers is in sync, and any conflicts that exist are reported or resolved according to a predefined set of rules.

Merge replication is most useful in environments using the multiple-publisher/multiple-subscriber or single-subscriber/multiple publisher model, or in those where conflicts (changing the same data on two servers between replication intervals, for example) are not expected. For example, in a situation where many sites will publish information and also receive information from other sites (see Figure 12-8), merge replication can be used to periodically synchronize all the sites and ensure that they all have the same data. Using merge replication, all participants will have the same set of data even though it may not arrive at its destination in the same way. In other words, transactional changes are not applied, so only the end result of the transactions is available.

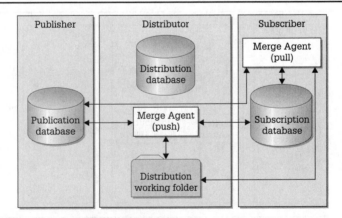

Figure 12-8.   Merge replication type

Like transactional replication, merge replication requires an initial snapshot to ensure that both the subscriber and publisher have the same set of synchronized data to begin with. Following this snapshot, the Merge Agent will periodically, or on demand, merge changes from all participants to come at a synchronized database when the merge is complete.

Designing and Planning Replication

Now that you know about the various replication models and types, you should know that the key to a successful replication strategy is proper planning. You need to answer several questions to determine the best model and type to use.

What Data Should be Published

Before you replicate data, you need to decide what databases and tables will be replicated. The easy thing to do might be to publish all the tables in a single publication and let people pick and choose those articles they want. However, this can create additional strain on the distribution server and require much more space for the **distribution** database. Carefully determining what needs to be published will reduce the overhead of replication.

You also need to consider how articles should be grouped. Will you publish all the data in the table, or will you vertically or horizontally filter the data? Will you create one publication for data that all subscribers will need, and additional publications for only certain subscribers? Or will you create publications for each subscriber containing both the global and individual data for that subscriber? The advantage of creating one global publication along with individual subscriber-specific publications is that changes to the global publication can be made once, and then automatically propagated to the subscribers. The disadvantage is that you might give out too much information to certain sites, and cause more work for the distributor. You can simplify adding or removing individual articles for a subscriber by sending all data to a subscriber in one publication. But if the same table needs to go to many subscribers, it requires more administrative work. The business requirements and security concerns may decide this for you.

12

Who Receives the Data and How Often

What servers will subscribe to the data, and are these SQL Servers or ODBC data sources? If the subscriber is a SQL Server, will it also publish the information back? If so, how will conflicts be resolved? Typically, once the question of "what" is answered, the "who" is quite easy. However, if ODBC data sources will participate in replication, you must keep in mind the capabilities of those sources. Publications should reflect the data types supported by all subscribers, or different publications should be set up to accommodate the differences.

The second part of this question deals with selecting the appropriate replication type: snapshot, transactional, or merge. After you select a type, you need to determine how much time should be allowed between data transfers. SQL Server supports nearly 100 percent real-time replication for transactional replication. In other words, as changes are made to tables included in publications, those changes are sent to the subscribers. However, for snapshot and merge replication, a schedule (hourly, daily, weekly, or another internal) must be configured for each, or all, subscribers. You must decide if changes to the subscription databases will be allowed with snapshot and transactional replication, and, if so, choose which updating subscriber mode—immediate, queued, or both, for transactional replication.

Considering Physical Network Characteristics

To decide on the type and frequency of replication, you also need to consider the physical characteristics of the underlying network. For example, are all the nodes (servers) that are participating in replication always available and reachable, or are there times when they cannot accept changes? If they are all available, transactional replication can be used and scheduled to always occur. However, if some nodes are down sometimes, you may wish to use merge replication or snapshot replication to send changes only at certain times, or implement queued updating subscribers. You may also configure transactional replication to take place at certain hours of the day. Keep in mind, however, that this may increase the disk space requirements of the **distribution** database. Generally, if the network is always available, and all nodes are always up, transactional replication will work well. If this is not the case, consider merge or snapshot replication. They may have a higher latency, but the data will be up-to-date when the merge or snapshot is complete.

Another issue to address is the speed and capacity of the network. If all nodes are in the same building, and you are using a Fast or Gigabit Ethernet, you can replicate more data, and performance will be good. However, if wide area network links exist, you might have to filter or partition the data to minimize the amount of network traffic. You also need to think about other applications making use of the wide area network and the effect of replication traffic on other business activities. If the network is busy during the day, but relatively idle at night, consider scheduling replication to occur at off-peak periods.

Finally, you need to consider how reliable the network is. In North America we tend to be relatively spoiled by our communications infrastructure and assume that in the event of a power outage or other anomaly, the phone lines will still work. We have an "expectation of dial tone" and don't see why we shouldn't. However, especially if your organization is international, this same expectation may not hold true. We have all heard stories of unreliable phone lines in certain parts of the world. If this applies to servers in your replication scenario, plan accordingly. For example, make sure that the **distribution** database has sufficient storage space to keep transactions for those nodes affected by poor communications infrastructure, so that they may be applied when the network is back up. The physical characteristics of the network will play a role in determining the type and frequency of replication, and must be considered in the planning process.

Choosing the Type and Number of Subscribers

Microsoft SQL Server supports three types of subscribers: local, global, and anonymous. Only the publisher knows the local subscribers, which is the default. This ensures that no other servers are aware of who else is receiving the information, thereby avoiding a potential security hole. For example, an administrator at the head office of a corporation could configure replication of sales data to certain branch offices, but might not want all branch administrators to know who is getting the data, and who is not. This can be used to prevent smaller branch offices that have servers incapable of handling the volume of data this replication would entail from saying, "Why can't I get this data if the other guy can?" It is security from the standpoint that branch administrators, who may not be fully trusted by the head office, can't ask about what they don't know about. In old spy movies, this was sometimes referred to as a "need to know" basis. If you don't need to know, you won't know.

Global subscribers are known to all servers participating in replication. This is typically used in organizations where the data to be published must be available to a large number of people and is not of a sensitive nature. Because the subscriber is known to all other servers participating in replication, that subscriber may leave itself open for someone to tamper with the configuration. Hence, this setting for a subscriber is not recommended in most environments.

Subscribers can also be configured as anonymous. Anonymous subscribers are known to the publisher only while they are connected. This is useful in situations where you publish to the Internet. An example of this might be an organization with salespeople on the road. These individuals may have notebook computers running the desktop version of SQL Server on Windows XP Professional. Using replication, the field sales force can use the Internet to receive updates on the status of their orders, or other information such as new product offerings and the like. While connected, they are known to the publisher. This configuration assumes that anyone can be a subscriber and replicate, so it should not be used for sensitive data unless other security mechanisms are implemented, such as protecting the FTP location for the subscribers with Windows security.

Considering Storage Space

Replication requires that storage space be considered from both the **distribution** database and the replication distribution directory. The factors to consider when determining space requirements for replication include the following:

- The number of articles and publications
- The replication frequency
- Replication latency
- Type of replication

The number of articles and publications will have a direct impact on the size of the **distribution** database. The larger the number of publications and articles, the more disk space required to store changes to those articles in the **distribution** database. When you're setting the size of the **distribution** database, you need to consider articles, publications, and the number of publishers that will use the distributor.

All data to be forwarded on to subscribers in a replication scenario is located in the **distribution** database. This is especially important in transaction-based replication where changes to publications and articles are sent to the distributor as they occur. If the number of changes is large, and distribution to the subscribers is infrequent, the **distribution** database must store all those changes until subscribers are ready to receive them. This may require significant disk space in a very busy database. When replication is frequent, less space will be required because changes can be forwarded to subscribers more often, thereby reducing the amount of disk space used on the distributor.

Note that the **distribution** database is like any other database with a data and log component. As with any other database, the **distribution** database must be backed up, and the transaction log cleared out. If the **distribution** database receives a large number of changes from publishers on an ongoing basis, you'll want to implement a backup strategy that periodically backs up the transaction log of the **distribution** database so that its transaction log does not completely fill up, which would cause replication either to fail or pause for a period of time.

To calculate storage requirements for the **distribution** database, you factor in the number of rows replicated, the size of those rows, and the frequency of changes sent to the distributor. It is often better to over-allocate space for the data and log portions of the **distribution** database than to under-allocate. Granted, this may waste disk space, but it may also prevent replication failure should the log or data portion become full.

For each article in transactional replication, consider the number of INSERT and UPDATE statements, the number of transactions (per hour or between backups of the **distribution** database and/or log), and the size of the average transaction. Add up these figures for all articles, and you should have a rough idea of the space requirements of the **distribution** database. Also, remember that not all subscribers may be able to pull or have data pushed to them all the time, so there may be a need to keep data in the **distribution** database for several minutes or hours before it is delivered to a subscriber. For those subscribers that are not receiving real-time replication data, allocate additional storage for the period prior to data delivery.

Other storage considerations center on the type of replication scenario used. If you use transactional replication, the **distribution** database requires more storage. However, snapshot and merge replication place the disk storage burden on the file system of the distributor by placing snapshots of publication tables in the distribution working folder (located at \\<*servername*>\C$\ Program Files\Microsoft SQL Server\MSSQL\REPLDATA for a default instance of SQL Server 2000 in the default install location). The amount of data to be stored in this folder is directly proportional to the size of the snapshot or merge job. Because this type of replication transfers all the data from the publisher to the distributor, and then from the distributor to the subscriber, if a publication is defined to take all the data from a database, the storage space required will be the size of all the data plus some overhead. If the same distributor is responsible for servicing multiple publishers, the disk storage requirements for this folder may be quite large. To ensure that SQL Server replication does not run out of disk space, you can relocate this folder to a hard drive with more disk space. As long as the new location of this folder is available to each of the subscribers, this should not present a problem, but it will solve the issue of snapshot or merge replication failing due to lack of disk space.

Data Definition Considerations

During replication, the data types used within the articles and publications also need to be considered. Use of certain data types require that changes be made during the establishment of replication between a publisher and subscriber.

Using timestamp, uniqueidentifier, and Other User-Defined Data Types in Replication

When planning replication, you should note that certain data type considerations must be made. First, a **timestamp** data type must be converted on the subscriber to a **binary** data type. The **timestamp** data type on the publisher indicates the date and time a row was inserted in the published table. When this is replicated, if the same data type exists on the subscriber, the time reflected in the data on the subscriber will show when the record was inserted in the subscriber database. As there is latency between the publisher inserting data and the subscriber receiving the same row, this will cause different values on the publisher and subscriber. Because this would create a data inconsistency, the **timestamp** data type must be converted to one that can store the same value, without changing the value. Therefore, SQL Server automatically converts a column defined as a **timestamp** data type on the publisher to a **binary** data type on the subscriber.

12

Second, the **uniqueidentifier** data type, which creates a Globally Unique Identifier (GUID) and is used with the NEWID function (which actually generates the identification number), cannot be fully replicated. The data type itself can be replicated between a publisher and subscriber, but it is not possible to replicate the function because a subscriber may combine data from several different publishers in the same subscriber database.

Finally, any user-defined data types cannot be replicated unless the exact same user-defined data type already exists in the subscriber database. To get around this problem, creation of the user-defined data type on the subscriber database needs to take place before the start of replication. This ensures that all data and all data types are properly replicated, and users will see the same information in the published and subscribed databases.

The IDENTITY Property

SQL Server automatically converts columns with the IDENTITY property set into their respective data types (normally **int**) and replicates the values, but not the property, from the publisher to the subscriber. In this way, the data on both the publisher and subscriber will have the same values, even though gaps may exist in the subscriber's data, if horizontal partitioning has been enabled.

The NOT FOR REPLICATION Option

In SQL Server 7 and 2000, you can set the NOT FOR REPLICATION option on a table to tell the server not to bother enforcing certain elements such as CHECK constraints, the IDENTITY property, and triggers on the table, when data is received at the subscriber as a result of replication. This ensures that the data sent to a subscriber from the publisher will not have these elements checked, but, for any data modified on the same server as a result of user activity, the server will verify the CHECK constraint, run the triggers, and maintain the IDENTITY property. This maintains good data integrity on databases and tables that are created as a result of replication or by concurrent user activity, thus providing the best of both worlds and ensuring that the data makes sense and is consistent.

Proper planning is required to ensure that IDENTITY property values take into account that data might come from the publisher, as well as be entered by a user. An example of this is the partitioning of data newly added by user activity through the use of a larger starting point on the IDENTITY property of a table. For example, if the same table includes both replicated data and data entered through user activity, the IDENTITY property on the column in the subscription database could be set to start at 100,000 for new additions by a user, and all lower values can then be used by replication (assuming the publisher will not have 100,000 rows replicated to the subscriber). This is especially important if the column with the IDENTITY property is the PRIMARY KEY in a table, which is often the case.

This could be used when the replication type is multiple-publisher/multiple-subscriber (all data from one site is sent to all other sites and also received from all other sites). The data to be replicated is horizontally partitioned, but because users will be INSERTing and UPDATEing on each server, you might want to define a CHECK constraint to ensure that the data being entered into any one server contains the region code for that server. This ensures that salespeople in a region enter only orders from customers in that region, yet it still allows all servers to see all orders for all customers. The NOT FOR REPLICATION option would ensure that the CHECK constraint was enforced for locally entered data, but not for data received and entered as a result of replication.

Configuring SQL Server Replication

Once you have planned SQL Server replication and made all decisions regarding the replication model and type to use, whether push or pull subscribers will be configured, and whether or not a remote distributor is needed, the actual process of configuring replication almost seems anti-climactic. You typically configure replication using SQL Enterprise Manager, although you can use system stored procedures to accomplish these tasks.

Configuring a Distributor

Before you can configure a publisher and publish your data, you must configure one of your SQL Server instances as a distributor. In fact, if you attempt to configure publishing on a SQL Server, you will be asked first to specify whether you will use a local or remote distributor. If you specify local, a distributor will be configured and a **distribution** database will be created.

The two most common ways to configure a SQL Server instance to be a distributor are by using SQL Enterprise Manager and selecting Configure Publishing, Subscribers, And Distribution from Tools I Replication (see Figure 12-9), or by using system stored procedures. Unless you have a reason to use the system stored procedures, you will, like over 90 percent of the DBAs out there, use SQL Enterprise Manager. Table 12-1 lists the system stored procedures available for configuring and managing a distributor in SQL Server 2000, although their syntax, which can be found in SQL Server Books Online, will not be described in detail here (because almost everyone uses SQL Enterprise Manager).

12

NOTE *You can also use SQL Distributed Management Objects (SQL-DMO) to configure replication. SQL-DMO allows you to incorporate setting up and managing replication within a Microsoft Visual Studio-based application, or a web site using ASP or ASP.NET.*

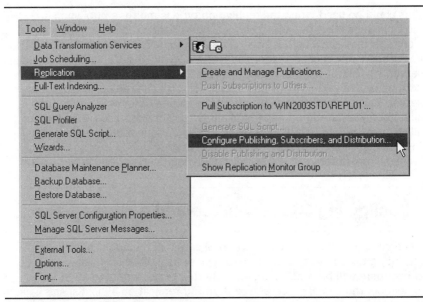

Figure 12-9.   Using SQL Enterprise Manager, you configure replication from the Tools menu.

Stored Procedure	Purpose/Description
sp_adddistributor	Adds an entry in the **sysservers** system table in the **master** database to indicate that the specified server is a distributor for replication.
sp_changedistributor_property	Changes the heartbeat interval (maximum number of minutes an agent can run without logging a status message) on the distributor, and may include other properties.
sp_dropdistributor	Removes the current SQL Server as a distributor. You must drop all **distribution** databases before executing this procedure.
sp_helpdistributor	Lists information about the **distribution** database, working path, SQL Server Agent logon account, and other details on the current SQL Server instance configured as a distributor.
sp_adddistributiondb	Creates a **distribution** database and installs all required objects in the database to support distribution. The database name can be specified, although **distribution** is typically used.

Table 12-1.   System Stored Procedures Used to Manage Publishers

Stored Procedure	Purpose/Description
sp_changedistributiondb	Changes properties of the **distribution** database including retention period and other values.
sp_dropdistributiondb	Drops the **distribution** database from the SQL Server instance. You should make certain that no publisher is using the database before dropping it.
sp_helpdistributiondb	Displays properties of the specified **distribution** database including log and data file sizes, retention settings, and others.

Table 12-1. System Stored Procedures Used to Manage Publishers (*continued*)

Important parameters you may need to specify as you configure a distributor include the startup account the SQL Server Agent service will use, and the location for snapshots. In order for the distributor to be able to communicate with both publishers and subscribers, the SQL Server Agent startup account that will be used cannot be the Local System Account, which has no permissions outside of the local computer. For this reason, you need to create a domain-level SQL Server Agent startup account and make it a member of the Administrators local group on each SQL Server that will be a distributor, publisher, or subscriber in replication.

The account you will use does not need to be a member of the Domain Admins global group, but it needs to be configured with all logon hours enabled and password never expires, and it needs to have the ability to log on to each computer that will be part of your replication scenario. Furthermore, make sure the account is granted the Logon as a Service right so that it can successfully start up the SQL Server Agent service. Most of this, with the exception of creating the startup account, is accomplished by the Configure Publishing and Distribution wizard that configured publishing and distribution on the server. Failing to perform these tasks could cause replication to fail or stop working.

12

Because snapshots are used to initiate all types of replication, subscribers need to be able to access the Snapshot folder to download the files and start the process. The default location for a Snapshot folder is via the administrative share (C$, D$, and so on) where SQL Server is installed. When configuring distribution using the Configure Publishing and Distribution wizard, you are prompted for the location of the Snapshot folder (see Figure 12-10). Specifying a shared folder on the network that does not require administrative permissions is a better idea. By using a nonadministrative share, you can grant the SQL Server Agent account membership in a group other than Domain Admins, thereby decreasing any security threat, and still allowing replication to take place. You would then set appropriate permissions

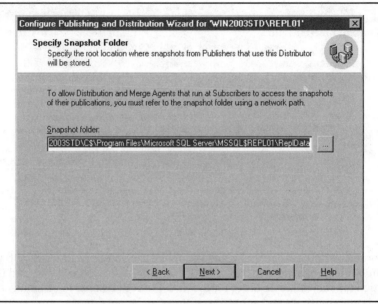

Figure 12-10. Specify a location for the Snapshot folder when configuring a distributor.

on the Snapshot folder share for all accounts and groups that need it. You can even place the Snapshot folder share on a network attached storage (NAS) device and reduce some of the workload of the distributor.

Running the Configure Publishing and Distribution wizard, you will be asked to choose whether to configure distribution using the defaults or to specify each required option. If you choose to specify the options, you can configure the name, data file, and log file location of the **distribution** database (see Figure 12-11). Notice that you cannot specify the size using the wizard, although you can do so afterwards using SQL Enterprise Manager or the ALTER DATABASE command—just as you can for any database. The Configure Publishing and Distribution wizard will ask you to specify which publishers can use this distributor, and then begins the process of configuring a publisher.

If you do not want to make the current SQL Server instance a publisher, you can click Next without selecting any servers or databases and your server will only be a distributor. The wizard will show a dialog box indicating the status as each required step is performed. You will also be informed that SQL Server Replication Monitor has been installed in the console tree for the distribution server.

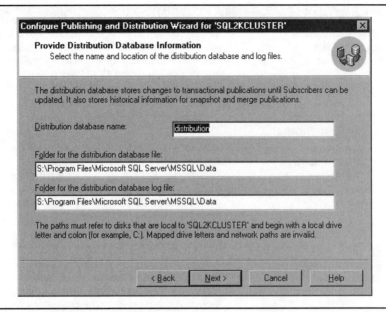

Figure 12-11. Specify the name, data file, and log file locations for the distribution database.

Configuring Publishing

Once you have configured a SQL Server as a distributor, you can configure the same, or a different, instance of SQL Server as a publisher. You can use SQL Enterprise Manager or any of the system stored procedures listed in Table 12-2 to manage a publisher and its publications. The steps involved in managing a publisher include the following:

1. Configure the computer as a publisher and specify a distributor to use.

2. Select databases to be published.

3. Determine which tables will be published and whether or not filtering is required (define the articles for your publications).

4. Create publications in the database by specifying one or more articles.

5. Specify who will be allowed to subscribe to the publications and whether or not publications will be pushed or pulled.

12

Stored Procedure	Purpose/Description
sp_adddistpublisher sp_addpublisher (SQL Server 6.x)	Configures the indicated publisher to use a specific distributor. You specify the publisher and distributor instance name, as well as authentication security between them (Integrated or SQL Server authentication), and so on. Execute this system stored procedure on the distributor.
sp_changedistpublisher	Modifies the properties of the publisher at the distributor, such as active status, for example.
sp_dropdistpublisher sp_droppublisher (SQL Server 6.x)	Executed on the distributor, drops the specified publisher from the **distribution** database, and optionally verifies that the publisher has dropped references to the distributor.
sp_helpdistpublisher	Returns information on a publisher acting as its own distributor.
sp_addpublication sp_addmergepublication	Adds a publication on the local publisher. Note: For merge replication, all system stored procedures to be used include the keyword *merge* within the procedure name, and have different parameters.
sp_changepublication sp_changemergepublication	Modifies the properties of a publication.
sp_droppublication sp_dropmergepublication	Removes a publication and its associated articles from the publisher.
sp_addpublication_snapshot	Creates a Snapshot Agent for a snapshot or transactional replication publication.
sp_helppublication sp_helpmergepublication	Displays information on the properties of a publication.
sp_addarticle sp_addmergearticle	Creates and adds an article to an existing publication.
sp_articlecolumn	Specifies the column to be added to an article in transactional and snapshot replication. Merge replication has no corresponding procedure.
sp_articlefilter	Specifies the filter (WHERE condition, for example) to be applied to the article in snapshot and transactional replication. Changes to the filter can only take place if no subscribers are currently configured for the article.
sp_addmergefilter	Specifies a join condition filter to be applied for an article that has a FOREIGN KEY reference to a published PRIMARY KEY table, and the PRIMARY KEY is filtered in the article. This procedure determines which rows in the FOREIGN KEY table to add to the subscription.

Table 12-2.   Publication-Related System Stored Procedure in SQL Server 7 and 2000

Stored Procedure	Purpose/Description
sp_articleview	Creates the view that will be used to synchronize data for articles filtered horizontally or vertically. No subscribers can exist for the article when executing this stored procedure.
sp_articlesynctransprocs	Creates procedures at the publisher called by immediate or queued updating subscribers in transactional or snapshot replication.
sp_changearticle sp_changemergearticle	Modifies the properties of an article.
sp_changemergefilter	Changes the filter name or join clause for an article filter in merge replication.
sp_droparticle sp_dropmergearticle	Removes an article from a publication.
sp_dropmergefilter	Removes a filter in merge replication.
sp_helparticle sp_helpmergearticle	Displays information about an article.
sp_helparticlecolumns sp_helpmergearticlecolumn	Displays information about columns in an article.
sp_helpmergefilter	Returns information on the filter for a merge publication.
sp_replicationdboption	Sets a replication option for the specified database on the current publisher.
sp_helpreplicationdboption sp_helpreplicationdb (SQL Server 6.x)	Displays databases that have publishing enabled on the current server.
sp_helpreplicationoption	Shows types of replication available on the server.

Table 12-2.   Publication-Related System Stored Procedure in SQL Server 7 and 2000 *(continued)*

Configuring publishing using the Configure Publishing and Distribution wizard is quite easy, but you need to plan ahead. You need to identify what you will publish, what type of replication will be used, how the data will be filtered, and who will be allowed to subscribe to it.

To configure publishing on a SQL Server, you follow the same steps as in configuring a distributor, but you specify a remote distributor. If you have configured the local server as a distributor, when you invoke Configure Publishing, Subscribers, and Distribution from Tools | Replication, you will be presented with a Properties dialog box for replication. Click on the Publisher's tab to display a list of SQL Servers registered with SQL Enterprise Manager (including the current server) and select which one will be allowed to publish to the current distributor. This will also configure publishing on the local server if it was selected from the list. To complete the configuration of the publisher on the local computer, specify the security mechanism,

Snapshot folder, and **distribution** database to use, as shown in Figure 12-12. You can also register new servers to allow them to publish to the distributor.

Once you have enabled publishing, use the Create and Manage Publications option from Tools | Replication to create or manage publications. Select a database, then click Create Publication to invoke the Create a Publication Wizard, or select an existing publication to modify or delete. When you create a new publication using the wizard, you can select the following options: the replication type (snapshot, transactional, or merge); whether or not to support updating subscribers (immediate, queued, or immediate and queued); which types of servers will be subscribers (SQL Server 2000, SQL Server 7, or other ODBC data sources such as SQL Server 6.x, Oracle, Microsoft Access, or others); articles to be created and the types of objects (table, view, or stored procedure in SQL Server 2000) publications can be based on; and any horizontal or vertical filtering to be applied. Depending on your choices, the wizard will execute the appropriate system stored procedure to create your publication and its associated articles. Once the publication has been created, the icon for the database on which the publication was created will change to include a sharing hand under the disk icon, and a new Publications folder will be available in the database context, as shown in Figure 12-13. You can delete publications or create new ones from the Publications folder, or modify the properties of a publication.

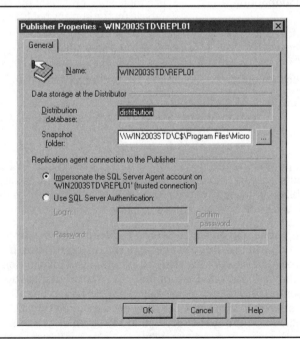

Figure 12-12.   Specify properties on the local server to configure publishing.

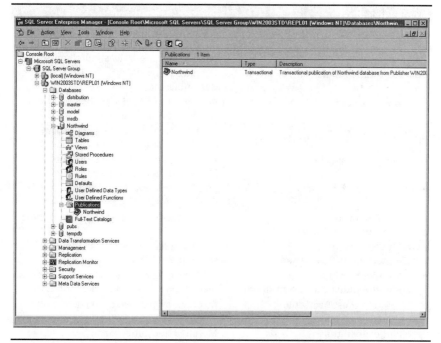

Figure 12-13. SQL Enterprise Manager indicates which databases have
publications and creates a folder to manage them from.

Configuring Subscribers

After you have created a publication on a SQL Server, you can then create
push subscriptions to get the data out to whom you know should have it,
or allow other DBAs to define a pull subscription to your publication. This
can also be accomplished using SQL Enterprise Manager or through system
stored procedures (see Table 12-3). No matter which method you choose,
when configuring a pull subscription you must have been granted
permissions at the publisher to pull a subscription from the server, or the
Anonymous Subscriber option needs to have been enabled. If neither of
these is true, you will not be able to configure a pull subscription. In order
to configure a push subscription, you need to be granted the **sysadmins**
role on the subscribing server to create the subscription.

To configure either a push or pull subscription using SQL Enterprise Manager,
you can use Push Subscriptions to Others and Pull Subscription to *severname*
options from Tools I Replication. Make sure that the server you are pulling
subscriptions to is not called "(local)" because you will need to change the
name in SQL Enterprise Manager to allow subscriptions to be configured.
You can also pull a subscription by right-clicking on the database that will be
the target for the subscription and selecting New I Pull subscription. For a
push subscription, if you right-click on the publication and select Push New
Subscription, you can also configure a push subscription. To specify who is

12

Stored Procedure	Purpose/Description
sp_addsubscriber	Adds the specified server as a subscriber on the publisher allowing it to receive publications, as well as pull them.
sp_changesubscriber	Modifies properties for the subscriber at this publisher.
sp_dropsubscriber	Removes the specified subscriber from the list for the publisher.
sp_helpsubscriberinfo	Provides information on subscribers configured at the current publisher.
sp_addsubscriber_schedule	Adds a schedule for the Distribution or Merge Agent to create snapshots.
sp_changesubscriber_schedule	Modifies a schedule for the Distribution or Merge Agent to create snapshots.
sp_addsubscription sp_addmergesubscription	Adds a push subscription to a subscriber.
sp_addpullsubscription sp_addmergepullsubscription	Creates a pull subscription on the subscriber.
sp_addpullsubscription_agent sp_addmergepullsubscription_agent	Adds an agent to the subscriber database used to pull data from the distributor.
sp_changemergesubscription	Modifies properties of a push or pull merge subscription.
sp_changesubstatus	Modifies the status of a subscription in transaction or snapshot replication.
sp_attachsubscription (SQL Server 2000)	Allows you to attach a subscription database from one subscriber to another. This is similar to **sp_attach_db**. It can be useful when two SQL Servers in the same location require the data, and establishing replication with the publisher would take too long because of slow network links, for example.
sp_dropsubscription sp_dropmergesubscription	Drops a subscription to one or more publications or articles from the publisher.
sp_droppullsubscription sp_dropmergepullsubscription	Drops a pull subscription at the subscriber.
sp_helpsubscription sp_helpmergesubscription	Provides information on the status and configuration of a subscription on the publisher.
sp_helppullsubscription sp_helpmergepullsubscription	Provides information on the status and configuration of a subscription on the subscriber.

Table 12-3. System Stored Procedures for Configuring and Managing Subscriptions

allowed to initiate pull subscriptions, go to Tools | Replication and select Configure Publishing, Subscribers, and Distribution (or via the Replication tab of the current SQL Server properties dialog box). Then, click the Subscribers tab (shown in Figure 12-14) and select which of the registered SQL Servers can pull subscriptions, and set security on the subscriber and create new known subscribers.

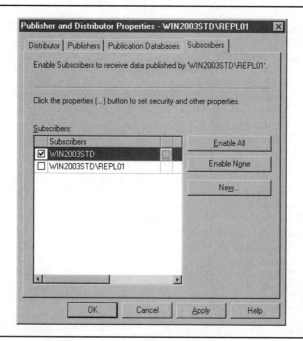

Figure 12-14. Check which servers can initiate pull subscriptions on the Subscribers tab.

NOTE *While you may trust SQL Enterprise Manager to do all the work for you in configuring replication, or be quite adept at writing the scripts to call appropriate system stored procedures to manage replication, a method that is easy and useful in re-creating replication in the event of failure is scripting. You can, for each publication and subscription, generate scripts to create and remove the publication or subscription. From Tools / Replication, you can also script the configuration of your publisher or distributor, as well as create scripts to remove this functionality. Look for the Generate SQL Script option, and then save the results to a file every time you make changes.*

Monitoring Replication

Once replication is up and running, your best bet for monitoring its activity and performance is using Replication Monitor in SQL Enterprise Manager. Replication Monitor will be installed as a context item on any server configured as a distributor, as shown in Figure 12-15. Using Replication Monitor, you can view the configured publishers and publications, as well as the current status of each subscriber. You can monitor the status of each agent as well as configure replication alerts that can notify you of any problems that may have occurred. Replication Monitor is the preferred tool when you need to find out what is happening with replication.

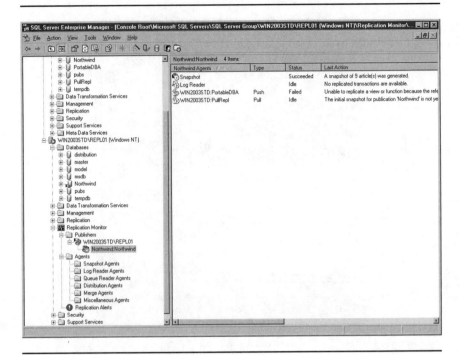

Figure 12-15.   Replication Monitor provides status on agents, publishers, publications, and subscriptions.

You can use the System Monitor and Performance tool to view performance of replication. When you install SQL Server, several performance objects starting with "SQL Server: Replication" can be used to get information on agent activity (SQL Server: Replication Agents), distributor activity (SQL Server: Replication Dist), log reader activity (SQL Server: Replication Logreader), merge replication activity (SQL Server: Replication Merge), and snapshot activity (SQL Server: Replication Snapshot). If these counters do not provide the information you require, you can use one of the user-defined performance counters (SQL Server: User Settable) by modifying one of the **sp_user_counter*n*** system stored procedures and adding code to satisfy your specific requirements.

Chapter 13

Managing Distributed Databases

As companies continue to collect more and more data, accessing and using this data is becoming increasingly important. However, this data often exists in different databases and these databases may be on any number of servers. The data might also be stored in data sources other than SQL Server (such as in Access or Oracle databases). All of this data is referred to collectively as distributed data. It is not always possible (or desirable) to gather this information together into one location, but your users may ask you to make this distributed data available to them. Luckily, Microsoft SQL Server includes the ability to query and manipulate distributed data.

Working with Distributed Data

The key point to remember in any discussion of distributed data is that the data you are working with is not physically moved from its source location. The computer where you issue the distributed command will send a request to the remote server, and the remote server will send the results of that command back. However, the results will not be permanently stored on your computer. Because data sources can be heterogeneous (that is, from different databases), SQL Server performs distributed operations via an OLE-DB provider. Therefore, in order for SQL Server to access a distributed data source, it must be reachable via an OLE-DB provider. There are a number of OLE-DB providers that have been tested with SQL Server. These are listed in Table 13-1.

Provider Name	Data Source
SQLOLEDB	The OLD-DB provider used by SQL Server 7 and 2000.
MSDAORA	The OLE-DB provider for Oracle (Oracle 7.x and later).
Microsoft.Jet.OLEDB.4.0	The OLE-DB provider for Microsoft Jet databases, particularly Microsoft Access.
MSDASQL	The OLE-DB provider used to access ODBC data sources. This provider allows you to connect to any ODBC-accessible data source. With this provider, you must also supply a locally configured DSN value.
DB2OLEDB	The OLE-DB provider used to access IBM DB2 databases.

Table 13-1. OLE-DB Providers Used with SQL Server

13

SQL Server supports two types of distributed operations:

- Ad hoc queries
- Linked server operations

In order to perform either type of operation, you will need to supply the following information:

- The name of the remote data source
- The OLE-DB provider name

Depending on the remote data source, you may be required to pass additional information. For example, if you are connecting to a remote SQL server, you must supply the server name and authentication credentials, whereas if the remote data source is Microsoft Access, you will provide the full path to the MDB file and only need to provide authentication credentials if you've implemented security on the Access MDB file. You may need to provide additional information when connecting to non-SQL Server databases. The distributed-data features discussed in this chapter are only available for SQL Server 7 and 2000. SQL Server 6.5 does not support these features. SQL Server 6.5 databases were able to perform distributed queries with other SQL Server databases using the **sp_addserver** stored procedure. This procedure still exists in SQL Server 7 and 2000; however, it is only maintained for backward compatibility. New distributed methods in SQL Server 7 and 2000 replace and expand the capabilities provided by this stored procedure.

Working with Ad Hoc Queries

As the name suggests, ad hoc queries are used when you need to periodically retrieve information from a remote data source. Only queries can be issued using this method. You cannot issue INSERT, UPDATE, or DELETE statements in an ad hoc query. You also cannot perform ad hoc execution of stored procedures on remote servers.

Ad hoc queries are performed using the OPENROWSET function. This function is used in the FROM clause of Transact-SQL queries. The syntax for this function is as follows:

```
SELECT [* | colx, coly ...]
FROM OPENROWSET ( 'provider_name',{ 'datasource' ;
['user_id' ; 'password' | 'provider_string'] },
{ [ catalog. ] [ schema. ] object | 'query' })
```

There are three basic parts to this statement. In the first part, you must supply a provider. The provider must be one supported by SQL Server and dictates what additional information is required by the function. There is no default provider and you will receive an error if one is not provided.

The second part of the statement identifies the data source (such as a specific SQL Server database or Access MDB file). Again, the provider dictates what information is required in this section. Depending on the provider, this section can optionally require authentication information. Remember that when you work with distributed servers, you must have the appropriate permissions on the remote server for the operation to complete successfully.

The third and final part of the statement indicates the remote data that you want to access. This can be the name of a table or the result of a query executed against the remote data source. It is a good practice to avoid returning the full contents of a table if only a small subset of that table is required. Whenever you call the OPENROWSET function, all of the data it returns is sent across the network. If a table contains thousands of rows of data, and you only need a few of those rows, you will bring a large amount of data across the network only to have it discarded when the remainder of the query is executed. Clearly it is better to eliminate the unwanted data on the remote server. The embedded query can include a WHERE clause to limit the number of rows returned by the OPENROWSET function.

To better understand the variable elements of this function, let's look at some examples.

If you wanted to view the name and price of all discontinued products from the products table in a database on a remote SQL Server 2000 server called SalesReporting, you would use the following query:

```
SELECT * FROM OPENROWSET('SQLOLEDB', 'SalesReporting'; 'RemoteUser';
'remotepwd', 'SELECT productname, unitprice FROM
northwind.dbo.products WHERE discontinued = 0')
```

Notice that in this query you are using the SQLOLEDB provider to connect to the remote SQL server. When using this provider, you must provide the server name and authentication credentials. In this example, the RemoteUser login must exist on the SalesReporting server and must have SELECT permission on the **northwind** database. Note that in the query, you must supply the fully-qualified name for the table. This is because you don't pass the database name as part of the connection string. If you don't supply the fully-qualified name, SQL Server will default to the default database that is associated with the login you specified. The fully-qualified name allows you to uniquely identify an object on a server. It is represented as: [server].database.object_owner.object.

The syntax would be different for an Oracle data source. In the following example, you need to access the name and telephone numbers of all customers in New York and New Jersey on an Oracle server called OraSales. The syntax would look like the following:

```
SELECT * FROM OPENROWSET('MSDAORA','OraSales.haunting.com';
'sys'; 'password', 'SELECT name, telephone From
OraSales WHERE city in ('New York', 'New Jersey')'
```

13

This query looks similar to the query that accesses the SQL server with one difference. Instead of the server name, you need to supply the TNS name of the database. In order for this query to work, you must have the Oracle network client (SQL*Net, Net8, and so on) installed and configured on the computer where this query is being executed.

Finally, the following query returns rows from the SalesResults table in an Access database called sales.mdb:

```
SELECT * FROM OPENROWSET('Microsoft.Jet.OLEDB.4.0',
'c:\mydatafiles\sales.mdb'; ; , 'SELECT * FROM SalesResults')
```

In this example, you are providing the path to the file. Note that the MDB file is not password-protected. However, the OPENROWSET procedure still expects a value for the user id and password. By including the semicolons, the function has the correct number of arguments, and a blank user id and password are sent to Access. If you omit these semicolons, the arguments will not match properly and the query will not execute.

Configuring and Managing Linked Servers

Executing ad hoc queries using the OPENROWSET function is fine when users need to connect infrequently to a remote data source. However, if your users are constantly accessing a remote server, you may consider creating a more permanent link. In SQL Server, this permanent link is known as a *linked server*. Unlike the OPENROWSET function, linked servers connect directly to a database on the remote data source rather than to a recordset returned by a query. This allows you to issue INSERT, UPDATE, and DELETE statements on the remote server, in addition to executing stored procedures. In order to create a linked server on SQL Server 7 and 2000, you must have been granted either the System Administrators or Setup Administrators server roles. You will also need permission to access the remote data source.

Linked servers work in a very similar manner to the OPENROWSET function. They connect to remote data sources using a valid OLE-DB provider and must be provided with all connection information when they are created. Unlike the OPENROWSET function, however, this information is written to the **sysservers** system table in the **master** database and permanently stored. Once the entry is added in this table, you can reference a remote data source simply by referring to its fully-qualified name, so you are not required to reenter the connection information. You can use either of two methods for creating a linked server: Enterprise Manager or the **sp_addlinkedserver** stored procedure.

Creating a Linked Server with sp_addlinkedserver

This stored procedure requires many of the same arguments as the OPENROWSET function. In particular, it needs to know the OLE-DB provider required to connect to the remote server type and the connection information for the database. The full syntax is as follows:

```
sp_addlinkedserver [ @server = ] 'server name',
[ [@srvproduct = ] 'product name' ],
[ [ @provider = ] 'provider name' ],
[ [ @datasrc = ] 'data source' ],
[ [ @location = ] 'location' ],
[ [ @provstr = ] 'provider string' ],
[ @catalog = ] 'catalog' ]
```

You will notice the only value that is mandatory is the server name. If you supply only a server name, SQL Server will assume that the remote server is also a SQL Server and will use the SQLOLEDB provider to connect to it. It will also use the server name in the datasrc field and look for a server of that name. If the remote server is not a SQL Server 7 or 2000 server, you must provide more information. Not all information is required. Each of the parameters is explained in Table 13-2.

Option	Description
@server	The name of the linked server that will be registered in **sysservers**. For most data sources, it is simply a friendly name, but for remote Microsoft SQL Servers, it must be the name of the server (or named instance) to which you are planning to link.
@srvproduct	The type of data source used by the linked server. This value is parsed when the stored procedure is executed and written into **sysservers**, and has no bearing on the execution because the provider determines the server type.
@provider	The OLE-DB provider used to complete the connection. This value must contain a valid provider name (see Table 13-1 for a list of provider names).
@datasrc	This parameter defines the physical location for the data source. If the data source is a SQL Server, it will contain the server name or the instance name. If the remote data source is Microsoft Access, this parameter must contain the full path to the MDB file. If the remote source is Oracle, this parameter will contain the SQL*Net alias for the Oracle server. If the data source is ODBC, it must contain the name of the System DSN used by the ODBC connection.
@location	The location of the remote data source. This value is recorded in the **sysservers** table but is not used to create the link.
@provstr	This parameter contains provider string details. It can contain the connection string details for ODBC clients. It is not used when connecting to most data sources.
@catalog	This parameter contains the database name on the linked server. This value is only used by the SQL Server and IBM DB2 providers. If it is left blank, the linked server will default to the default database for the login used to connect.

13

Table 13-2. The sp_addlinkedserver Parameters

Let's look at some specific examples. If you wanted to connect to a SQL Server 2000 server called CorpSrv2, you could use the following statement:

```
EXEC sp_addlinkedserver @server = 'CorpSrv2',
@srvproduct= 'SQL Server'
```

Notice that you don't need to include a provider string for this statement. When you specify SQL Server as the product, the SQL engine automatically uses the SQLOLEDB provider and sets the @server value as the data source value. You don't need to provide any more information. If the remote SQL server was a named instance, you would need to supply the full name (server name\instance name).

If you were to link to another type of data source, the query would be quite different. Suppose, for example, that you wanted to connect to a SQL 6.5 server called HRData using an ODBC DSN called SQL65.dsn. You would use the following syntax:

```
EXEC sp_addlinkedserver @server = 'HR Data',
@srvproduct= 'SQL Server 6.5', @provider = 'MSDASQL',
@datasrc = 'SQL65'
```

In this example, the @srvproduct parameter has no effect on configuration. SQL Server doesn't recognize this type, so it records the value supplied, but otherwise ignores it. You must, in this case, supply an OLE-DB provider. The ODBC provider also requires either a System DSN or a connection string. In this example, you have a System DSN already created so you can include it as the value for the @datasrc parameter.

NOTE   *You must create the System DSN before you can execute this query.*

If you are connecting to an Oracle database, the procedure is similar to the previous example. Suppose you wanted to connect to the RDdata dat

```
EXEC sp_addlinkedserver @server= 'RData',
@srvproduct = 'Oracle 9i', @provider= 'MSDAORA',
@datasrc = 'RData.haunting.com'
```

In this example, you need to provide a different provider name (because it is a different kind of data source). In this case, the value in the @datasrc parameter is the SQL*Net alias name rather than the DSN name. You must also have the Oracle network client installed and configured on the local computer to connect to Oracle.

Creating Linked Servers Using Enterprise Manager

Enterprise Manager simplifies the creation of linked servers by providing a GUI tool. Linked servers are created and managed under the Security folder. To add a new linked server in SQL Server 7 or 2000, use the following steps:

1. Expand the Security folder in the Explorer pane in Enterprise Manager.

2. Right-click on the Linked Servers icon.

3. Select New Linked Server from the pop-up menu.

The Linked Server Properties is useful because it grays out fields that are not required based on which provider you have chosen. Also, in SQL Server 2000, as you click on each text box, a legend in the bottom of the window tells you what each box is used for (see Figure 13-1). You'll also notice from Figure 13-1 that you can set security and configuration settings on the same properties form. These options will be discussed later in the "Configuring Linked Server Security in Enterprise Manager" and "Configuring Linked Server Settings" sections of this chapter.

Securing Linked Server Connections

To create a linked server, you must have been granted the System Administrators or Setup Administrators role. However, to use a linked server to access data on a remote data source, you must have permissions to access the remote source. When you connect across a linked server connection, the local SQL Server passes your credentials to the remote server. The remote server must accept those credentials before you are

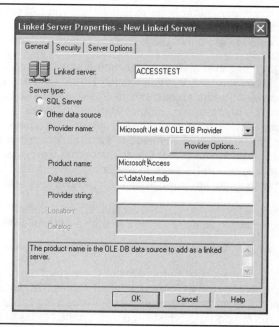

Figure 13-1. Adding a linked server in Enterprise Manager

allowed to connect and retrieve data. SQL Server allows you to configure how you will authenticate to the remote server. In Transact-SQL, this is done using the **sp_addlinkedsrvlogin** stored procedure.

To execute this command, you must have been granted the System Administrators or Security Administrators server role. The Setup Administrators role, while able to create a linked server, is not able to issue the **sp_addlinkedsrvlogin** stored procedure.

The syntax for this procedure is as follows:

```
sp_addlinkedsrvlogin [ @rmtsrvname = ] 'Linked server name'
  [ , [ @useself = ] {True | False} ]
  [ , [ @locallogin = ] 'local login Account' ]
  [ , [ @rmtuser = ] 'Remote User account' ]
  [ , [ @rmtpassword = ] 'password' ]
```

In this procedure, the @rmtsrvname parameter defines the linked server for which you are configuring security. In order to execute this statement, the linked server name that you supply must already exist on the local server. The @useself parameter is a Boolean value that defines whether or not a user's credentials will be passed to the linked server when that user connects. If this value is set to True, SQL Server will determine the SQL Server login and password, or the Windows login name, of each user who connects to the linked server, and will pass those credentials to the remote server. You must create logins on the local server for each user who will access the linked server. If this parameter is set to False, then you can set an alternate set of credentials for the user when connecting to the linked server. The final three parameters are only used if @useself is set to False.

The @locallogin parameter is used to determine which logins are allowed to access the linked server. If this value is left NULL, then any user with a valid SQL Server login can access the linked server. The @rmtuser and @rmtpassword allow you to set a single set of login credentials that will be used every time a user connects to a linked server. The advantage of using remote credentials is that you only need to maintain one set of credentials on the remote server. It also allows you to limit what users can do on the remote data source by limiting what the remote login is able to do. One caveat with this method, however, is that the password is sent in clear text.

As an example, to specify that SQL Server should use the user's credentials on a linked server called SalesServer, you would use the following statement:

```
EXEC sp_addlinkedsrvlogin @rmtsrvname= 'SalesServer', @useself = True
```

Make sure not to place single quotes around the value True or you will receive an error. When users access the linked server, SQL Server will look up the credentials of the user (that is, the user accessing the linked server, not the user who created it). If the user doesn't have access to the remote data source, the connection will fail.

Suppose you want to make linked server called HRArchive available to all members of the HR Windows group (which has been configured with a SQL Server login), using a single remote account. You could use the following statement:

```
EXEC sp_addlinkedsrvlogin @rmtsrvname= 'SalesServer', @useself = False
, @locallogin = 'HR', @rmtuser = 'myRemoteUser', @rmtpassword = 'password01'
```

In this case, only members of the HR group will be able to access this linked server. The user will never see the user id and password that was used to authenticate. Members of the HR group will simply issue a query against the linked server and the local SQL Server will retrieve the login credentials from the local system table and send them to the remote sever.

Configuring Linked Server Security in Enterprise Manager

Security settings can also be set using the Security tab of the Linked Server Properties window in Enterprise Manager (see Figure 13-2). You can set security when you create the linked server, or you can configure security for an existing linked server by right-clicking the linked server and selecting Properties from the popup menu.

As you can see, the top half of the Properties window allows you to set which users can access the remote server. This is the same as the @locallogin setting. If you leave this table blank, it's the same as supplying a NULL for

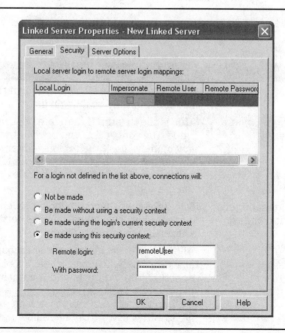

Figure 13-2. Setting linked server security

the @locallogin parameter. That is, all users can access the linked server. Notice that if you choose to limit access, you can set a remote user and password for the local login account.

You can set the default connection options with the radio buttons on the lower part of the Properties window. The four options are described in Table 13-3.

Configuring Linked Server Settings

Once you have created your linked servers, you can further configure the behavior using the **sp_serveroption** stored procedure or by accessing the Linked Server Properties window in Enterprise Manager. In order to execute this stored procedure, you must be a member of the System Administrators or Setup Administrators role. The syntax for this procedure is as follows:

```
sp_serveroption [@server =] 'linked server'
,[@optname =] 'option name', [@optvalue =] 'linked server option'
```

There are a number of options that can be set using this stored procedure as part of the @optname parameter. They are listed in Table 13-4.

To execute this procedure, you must specify the name of the option you want to set. You can only set one option with each execution of the stored procedure. For example, to turn collation compatibility off and set a query timeout of five seconds, you would execute the following statement:

```
EXEC sp_serveroption 'RemoteSQL', 'query timeout', 5
GO
EXEC sp_serveroption 'RemoteSQL', 'collation compatible', False
GO
```

Option	Description
Not be made	This option blocks all connections if the user is not listed in the Local Login list.
Be made without using a security context	This is the default. If there are no local logins listed, the connection will be made without any credentials. If the remote server requires authentication, the connection will fail. This option requires that a guest login exist on the remote server.
Be made using the login's current security context	SQL Server will send the login credentials of the current user. This is the same as setting the @useself parameter to True.
Be made using this security context	Allows you to set a remote user account that all local users will impersonate. This is the same as setting the @rmtuser and @rmtpassword parameters. The username and password that you enter in the text box must match an existing user name and password on the remote data source.

Table 13-3. The Enterprise Manager Security Options

Option Name	Description
collation compatible	This is a Boolean value that indicates if a remote server uses the same collation as the local SQL server. If the collations are different, character data might not display properly.
use remote collation	This is a Boolean value. If it is set to True, SQL Server will use a different collation when connecting to the remote server. The remote collation must be listed in the collation name parameter. If it is set to False, SQL Server will use its own collation when interpreting remote character data. This option is not available in SQL Server 7.
collation name	Name of the remote collation (if the use remote collation value is true). This value must be a collation recognized by SQL Server. This option is not available in SQL Server 7.
connect timeout	Determines how long a connection will remain open. The default is 0 (no timeout).
data access	Allows you to enable or disable a linked server for query access by setting the value to True or False.
lazy schema validation	Boolean value. If it is set to false, SQL Server checks the remote schema each time the linked server is accessed. If it is set to true, schema checking is skipped when a remote query is executed.
query timeout	Sets the maximum amount of time a query can run against a remote server. The default is 0 (unlimited).
rpc	Enables remote procedure call (RPC) requests from the remote data source.
rpc out	Enables RPC requests from the local server to the remote data source.

Table 13-4.   The Options for sp_serveroption

You can also set a limited number of options in the Enterprise Manager by accessing the Properties window of the linked server and clicking on the list of options on the Server Options tab (see Figure 13-3). If you want to set a property that is not listed in the Enterprise Manager properties window, you must use **sp_serveroption**.

Accessing and Manipulating Remote Data

Once you have configured your linked server, you can access the remote data on your local server. If the remote data source is a SQL Server 7 or 2000 server, you can simply use the fully-qualified name. The fully-qualified object name is Server.Database.ObjectOwner.Object. For example, if you had created a linked server connection to a server called DataSrv3, and you

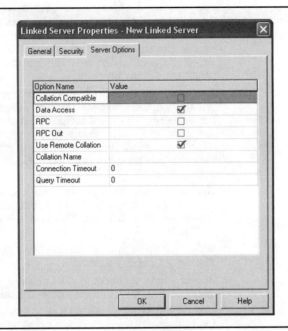

Figure 13-3. Configuring linked server options in Enterprise Manager

wanted to access the SalesDetails table in the CorpSales database, you could use the following query:

```
SELECT * FROM DataSrv3.SalesDetails.dbo.CorpSales.
```

When processing this query, SQL Server will locate the server in **sysservers** and make the appropriate connection to retrieve the required data.

You can also issue other DML statements through a linked server. For example, if you wanted to update a record in the remote SalesDetails table, you could issue the following query:

```
UPDATE DataSrv3.SalesDetails.dbo.CorpSales
SET ClosedDate = '2003-5-18'
WHERE SalesOrderID = 12343
```

This is a normal update statement and will execute as expected on the remote server as long as you are connected with an account that has update permission on the table.

You can even execute remote stored procedures across a linked server connection. All you need to do is provide the fully-qualified name of the remote stored procedure. For example, to enumerate the details of a table on the remote database, you would use the following statement:

```
EXEC Remoteserver.master.dbo.sp_help <remote table name>
```

NOTE *This stored procedure will execute on the remote server and only pass the results back to the calling server. It is not possible to execute a remote stored procedure on the local server.*

If you want to retrieve data from a non-SQL Server 7 or 2000 linked server, you must use the OPENQUERY function. This function allows you to access a linked server and pull data from the remote data source. Consider the following situation. Suppose you create a linked server called AccessTest that points to a Microsoft Access database, and you want to retrieve data from a table called test1. You could use the following query:

```
SELECT * FROM OPENQUERY(AccessTest, 'Select * from test1')
```

In this query, the OPENQUERY function accesses the remote server through the link and retrieves the information required as a recordset. Notice that you do not have to provide any connection or authentication information. All of this information is contained within the definition of the linked server.

Finally, SQL Server provides a number of system stored procedures that allow you to query information about the schema of a remote data source. These procedures are described in Table 13-5.

Executing Distributed Transactions

As you saw in the previous section, it is possible to issue an INSERT, UPDATE, or DELETE statement against a linked server. These statements run as transactions, and the transactions are controlled by the remote server. SQL Server can also run transactions that span servers. In order to run distributed transactions, the Distributed Transaction Coordinator service (DTC) must be running on at least one server. DTC performs what is referred to as a two-phase commit. It sends the transaction to each server and waits for each server to report back that the operation was successful. The remote servers do not commit their respective transactions until they are instructed to do so by the DTC. The DTC will not instruct the individual servers to

Stored Procedure	Description
sp_linkedservers	Returns a list of all linked servers configured on the local server
sp_indexes	Returns a list of indexes for a specified remote table
sp_catalogs	Returns a list of databases located on the remote server
sp_primarykeys	Returns a list of columns comprising the primary key for a remote table
sp_foreignkeys	Returns a list of FOREIGN KEY columns on a remote table
sp_tables_ex	Returns a list of information about a remote table
sp_columns_ex	Returns a list of information about a specified column in a remote table

Table 13-5. Information-Gathering Stored Procedures for Linked Servers

13

commit transactions until each member of the distributed transaction reports back that they are ready to commit.

In order to execute a distributed transaction, you must execute the following two statements:

```
SET XACT_ABORT ON
Begin Distributed Transaction
```

The **XACT_ABORT** session option instructs DTC to roll back all operations on all servers if a rollback is called by any server. If this option is not set, the rollback will only take place on the local server where the transaction fails. The Begin Distributed Transaction statement instructs SQL Server to use DTC to control the transaction.

Consider the following example. Suppose one of your users wanted to execute two updates as part of a single transaction. The operation involves a money transfer between two servers. The transaction takes the form of two UPDATE statements: the first statement removes the money from one account on one server and the second statement adds the money to an account on the other server. The statement would look something like the following:

```
SET XACT_ABORT ON
Go
Begin Distributed Transaction
UPDATE linkedsrv.AccountDB.dbo.Sourcetable
SET balance = balance - 1000
WHERE Accout_number = 123345
UPDATE localserver.account2.dbo.desttable
SET balance = balance + 10000
WHERE Account_number = 545346
Commit Transaction
```

Remember that as an administrator, you must make sure that the DTC service is running, and that the users have update permission on the appropriate tables in order to execute this statement.

Chapter 14

Clustering and Log Shipping

When you come right down to it, DBAs spend a lot of their time dealing with two major issues: performance and availability. Performance ensures that the database is operating at levels that are acceptable to users in terms of query response time and throughput. Availability is as important, if not more important, than performance, because it deals with the first part of what performance means—it ensures that the database is operating.

SQL Server offers a number of solutions to address availability issues, such as performing backups on a regular basis, replicating data to another server so a copy exists, and the two that we will discuss here: clustering and log shipping. In the case of a failure of a CPU, motherboard, or whole computer, clustering prevents your databases being unavailable by having a different host take on the databases from the failed computer. Configuring clustering requires that you configure Windows properly first, and that you have the supported hardware. With clustering, when a failure does occur, no intervention is needed by the DBA to allow users to continue to work on their databases—it's automatic.

Log shipping allows you to keep a standby server around that will take over should the computer hosting the main server fail for any reason. Configuring log shipping is easier than configuring clustering and requires no specialized hardware. However, when a failure occurs, the DBA will need to bring the standby server online, which will cause a slight disruption to user activity.

Clustering SQL Server

Microsoft Cluster Server (MSCS) was introduced as a component of Windows NT Server 4.0 Enterprise Edition to allow for automatic failover of applications and services between two nodes if one becomes unavailable. In all fairness, this first rendition of clustering by Microsoft did not work as well as hoped, and many applications that were supposed to use it, such as SQL Server 6.5, did not work very well when clustered. Jump ahead to 2003. Windows Cluster Service is an integral component of Window Server 2003 and works very well with SQL Server 2000, offering excellent support for clustering. Today, clustering SQL Server makes sense, and, because of price reductions in hardware, is no longer as cost-prohibitive as it once was.

In Windows Server 2003 clustering, anywhere from two to eight computers (nodes) can be part of a cluster (the limit was four nodes with Windows 2000 Server Datacenter Edition). The most common implementation is a two-node

14

cluster. Going beyond two nodes requires even more planning and configuring, which is why this chapter looks only at configuring a two-node cluster. Besides, I can speak from experience on two-node clusters in Windows 2000 and Windows Server 2003, but have yet to get my hands on a four- or eight-node cluster.

In clustering, both nodes must share a common hard disk array or drive, and are addressed as a unit by a virtual server name. Any user accessing network resources on the cluster will use this virtual server name for the entire cluster. The user does not need to know the names of the individual nodes on the cluster, only the UNC name of the cluster. Because of this, adding or removing nodes and reorganizing the cluster does not impact the user's ability to access SQL Server data on the cluster.

All applications that run on either node of the cluster are accessible to all users of the cluster. Should one node in the cluster fail, the other will take over the task of running an application configured within the cluster. This provides true hot-standby capability as the network resources configured on the cluster are still available, should a hardware failure occur.

For the configuration of SQL Server in a cluster environment, two failover options are available: an active/passive configuration and an active/active configuration. You should only cluster SQL Server 2000. SQL Server 7 had some issues with clustering and SQL Server 6.5 just did not work at all (or, if you got it working, it did not stay up for long). Neither SQL Server 6.5 nor SQL Server 7 supported an active/active clustering scenario because only one instance of SQL Server could run per machine. SQL Server 2000 supports both active/passive- and active/active clustering. In the case of a four- or eight-node cluster, each node can be either active or passive, provided you properly configure the failover scenarios.

In an active/passive failover configuration, SQL Server services are automatically started on only one node of the cluster (the primary node), while the other node (the secondary node) has the services configured to start manually. In this case, users will use the resources of only one machine on the cluster for accessing data. The other machine does not service user requests (it is passive). Should a failure on the primary node occur, MSCS starts the SQL Server services on the secondary node and brings the databases online. Users will have to reconnect to access the data in the databases of SQL Server, but the amount of time for the switchover will cause only a minimal disruption in service. Until the primary node comes back online, the secondary node will continue to provide users with access to SQL Server and its databases.

In an active/active failover configuration, SQL Server is installed and started on both nodes in the cluster. Also, in this configuration, two virtual servers are configured on the cluster to allow both SQL Servers to provide database access to their own respective data, to users. In essence, in an active/active configuration, both Windows Servers in the cluster are operating as individual servers and can be addressed individually for accessing SQL Server data.

However, should one of the nodes fail in an active/active configuration, the other will grab control of the shared databases and continue to provide services to users. In this case, the single remaining node in the cluster will operate as both virtual servers, allowing users of each SQL Server to access their data, even though one machine is no longer physically available.

An active/active configuration requires that each SQL Server be configured as a primary, specifying the other node in the cluster as the secondary. In the case of a hardware failure, the databases to be failed over must be stored on the shared drive of the cluster in order for both nodes to access them and continue operating when something goes wrong. Configuring an active/active failover scenario using MSCS requires a little more work than configuring an active/passive failover scenario. But, it allows for better utilization of server hardware because both machines service users. One machine takes on the full load only if something should happen to its partner node.

When deciding whether or not to use MSCS with SQL Server, you need to keep in mind that MSCS has very stringent hardware requirements. Consult the Microsoft Windows Hardware Compatibility List (HCL) for Microsoft Cluster Server to determine if the hardware to be used in your cluster is supported. Furthermore, even though it is possible to use differing hardware configurations for each node in a cluster, it is quite likely that doing so may cause problems in cluster performance, and may even cause the cluster to fail. The best configuration to use consists of two *identical* servers with *identical* hardware peripherals, BIOS versions, versions of Windows, and everything else. Because this doubles the hardware investment, it may not be feasible for many organizations. However, MSCS can minimize downtime dramatically in a database critical to an enterprise's operation.

Installing SQL Server in a Clustered Environment

If you are planning to install SQL Server 2000 the first thing you need to do is configure the cluster (don't try this with SQL Server 6.5 or SQL Server 7). Make sure that at least one shared hard disk is available and attached to a SCSI (requires special cables and specific controller versions) or Fiber Channel controller (the preferred option), and that you have configured the public and private networks for the cluster. These should all be part of the default group in the cluster called Cluster Group in Windows Server 2003. The process of configuring a cluster is a bit more involved than can be covered in this chapter, so refer to Microsoft online help or pick up a copy of *Windows 2000 and Windows Server 2003 Clustering and Load Balancing*, by Robert Shimonski (McGraw-Hill/Osborne, 2003). It contains helpful tips on what's needed to configure a Windows cluster.

14

SQL Server Clustering Prerequisites

After you have configured your cluster, the next step is to add the Microsoft Distributed Transaction Coordinator (MS DTC) as a cluster resource to the default Cluster Group. You need to complete this on each node of the cluster in Windows 2000 by executing comclust.exe from a command prompt. This will install the MS DTC into the default Cluster Group and configure it to work properly in a cluster environment.

In Windows Server 2003 clustering you need to add the MS DTC to the Cluster Group as a resource, which will add it to both nodes of the cluster. To do this, in the Cluster Administrator program right-click on the Cluster Group and select New Resource. Next, assign a name (MS-DTC, for example) and select a resource type of Distributed Transaction Coordinator. You will then need to add the Cluster IP Address, Cluster Name, and one cluster disk resource as dependencies for the MS DTC. For the MS DTC, it is alright to use the cluster quorum disk, provided there is sufficient space for the MS DTC log files. When you are done, the default Cluster Group for your cluster should look similar to Figure 14-1, when viewed from Cluster Administrator.

The next step is to configure shared disk resources that will be used. When you configure clustering on Windows 2000 or Windows Server 2003 you must specify a shared disk resource to use as a quorum drive. This drive will be used by the cluster service to keep track of cluster resources and state, and for other cluster management purposes. The quorum disk should not be used for any SQL Server files, with the possible exception of the MS DTC log file, as indicated earlier. Because of this, you need to configure at

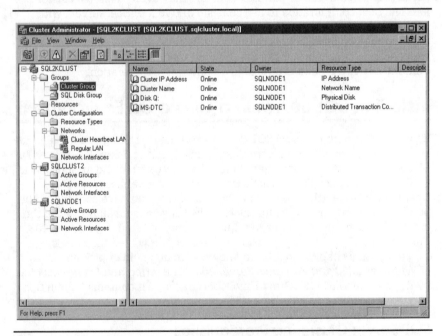

Figure 14-1. View the default Cluster Group in Cluster Administrator to confirm that MS DTC is configured.

least one additional disk resource that SQL Server can use to store data and transaction log files. If you have more shared disks, you can use them to place different data files on different drives, or separate data from log files. In clustering SQL Server, and for failover to work, all SQL Server data files, but not program files, must reside on shared cluster disks.

To configure shared disks, invoke the Cluster Administrator program and create a new cluster group by right-clicking on Groups and selecting New | Group. Name the group and specify which nodes the group can be assigned to. Click OK to save your group. In order to create the disk resource, right-click on the new group and select New | Resource. Select Physical Disk as the resource type, assign it to the appropriate nodes, and then specify which shared volume to use. If you do not see any shared volumes available on the drop-down list box, you need to configure and format the shared volume first, using the Disk Management MMC snap-in. Otherwise, you may have hardware issues. Correct any of these issues before installing SQL Server.

Once you have configured all of the shared disks, verify that the appropriate Windows services are started. While this generally is handled by Windows, when you first configure the cluster, make sure that in Windows 2000 the following Windows services are started on both nodes and set to start automatically (in Windows Server 2003 required services will be configured by the Cluster Administrator):

- Alerter
- Cluster Service
- Computer Browser
- Distributed File System
- Distributed Link Tracking Client
- Distributed Link Tracking Server
- DNS Client
- Event Log
- IPSEC Policy Agent
- License Logging Service
- Logical Disk Manager
- Messenger
- Net Logon
- Plug and Play
- Process Control
- Remote Procedure Call (RPC) Locator
- Remote Procedure Call (RPC) Service
- Remote Registry Service
- Removable Storage
- Security Accounts Manager
- Server
- Spooler
- TCP/IP NetBIOS Helper
- Windows Management Instrumentation Driver Extensions
- Windows NT LM Security Support Provider
- Windows Time Service
- Workstation

14

Finally, you will need to know the usernames and passwords of two critical user accounts during the setup process: the Cluster Administrator account and the startup account for SQL Server services. If you have not created a domain user account to start SQL Server services, do so now and make the account a member of the Administrators local group on each node of the cluster. Making the SQL Server startup account a member of the Domain Admins group will also work, but will introduce a potential network security hole that may not be acceptable.

Running SQL Server Setup on a Cluster

Once you have configured your Windows computers for clustering and created the necessary group and disk resources for SQL Server, you can begin installing SQL Server 2000 on the cluster by running the SQL Server Setup program like you would on any computer. Remember that only SQL Server 2000 Enterprise Edition (or Developer Edition) can be installed on a cluster, so make sure you have the correct version. Insert the CD-ROM into the drive of one of the cluster nodes and start the setup program from the AutoRun menu that appears, or by invoking SETUP.BAT from the CD.

If you are running the SQL Server Setup program on Windows Server 2003, you will see a warning indicating that Windows Server 2003 requires SQL Server Service Pack 2 or later. This warning can be ignored, but you should install SQL Server Service Pack 3 or later after you have configured SQL Server on the cluster. Failing to do so may cause SQL Server to stop working or generate errors during operation.

The setup program will launch the introductory screen. Click Next and you will see a dialog box, similar to Figure 14-2, asking where to install SQL Server. Notice the new option to install SQL Server 2000 on a virtual server. This option is available because the SQL Server 2000 Setup program is cluster-aware and knows that you are running it from a cluster node. In the text box provided, enter the name of the virtual server that will access SQL Server 2000 on the cluster. This name needs to be different from the cluster name or the name of any other computer on the network, including the cluster nodes.

After accepting the license agreement, you will be asked for the IP address of the virtual server that you created earlier. This cannot be the same IP address as the Windows cluster virtual server or any other computer on the network. The IP address will be used to resolve the SQL Server virtual server name and allow clients to connect to it, no matter on which node on the cluster the SQL Server is active. Specify the IP address, network mask, and the cluster network interface that will be used for communication, and click Next.

You will see a dialog box similar to the one in Figure 14-3 that asks you to select a disk resource to store data files on. The SQL Server Setup program only allows you to select one disk resource when installing SQL Server, but you can add more disk resources to the Cluster Group using the Cluster Administrator. Having multiple-cluster disk resources configured for the group allows you to place database and log files on separate drives for performance and other redundancy reasons. Having data files on the

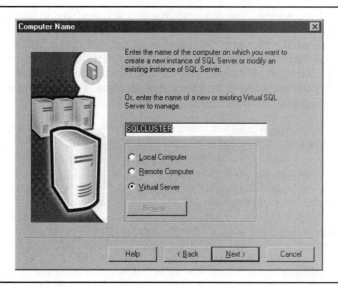

Figure 14-2. Name the virtual server.

shared-cluster disk allows for another node to easily take control of the failed nodes databases by having access to the data and log files. All data files for all databases, including the system databases such as **master, msdb, temp**, and others, must reside on the shared-cluster disks because the failed SQL Server instance will be started on another cluster node and take the place of the instance that failed.

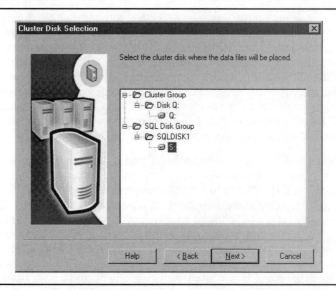

14

Figure 14-3. Select a cluster disk resource for SQL Server data files.

Once you have selected the disk resource, you will see a list of cluster nodes on which SQL Server will be installed. These nodes will be responsible for failover in case the primary node, the one currently running SQL Server services for the instance being installed, fails. By default, the setup program will list all nodes on the cluster that are available as configured nodes. You can remove the ones you do not want, but should list at least two nodes for failover processing to occur. Click Next when done.

When configuring a SQL Server instance on a cluster, SQL Server Setup needs to know the name and password of the Cluster Administrator account. During the installation of SQL Server files, the setup program performs a local install on the computer on which it runs, as well as a remote install of SQL Server on the other cluster nodes selected. This way, all program files reside on all nodes, and are the same version. This ensures that after the installation of SQL Server, you are running in an active/passive cluster scenario with the installed instance, and can perform a failover right away. This also makes the entire install process easier than in previous SQL Server releases.

The next screen will ask you to specify whether a default or named instance of SQL Server is to be installed. If an instance of SQL Server already exists on the cluster, you will be required to specify an instance name. Otherwise, you can install a default instance. If a copy of SQL Server running the default instance already exists on one of the other nodes, but is not cluster-aware, the setup program will fail. For this reason, before upgrading any Windows 2000 or Windows Server 2003 computer to be a node in a cluster, all instances of SQL Server should be removed. There is no way to upgrade a currently running single-node instance of SQL Server to a cluster-aware instance without uninstalling and re-installing SQL Server. Before doing so, back up all your databases so that you can install them on the cluster afterwards.

Finally, after selecting the instance to install, you get the SQL Server 2000 dialog box requesting you to select a setup type: Typical, Minimum, or Custom. Notice that the data file location points to the cluster disk resource you selected earlier, while the program files destination is the local hard drive of the node—not a shared-cluster drive. This is how SQL Server should be installed on a cluster so that a single copy of the data files exists but multiple copies of program files local to each node are also available. This will let alive nodes load SQL Server services when failing over data on the shared drives from failed nodes in the cluster.

When prompted, specify the domain account to use to start the SQL Server services on each node. Specify a different account for each SQL Server service, if desired (you typically use one account for all services). Following this, select the authentication mode (Windows only or Mixed), as well as other standard choices such as collation and network libraries if you selected the Custom setup type. Finally, licensing needs to be specified. Then, the SQL Server Setup program will perform the installation of the necessary files, create the other cluster resources in the cluster group where the disk resource is located, and start the necessary services. If the services do not start right away (as is the case in Figure 14-4), you can

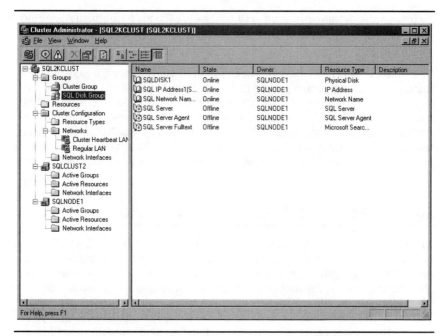

Figure 14-4.   SQL Server resources display for the selected group in
Cluster Administrator

bring them online using the Cluster Administrator. Right-click on the
service and select Bring Online.

Installing SQL Server Service Packs

Once you have installed SQL Server 2000, it is a good idea to upgrade to
the most current release—and make it work on Windows Server 2003. This
process is similar to installing SQL Server, and will ensure that all binaries
for the nodes in the cluster are updated to the service pack release. This
way, no problems should arise during failover. You will be asked to reboot
the node on which you ran the install program after the service pack setup
completes. You can do so at the time of the install, or reboot later when user
load is lighter.

Running Multiple SQL Server 2000 Instances

Just like on a single-node install of SQL Server, it is possible to run more
than one SQL Server instance on a cluster. Each instance can be configured
to run on a separate node by default, and then have another node for failover.
This allows SQL Server 2000 to operate in an active/active scenario with
multiple instances running on separate nodes, allowing other nodes to
assume responsibility in the case of failure. If your configuration will be
like this, ensure that each node in the cluster has sufficient memory for the
worst-case scenario—all instance of SQL Server running on a single node.
When failover occurs, if sufficient RAM is not found on each node (the

14

recommended implementation is to configure all nodes identically), paging can take place thereby reducing performance for all SQL Server instances.

Unlike SQL Server 2000, SQL Server 7 does not support named instances. Therefore, if using SQL Server 7 in a clustered environment, you cannot install more than one instance of SQL Server on the cluster. If you need to run SQL Server 7 on the cluster, you can install additional SQL Server 2000 named instances while keeping the SQL Server 7 instance running. This can also provide an upgrade path by allowing you to run SQL Server 7 and use the Copy Database Wizard to re-create the databases on the SQL Server 2000 named instance. You can then test to make sure everything works as expected.

Administering SQL Server in a Cluster

The nice thing about clustering SQL Server is that administering SQL Server on a cluster is not much different from administering it on a single node. To create databases you can still use Query Analyzer or SQL Enterprise Manager. The major difference is that you connect to the virtual server name you created when installing SQL Server, and not to the actual node running the software. Also, when creating databases, you need to make sure that you specify the cluster disk resources as the location of all data and log files, if you want failover to work properly. There are no real changes to the way SQL Server works when running it on a cluster with regard to backups, automating SQL Server management using tasks and alerts, and all other aspects of configuring and running SQL Server. The main difference is in how you configure the SQL Server resources to operate on the cluster using the Cluster Administrator program.

Administering SQL Server on a cluster encompasses many tasks, including ensuring disk resources are assigned to the SQL Server Cluster Group, failover and failback configuration are properly performed, node preferences are established, dependencies maintained, and so on. All of these are accomplished using the Cluster Administrator program. When running on a cluster, SQL Server becomes another cluster resource that must be managed in the same way as other cluster-based applications such as DHCP or DNS services.

Configuring Node Preferences and Failover/Failback

When you install SQL Server 2000 on a cluster, the SQL Server Setup program asks you to specify the list of nodes that will be configured to run SQL Server. In the setup program you *cannot* specify which node should be running the SQL Server services by default, and which one will be used for failover. You also cannot specify the failover thresholds, or whether SQL Server should fail back to its preferred node once it becomes available. To do this, you need to view the properties of the SQL Server Cluster Group in Cluster Administrator, as shown in Figure 14-5.

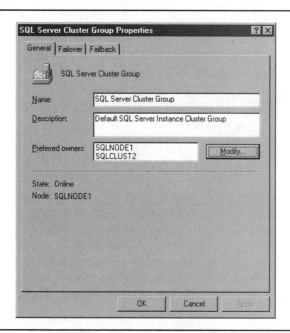

Figure 14-5. Use the cluster group Properties dialog box to configure preferred nodes and failover and failback settings.

From this dialog box, you can click Modify to change the list of preferred nodes, as well as the order in which they appear. The node at the top of the list will be the one on which SQL Server services and other resources in the group will start. If this is different from where the resources are currently running, you can switch to the preferred node by right-clicking on the group name and selecting Move Group.

The default failover configuration for any cluster group is usually sufficient for SQL Server as well. By default, if the node on which resources are running fails, another node in the preferred node list will take over and start the services. During this process, clients will not be able to use SQL Server. After the switch, however, everything will work properly. Each resource within the group can also have different failover settings, as defined by its properties page (Figure 14-6). For the resource, you can configure the number of times to try to restart the resource on the failed node, as well as whether or not the failure should affect the group and cause all of its resources to fail over to a working node on the cluster. By default, all SQL Server resources (any SQL Server service or shared disk, etc.) will also fail the group and cause all of the group's resources to be restarted on the next node in the preferred list.

If a SQL Server resource fails and the group initiates failover, you have the option to allow the group to fail back to its original preferred node. By default, failback is disabled because it can cause a disruption to the system if servers

14

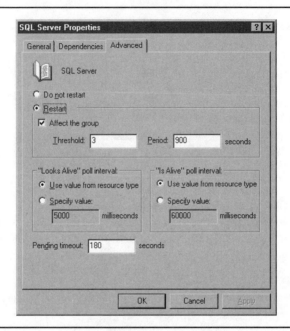

Figure 14-6. You can configure the failover settings for each cluster resource individually.

experience problems that make them fail repeatedly. You can configure the Cluster Group to initiate failback immediately after a preferred node higher in the list becomes available. Or, you can schedule the failback to occur at a specific time when the preferred node is available, by specifying these values on the Failback tab of the cluster group's property page, as shown in Figure 14-7. It is important to remember that the failback interval is a specific time period, such as between 1 A.M. and 5 A.M., as indicated in Figure 14-7. The benefit of setting a specific time period is that you can schedule the failback to occur when users are not on the system, and thereby minimize the impact to the organization.

Testing SQL Server in a Cluster and Other Administrative Tasks

It is important to be sure that SQL Server will failover if something goes wrong. The Cluster Administrator program provides facilities to test a failover scenario. It can also bring a resource or group offline for maintenance, or manually move it to the next preferred node in the list.

Right-clicking on a resource within the cluster group provides options to take the resource offline, initiate a failure scenario (to test what would happen when the resource failed), move it to another group, and delete or

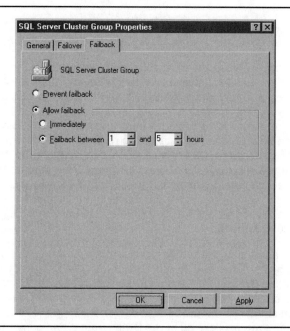

Figure 14-7. You can configure failback to happen immediately or within a specific time interval.

rename the resource. All of these functions can be performed for any of the SQL Server resources, or any depended upon resource. It is a good idea to initiate failure on SQL Server after you have installed it on the cluster, to make sure failover works. If you have configured failback, you will see the failure to the next preferred node, and then a quick failback (if configured immediately) or during the failback interval (if scheduled) to the original node. You should also test failover and/or failback whenever configuration changes occur on any of the preferred cluster nodes.

If you right-click on the cluster group hosting SQL Server (or any cluster group), you have the option to take the entire group and all its resources offline, move the group to another preferred node, as well as delete or rename the group. It is good practice to take a group offline when you are making major changes to the group configuration, such as changing the IP address or virtual server name (which is problematic for SQL Server—see Microsoft Knowledge Base article 307336), or performing maintenance on SQL Server. Taking the entire group offline makes any of its resources unavailable and tells the Windows Cluster Service that it should not worry if resources fail. It is important to remember to bring the group online after maintenance is complete.

14

Standby Servers and Log Shipping

While clustering provides the most consistent availability for a SQL Server configuration, the need for specialized hardware and the Enterprise Edition (Advanced Server for Windows 2000) of both Windows and SQL Server can make it a very expensive option for smaller organizations. At the same time, relying solely upon backups provides fault tolerance, but the time required to recover can be quite long if you need to replace hard disk drives, or even the entire server. Using RAID arrays can mitigate some of the downtime, but a restore will always take at least as long as the backup took, which can mean several hours of lost productivity. Clearly, this is not an acceptable solution for production databases in many small- to medium-size organizations. This is where standby servers and automated log shipping in SQL Server 2000 come in.

Log shipping and using a standby server is not a new concept. In fact, this solution can be implemented, in one way or another, in every version of SQL Server, from the very first one I worked on (1.11A) to SQL Server 2000. The idea is simple. Install SQL Server on another computer with a hardware configuration similar to the production server. Back up the database on the production system. Take all of the logins from it and copy them to the standby server. Restore the database on the standby server. Make sure no changes are made to the standby copy of the database, and, as changes are made to the production database, back up and restore each transaction log on the standby database. If the production system fails, switch all users so that they connect to the standby server, instead of to the failed production system. Fix the problem that caused production to fail and, once production is back online, reverse the process.

While performing all of these steps can be a nightmare if done manually, SQL Server 2000 allows the process to be automated and ensures that no changes are made to the standby copy of the database by leaving it in permanent recovery mode. Furthermore, it provides automated tasks that can be configured to send transaction log backups to the standby server and have them automatically applied. It will also monitor each database on a SQL Server 2000 instance configured for log shipping, and track its progress. SQL Server Agent must be running on both servers in order for this process to work. What you once had to do manually, SQL Server 2000 makes almost a no-brainer. Remember, I said *almost*. Before getting started, register both the primary and standby servers in SQL Enterprise Manager.

Configuring a Production Database for Log Shipping

Before you can enable log shipping on a SQL Server database, a number of prerequisites must be satisfied on the server. First, the SQL Server Agent service must use the same startup account on both the production and standby instances. This allows the SQL Server Agent to write and read transaction log backups as they occur. Second, both the production (primary) and standby databases must be configured for Full Recovery mode. Full Recovery mode ensures that transaction log entries of every transaction are created, and that the transaction log holds a complete record of all database changes. If this is not the case, you cannot enable log shipping. Finally, logins must be re-created on the standby server to match those that exist on the primary server. This process can be automated in SQL Server 2000 by creating a DTS package to use the Transfer Logins task and copy the logins from the primary server to the standby server to ensure no discrepancies exist.

Enabling a Database for Log Shipping Using the Database Maintenance Plan Wizard

The first few steps in configuring log shipping for a database are done outside of SQL Server. Because transaction log backups will need to be stored on disk somewhere, you need to create a folder on either the primary or standby servers, or a shared network drive, to hold the transaction log backups. The automated backup process on the primary server will place transaction log backups there that will be picked up by the restore process on the standby server. On the standby server you also need to create a second folder to hold transaction log backups that are in a pending state and ready to be applied to the standby database. The standby server recovery process copies the files that were originally backed up from the primary server, to this second folder.

After creating the necessary folders, you need to configure the primary server's database for log shipping. The easiest way to do this in SQL Server 2000 is to invoke the Database Maintenance Plan Wizard in SQL Enterprise Manager. You can invoke it from the Tools menu by either selecting Wizards... and then locating the Database Maintenance Plan Wizard by expanding Management, or by selecting Database Maintenance Planner from the Tools menu directly. You can also right-click on the database for which you want to configure log shipping to access it. After clicking past the initial welcome screen, you are presented with a dialog box, similar to Figure 14-8, which asks you to select the databases on which you want to perform maintenance. Selecting the check box next to "Ship the transaction logs to other SQL Servers (log shipping)" tells the Database Maintenance Plan Wizard that you are configuring tasks for log shipping.

After you select the database, which must be a user database and cannot be one of the default SQL Server databases, you proceed through the normal Database Maintenance Plan Wizard dialog boxes. Choose whether to check database integrity, perform a full backup, and so on. When you are asked to supply the transaction log backup location, you need to specify a disk location that is the same as the folder you created earlier for the primary server's transaction log backups. You will then be asked for the network share name of the transaction log backup location. The standby server requires this information to read the files and copy them to its holding area.

14

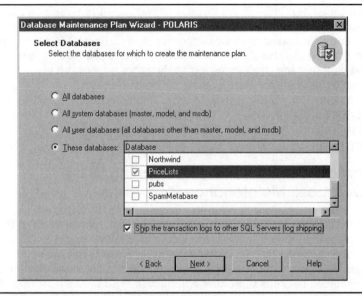

Figure 14-8.   You can configure all log shipping tasks with the Database Maintenance Plan Wizard in SQL Server 2000.

Click Add to get the dialog box for configuring a log shipping destination (shown in Figure 14-9). After specifying the network share of the backup folder, you can add servers to ship the logs to. More than one standby server can be configured for the same database, for additional redundancy. For each server, you can configure a holding folder (Transaction Log Destination Directory) and designate which database to restore the transaction logs to—you can create a new database or choose an existing one (creating a new one is the safer choice). If configuring a new database, verify the location of the data and transaction log files to make certain there is sufficient space for the volume of data. As you may have guessed by the server name in the figure, it is possible for log shipping to send data to a standby database on a cluster, or to configure log shipping of a cluster-based database to another node. When selecting the database load state, you should select Standby mode to keep the database in permanent recovery mode.

Once you have completed adding and configuring standby servers, you are prompted to either perform a backup of the primary database or use an existing backup. Backing up a database is preferred if the volume of data is not too large. Otherwise you can use an existing backup and then apply restores of transaction logs incrementally up to the time you enabled the standby server. This will get both databases in sync so transaction log backups will be applied successfully. When using an existing backup, it is important that you have all transaction log backups since the last full backup was performed.

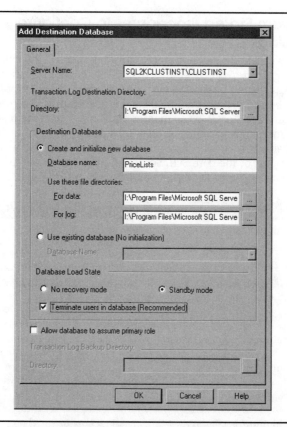

Figure 14-9.   Select the database and method to use for the standby server from this dialog box.

The next series of screens allows you to configure the frequency of transaction log backups and the log shipping schedule. You will need to specify which server will act as a log shipping monitor server and where and for how long to keep history information. Finally, give the log shipping maintenance plan a name and then start the process of configuring log shipping. If during the configuration an error is encountered, you may have to repeat the Database Maintenance Plan Wizard from the beginning, and put all the information in again. The best way to avoid errors is to ensure that the SQL Server Agent service on all nodes is using the same startup account and that SQL Server Agent can access the shared folders in read/write mode.

When configuring log shipping, if either of your servers is running in Mixed Security mode, a new login called **log_shipping_monitor_probe** is created to populate the log shipping tables in the database whenever an event related to log shipping takes place. This includes transaction log backups, restores, or copies.

14

Using System Stored Procedures to Configure Log Shipping

If you want to configure log shipping programmatically, you can execute a series of system stored procedures that the Database Maintenance Plan Wizard invokes during execution and configuration of log shipping. Unlike most system stored procedures, those used for configuring and managing log shipping are not stored in the **master** database, but in the **msdb** database instead. The main reason for this is that log shipping is essentially a series of jobs and tasks that are under the control of the SQL Server Agent service and not actually a part of the core SQL Server engine. Table 14-1 lists the stored procedures in SQL Server 2000 that can be used to configure log shipping.

Stored Procedure	Purpose
sp_add_log_shipping_database	Executed on the primary server, it takes a database name and maintenance plan as parameters and indicates that the specified database is configured for log shipping
sp_add_log_shipping_plan	Creates a new log shipping plan and inserts the appropriate entries in the **log_shipping_plans** table of the **msdb** database
sp_add_log_shipping_plan_database	Adds a database to a current log shipping plan that has been configured
sp_add_log_shipping_primary	Inserts a new row in the **log_shipping_plan_primaries** table in the **msdb** database to specify the name of a new primary database
sp_add_log_shipping_secondary	Inserts a new row in the **log_shipping_plan_secondaries** table in the **msdb** database to specify the name of a new standby database
sp_change_monitor_role	Switches the role in the log shipping monitor to make an existing secondary a primary database
sp_change_primary_role	Deletes a current primary database from a log shipping plan
sp_change_secondary_role	Moves a current standby database to a primary database in the log shipping plan
sp_create_log_shipping_monitor_account	Creates the log shipping monitor account to be used in Mixed Security mode and assigns it a password
sp_define_log_shipping_monitor	Configures the log shipping monitor account on the monitor server
sp_delete_log_shipping_database	Removes a current primary database from the **log_shipping_databases** table indicating it is no longer being log shipped

Table 14-1.   System Stored Procedures Used to Configure and Monitor Log Shipping

Stored Procedure	Purpose
sp_delete_log_shipping_monitor_info	Removes a primary and standby database combination from the log shipping monitor
sp_delete_log_shipping_plan	Deletes a log shipping plan from the **msdb** database
sp_delete_log_shipping_plan_database	Deletes a database from a current log shipping plan
sp_delete_log_shipping_primary	Removes a primary server from the **log_shipping_primaries** table in the **msdb** database
sp_delete_log_shipping_secondary	Removes a standby server from the **log_shipping_secondaries** table in the **msdb** database
sp_get_log_shipping_monitor_info	Returns current status information about a combination of primary and standby servers
sp_remove_log_shipping_monitor	Removes a log shipping monitor from the **log_shipping_monitors** table in the **msdb** database and disables it as a monitor
sp_resolve_logins	Compares logins from the primary server and standby server and ensures all logins in the primary are available on the standby server
sp_update_log_shipping_monitor_info	Updates log shipping monitor information about a primary and standby server pair
sp_update_log_shipping_plan	Writes changes to log shipping plans to the appropriate tables in the **msdb** database
sp_update_log_shipping_plan_database	Writes changes about a database that is part of a log shipping plan to appropriate tables in the **msdb** database

Table 14-1. System Stored Procedures Used to Configure and Monitor Log Shipping *(continued)*

Monitoring Log Shipping

Once log shipping has been configured, the best way to monitor it is using the Log Shipping Monitor utility from SQL Enterprise Manager. The monitor is automatically configured when you use the Database Maintenance Plan Wizard to enable log shipping of a database. It provides real-time status information on each log shipping pair of databases, and can alert you of errors.

Another way to monitor log shipping is to use the system stored procedures that monitor log shipping such as **sp_get_log_shipping_monitor_info**. A third way to monitor log shipping is to view the contents of tables in the **msdb** database that apply to log shipping, as outlined in Table 14-2.

14

Table Name	Purpose
log_shipping_database	Lists all primary databases and associated maintenance plans for log shipping.
log_shipping_monitor	Used by primary and standby servers to locate the name of the monitor server, which is stored in this table.
log_shipping_plan_database	Stores information about the primary and standby database, maintenance plan, and other parameters for each log shipping pair.
log_shipping_plan_history	Used to track status of processes during log shipping. This is a good place to look for any tasks that failed and the reason for failure.
log_shipping_plans	Stores information on each primary and standby server pair and the paths used for transaction log backups and other server-wide parameters.
log_shipping_primaries	Information on the maintenance plan on the primary server is stored here along with the associated options such as plan name, server name, database name, and so on,. The name of the last backup file is stored here as well.
log_shipping_secondaries	Information on the maintenance plan on the standby server is stored here as well as the associated options such as plan name, server name, database name, and so on. The name of the last backup file is stored here as well.
sysdbmaintplans	Holds information about all maintenance plans on the server, including those used for log shipping.
sysjobs	Data about each configured job on the server is stored here, including log shipping jobs.

Table 14-2.   Tables in the msdb Database Relating to Log Shipping

Switching Roles

The main reason to perform log shipping is so you can switch to the standby server in case something goes wrong with the primary server. To switch to the standby server, do the following:

1. Transfer all logins from the primary server to the standby server if they have changed since log shipping was established. You can use the DTS Transfer Logins task to do this.

2. Back up the transaction log of the primary server (if available).

3. Execute **sp_change_primary_role** on the primary server to tell it that it is no longer the primary.

4. Execute **sp_change_secondary_role** on the standby server to promote it to the primary for the specified database.

5. Execute **sp_change_monitor_role** to notify the monitor of the new primary server and database.

6. Execute **sp_resolve_logins** on the new primary (the old standby) to resolve any login account issues.

7. Restore the backup created in step 2 to the new primary (the old standby) to bring across the most recent transactions.

8. Configure client computers to use the new primary server, or configure the new primary with the IP address and computer name of the old primary. This way users will be able to connect to the new primary server.

If you want to reestablish the failed server as the primary again, configure log shipping between the new and old primary servers. You then perform the steps above to make the switch. Or take a complete backup of the databases on the new primary, restore them on the recovered server, and then bring it online. Make sure you configure user access to the recovered computer.

Removing Log Shipping

To remove log shipping, simply delete the Database Maintenance Plan associated with it, or, if you configured log shipping manually, delete the jobs from the **msdb** database. You can also execute the appropriate stored procedures listed previously in Table 14-1.

14

INDEX

INTERNATIONAL CONTACT INFORMATION

AUSTRALIA
McGraw-Hill Book Company
Australia Pty. Ltd.
TEL +61-2-9900-1800
FAX +61-2-9878-8881
http://www.mcgraw-hill.com.au
books-it_sydney@mcgraw-hill.com

CANADA
McGraw-Hill Ryerson Ltd.
TEL +905-430-5000
FAX +905-430-5020
http://www.mcgraw-hill.ca

GREECE, MIDDLE EAST, & AFRICA
(Excluding South Africa)
McGraw-Hill Hellas
TEL +30-210-6560-990
TEL +30-210-6560-993
TEL +30-210-6560-994
FAX +30-210-6545-525

MEXICO (Also serving Latin America)
McGraw-Hill Interamericana Editores
S.A. de C.V.
TEL +525-1500-5108
FAX +525-117-1589
http://www.mcgraw-hill.com.mx
carlos_ruiz@mcgraw-hill.com

SINGAPORE (Serving Asia)
McGraw-Hill Book Company
TEL +65-6863-1580
FAX +65-6862-3354
http://www.mcgraw-hill.com.sg
mghasia@mcgraw-hill.com

SOUTH AFRICA
McGraw-Hill South Africa
TEL +27-11-622-7512
FAX +27-11-622-9045
robyn_swanepoel@mcgraw-hill.com

SPAIN
McGraw-Hill/
Interamericana de España, S.A.U.
TEL +34-91-180-3000
FAX +34-91-372-8513
http://www.mcgraw-hill.es
professional@mcgraw-hill.es

UNITED KINGDOM, NORTHERN,
EASTERN, & CENTRAL EUROPE
McGraw-Hill Education Europe
TEL +44-1-628-502500
FAX +44-1-628-770224
http://www.mcgraw-hill.co.uk
emea_queries@mcgraw-hill.com

ALL OTHER INQUIRIES Contact:
McGraw-Hill/Osborne
TEL +1-510-420-7700
FAX +1-510-420-7703
http://www.osborne.com
omg_international@mcgraw-hill.com